Praise for *Mommy's Boy*

"Mommy's Boy *is a tender, compassionate story, . . . a great read for dog lovers; tender and heart-wrenching, readers will both laugh and cry as the story progresses. I loved it!*"

—Emily-Jane Hills Orford, Readers' Favorite

"Mommy's Boy *is an absolute must-read for dog lovers, but it's more than just a pet memoir. It's for anyone who's ever rebuilt themselves after heartbreak, found love in unexpected places, or realized that sometimes, the best relationships aren't the ones we're conditioned to chase. It's a book that makes you laugh, cry, and maybe even hug your dog a little tighter. If you've ever known the kind of love that only a dog can give, this book will feel like home.*"

—Literary Titan

"Mommy's Boy *is one of the most moving stories I have ever read. . . . It will make you smile and cry at the same time. . . . This is a heartfelt story about unconditional love, the importance of celebrating life, and the special relationships we build with our pets.*"

—Luwi Nyakansaila, Readers' Favorite

"Mommy's Boy *is a poignant love letter to a dog who was much more than "just a dog." Schaeffer reminds readers that sometimes the deepest connections come on four paws. For anyone who has ever had their heart stolen by an animal, this book will speak directly to the soul.*"

—Edward Sung for IndieReader

Mommy's Boy

How My Doggie Soulmate's Love Rescued Me

JENNIFER HUSTON SCHAEFFER

ISBN-13: 979-8-9922012-0-8 (hardcover)
ISBN-13: 979-8-9922012-1-5 (paperback)
ISBN-13: 979-8-9922012-2-2 (e-book)

Library of Congress Control Number: 2024927012

Quoted material used in this book comes from the following sources:

page vi: Billie Lourd (praisethelourd), "It has been two years since my Momby's death …" Instagram, December 27, 2018, https://www.instagram.com/p/Br4RgjPlHi-u/?img_index=1

page 78: "Raptor," Cedar Point, accessed July 24, 2024, https://www.cedarpoint.com/rides-experiences/raptor

page 90: Dr. Edward Bassingthwaighte, "Cytopoint for Dogs: Is It Really Safe?" last modified April 30, 2024, accessed July 24, 2024, https://www.dogsnaturallymagazine.com/cytopoint-for-dogs-not-safe/

page 243–244: "Takotsubo Cardiomyopathy," St. Vincent's Hospital Heart Health, accessed July 29, 2024, https://www.svhhearthealth.com.au/conditions/takotsubo-cardiomyopathy

page 244–245: *Grey's Anatomy*, season 20, episode 1, "We've Only Just Begun," directed by Kevin McKidd, written by Shonda Rhimes, Meg Marinis, Megan Chan Meinero, aired March 14, 2024, on ABC.

page 245: *The Guilt Trip*, directed by Anne Fletcher, written by Dan Fogelman and Jason Conzelman (2012; Hollywood, CA: Paramount Studios), Netflix.

page 254: Marion Roach Smith, "Some New Insights on The Memoir Project Algorithm," The Memoir Project Blog, January 2023, https://marionroach.com/2023/01/the-memoir-project-algorithm

Editorial Team: Debra Almgren-Horwitz and Steven Grundt

Book Cover Design and Interior Formatting by Melissa Williams Design

Cover photo, author photo, and interior photos copyright Brad and Jennifer Schaeffer

Published by White Dog Books, Westfield, IN

First Printing, March 9, 2025

For Benny Goodman Wrigley Ron Santo Huston Schaeffer,
my doggie soulmate.

You were and always will be my sunshine.

"Take your broken heart, and turn it into art."

—Carrie Fisher

Contents

Prologue

Around seven o'clock on Christmas morning of 1979, I woke up with adrenaline coursing through my veins, eager to see what Santa had brought me. Without waking my parents or my older sister Lori, I wiped the sleep from my eyes, stepped into my Snoopy slippers, and padded downstairs to the living room. The smoky vanilla aroma from my dad's pipe lingered in the air and mixed with the scent of pine from the Christmas tree, under which I found a letter from Santa, informing me that he'd left my present in the basement.

Wondering what Santa might've left me that couldn't be placed under the Christmas tree, I toddled my little seven-year-old butt down two more flights of stairs. (The house where I grew up in southern Michigan was a trilevel, so the basement was technically a fourth floor.) In the chilly, unfinished basement, I found my brother, Steve, who was nineteen at the time, snoring on the couch with a beige bundle of fur nestled on his chest. My heart began to pound with excitement as I realized Santa had brought me a furry friend. I nudged my big brother and said, "Wake up, Steve. Give me my Christmas present from Santa!"

After handing over the squirmy little pup, Steve grumbled, rolled on his side toward the back of the couch, and attempted to go back to sleep. With my golden-blonde, Cindy Brady pigtails bobbing up and down, I bounded up three flights of stairs, shouting, "Santa brought me a puppy! Santa brought me a puppy!" After that, my parents and seventeen-year-old Lori reluctantly stumbled out of bed and made their way to the living room to open presents.

I never told my family members, but that's the day when my belief in Santa started to unravel. As most kids do by that age, I'd had my suspicions. For one thing, I'd already come to the conclusion that Santa's handwriting bore a strong resemblance to my mom's. Plus, my cousin Crissy, who's two years older than me, had recently begun putting the idea in my head that the whole Santa biz might be a sham. And when I saw Arnold on Steve's chest that day, I started to put the pieces together.

That year, we'd spent Thanksgiving at the home of my Uncle Sonny and Aunt Carol, whose dog, Priscilla, had recently given birth to a litter of cockapoo puppies. When my cousins Vonda and her twin brothers, Bill and Mike, showed me the puppies, I oohed and aahed over the tiny creatures. One of the twins—don't ask me which one because I've never been able to tell them apart—asked which of the pups was my favorite. Most of the puppies were black, like Priscilla, but one was beige—or apricot in technical terms. The lighter-colored one was also a bit smaller than the others. Always a fan of the underdog, I pointed to him and said, "That one's my favorite."

"Nah . . . you don't want that one!" a twin exclaimed. "He's the runt!"

"What's a runt?" I asked, perplexed. After receiving a brief explanation, I said, "That's okay. I still like him the best."

Fast-forward to Christmas Eve. After spending the evening celebrating and opening gifts at my grandparents' house, my mom tucked me into bed and told me to go to sleep because Santa wouldn't visit our house if I was awake. But, naturally, I was too wired to sleep. What kid isn't on Christmas Eve?

I squeezed my eyes shut until I could see a kaleidoscope of glittery sparkles, which my mom always told me was the fairy dust that the sandman sprinkled into the eyes of children to help them sleep. Looking back, it sounds scary to imagine some strange dude coming into my room to sprinkle dirt into my eyes so I could fall asleep. But as a child, it seemed magical.

Frustrated that I couldn't sleep and worried that Santa would pass up our house, I turned on my side and clutched my favorite toy, a small, plush doll I called Baby Boy. Just then, I heard the clickety-clack of the garage door raising, so I sat up in bed and peered out the window. That's when I saw my dad's rust-colored 1973 T-bird pull out of the driveway and head toward Uncle Sonny's house, although I didn't realize it at the time. *Where's Daddy going this late at night?* I wondered. Soon after, the sandman's magical elixir began to take hold, and I drifted off to dreamland.

Later on Christmas Day, Lori, Steve, and I were in the basement, playing with the puppy, when our twenty-one-year-old sister, Denise, arrived with her boyfriend, Bernie, and asked what I was going to name him. I hadn't given it much thought, but looking up at the poster of pint-sized, chubby-cheeked Gary Coleman that I had hanging on the wall, which read, "My engine may be small, but look out for my steam," it suddenly came to me. "Arnold," I replied confidently. *Diff'rent Strokes* was my favorite TV show at the time, so I decided to name him after Coleman's precocious character.

"*Arnold?*" Lori scoffed. "What kind of name is Arnold for a dog? I think you should name him Pug. He has the cutest little pug nose."

I had no idea what a pug nose was, so being the stubborn little tyke that I was, I stood my ground. "He's *my* dog, and *I'm* naming him Arnold." But I conceded by making Pug his middle name.

I took my naming rights seriously, but I also took a lot of flak for naming him Arnold. In addition to Lori giving me the third degree over my choice of names, Crissy and her brother, Todd, who's a year younger than me, also teased me. "You named him Arnold?" Crissy taunted. "Like the pig from *Green Acres*?"

"No . . . I named him after Arnold on *Diff'rent Strokes*."

But all the mocking and chastising over the name Arnold eventually got to me. One day, shortly after returning to school following winter break, my bus driver, Mrs. Hough, asked me what I got for Christmas.

"Santa brought me a puppy!"

"Oh, that's wonderful! What did you name your puppy?" Mrs. Hough inquired.

I was always a shy kid, so when put on the spot like that, I froze up. I didn't want another person making fun of me or the name Arnold, so I quickly thought on my feet, "Uh . . . Lucky," I fibbed, crossing my fingers behind my back as if that would somehow negate my lie. "I named him Lucky." Lori had taken Crissy, Todd, and me to see *101 Dalmatians* over Christmas break, and Lucky was my favorite in the movie.

The next day when Lori was getting off the high school bus, Mrs. Hough said, "Give Lucky a pat for me."

"*Lucky?* Who's Lucky?" Lori wanted to know.

"Your new puppy . . . Jennifer said his name is Lucky."

"We don't have a dog named Lucky," Lori blurted out in sarcastic teenager fashion. "Jennifer named him Arnold!"

Busted!

Of course, Lori just *had* to tell Mom about it. Perhaps she was still mad at me for tattling that I'd found P-O-T in her purse a couple months earlier.

"Jennifer Lynn!" my mom called from the kitchen after I got home from school and sprinted upstairs to my room with Arnold on my heels.

Uh-oh, I thought. *She's calling me by my first and middle name.* That can't be good. I hesitantly trudged from my bedroom to the top of the stairs, my brown corduroys making an audible *zwert-zwoot, zwert-zwoot* sound as I crept down the hallway like a prisoner taking her last walk of freedom.

Mom was standing at the bottom of the stairs with her hands on her hips. "Did you lie to Mrs. Hough about Arnold's name?"

"Yes," I confessed, lowering my head dejectedly.

"Why?"

"Because everybody keeps making fun of his name and making me feel bad about it!" I cried out.

"Do you wanna change his name to Lucky?" Mom asked.

I slumped my shoulders, shook my head, and pushed out my lower lip. "No," I mumbled.

"Then if anyone makes fun of you, just ignore them. He's your dog, and you can name him whatever you want."

Easier said than done, I thought.

But after that, if anyone teased me about Arnold's name, I must've let it slide because I don't recall it ever happening again.

Whenever someone asked me his name, I would simply reply, "It's Arnold, like the character on *Diff'rent Strokes*." And they never questioned it. But I did have to apologize to Mrs. Hough and explain why I'd lied to her.

Arnold and I were instant best friends. For the next twenty-one years—yes, you read that correctly, twenty-one *human* years—we were practically inseparable. (Give me a plant, and I'll likely kill it. Give me a dog, and I'll love it and nurture it practically into the *Guinness Book of World Records*.) Arnold was my constant companion, following me everywhere I went. He let me dress him up in my baby clothes, waited by the door every day for me to get home from school, played board games with me when nobody else would, and ran alongside the pool, barking to cheer me on as I swam laps, often "accidentally" falling in to join me for a swim. He kept me company when I was lonely, paced the floor at night when I started dating, and licked away my tears whenever some stupid boy broke my heart.

In the fall of 1992, when I moved to Boston for a brief stint as a nanny, it was Arnold that I missed the most. I could talk to my parents on the phone, but in the days before FaceTime and Zoom, I couldn't even see Arnold. So when I later moved away for my last two years of college, I rented an apartment so Arnold could come along.

After Arnold passed away in November 2000, I cried for months yet put on a brave face in front of my family, friends, and coworkers. But deep down, I'd lost my moorings and was like a ship adrift at sea. I had literally spent three-quarters of my life with Arnold at that point. We'd grown up together, and I could scarcely remember life without him.

I knew I would get another dog eventually, but I also knew it would be a long, long time before I was ready to give my heart to a furry friend again. In fact, it would be more than a decade.

Chapter 1

Must Love Dogs and U2

"Maybe you should get a dog," my friend Nicole suggested in an effort to console me. It was two weeks before Christmas in 2010, and Nathan, my boyfriend of nine months had just dumped me. He was the first guy I'd dated since my mom had passed away five years earlier. Although he wasn't the man of my dreams, it still hurt to be rejected and lose the companionship of being a couple.

"*What?*" I questioned as Nicole and I sat on the couch in my apartment in Chicago. Through my tears, it came out more as a squeal than a coherent word. "Didn't you hear what I said? I just wanna put on my PJs, curl up into a ball, and never leave my apartment again."

"Yeah, I heard you," Nicole confirmed. "That's exactly why I think you should get a dog. It'll force you to get dressed and get out of your apartment every day."

"You know I love dogs, and I'll definitely get another one someday," I sniffled and wiped my cheeks. "But all I've ever wanted is to marry my soulmate and have his children, so right now, I need to concentrate on finding a man. My biological clock is ticking!"

"You have plenty of time to have children," Nicole assured me as she swept my blonde locks off my shoulder and embraced me in a side hug.

That's easy for you to say, I thought. *You're forty and have five kids!* "But now I have to start over from scratch, and I'm gonna be *forty*!" I wailed.

"In *two* years!" she responded.

"But it's just looming over me like some dark cloud. *Tick. Tick. Tick.* . . . What is wrong with me? Why doesn't anyone want me?" Our conversation was starting to sound like the scene from *When Harry Met Sally* when Meg Ryan's character finds out her ex-boyfriend is marrying someone else.

"There's nothing wrong with you. You just haven't found the right one yet."

Inside, I was rolling my eyes. I knew Nicole meant well, but I was so sick and tired of being spoon-fed platitudes.

"Having a dog will get you out of the house more often, so you'll have a better chance of meeting someone . . . someone who also loves dogs."

"I don't have time for a dog right now," I insisted, staring at Nicole through my tear-splattered glasses. "Besides, if I get a dog, he'll become my whole world and I won't wanna go out and socialize, so I'll never meet a guy."

The next night, when my friend Bill also suggested I get a dog, I told him the same thing. They didn't believe me, but I knew better.

"I just can't believe it's over! We were perfect for each other, and I thought we'd spend the rest of our lives together!" This time it wasn't me crying over a broken heart; it was Tommy, my boyfriend of two months.

I rubbed his shoulder soothingly, trying to comfort him, but I didn't know what to say. He was blubbering uncontrollably, and I'd never seen him like that before. My heart clenched and a twinge roiled in the pit of my stomach as I gazed at whitecaps crashing into the beach while we zipped down Lake Shore Drive. My budding relationship with Tommy seemed to have so much promise, but now it was clear that he was "emotionally unavailable."

It had taken a month or so after my breakup with Nathan, but eventually I'd put my profile back on Match.com, with the tagline "Must Love Dogs and U2." Unfortunately, my luck didn't really change. Then on November 11, 2011 (yes, 11/11/11), I met

Tommy, who I honest to God thought could be "the one." Boy, was I wrong.

During my dating hiatus, which began in the fall of 2003 when my mom was diagnosed with stage 4 lung cancer and ended in early 2010, a trend had developed where men had seemingly become incapable of having a conversation in person or over the phone, instead hiding behind their devices and letting their fingers do the talking. But Tommy was the exception. We had deep conversations that lasted for hours and communicated in a way I'd never experienced with any guy I'd ever dated. And he wasn't pushing the physical stuff, which I appreciated.

However, he was quite the homebody and didn't want to go out and do fun things very often. I'm an introvert too, so we spent a lot of time watching TV and movies and eating takeout—always at his apartment. He lived in a one-bedroom apartment in a high-rise building with a doorman in the Gold Coast, which sounds a lot swankier than it actually was. I lived in a spacious two-flat on a quiet, tree-lined street about a mile west of Wrigley Field. My place was literally only four or five miles away from his and still very much within the Chicago city limits, but he was so reluctant to visit my place (or anywhere outside his tiny bubble) that you would've thought I lived in Wisconsin. However, he had no qualms about driving up to Evanston (twelve miles from his apartment) to sit on the beach at Northwestern or go windsurfing on Lake Michigan. None of this really bothered me at first since we were in the beginning stages of dating, but that started to change in early 2012.

In late January, Mother Nature dumped about six or seven inches of snow on the Chicago area. It was nowhere near as much as the "Snowmageddon" blizzard of a year prior, when the city was pummeled with more than twenty inches of snow, but it was enough to venture outside for some sledding. I researched where to go nearby and found a nice hill at a park in Evanston. Known colloquially to locals as Mount Trashmore, the sixty-five-foot hill and surrounding area was once a landfill but had been converted to a city park in the 1960s.

Tommy agreed to an outdoor escapade, yet when I suggested sledding at Mount Trashmore, he balked at the idea because he'd once gone there with his ex-girlfriend. This should've been a red flag to me, but he seemed to have many other endearing qualities, so I kept my blinders on.

When we'd first started getting to know each other in November, he told me that he'd broken up with his longtime girlfriend over the summer. To me, five months to get over a five-year romance seemed a bit quick, but everyone grieves at their own pace and I figured maybe it had been going south for a while. So again, I gave him the benefit of the doubt. He told me she was a narcissist and he'd "hitched his wagon to the wrong horse" because they ended up dragging each other down in a codependent relationship.

At first, he convinced me that he was ready to move on, but over time, it became evident that he was still carrying a torch for her. Even so, in my naivety, I thought that with time, he'd get over her and realize I was the one he wanted to be with. Even his family hoped so.

He did eventually put on his big boy boots and go sledding with me at Mount Trashmore, and we had a great time—or at least I did. We made a few runs down the hill on innertubes, gliding along the slippery slope—even becoming airborne a couple times—and giggling like children all the way. It was exhilarating ... until he cried all the way home, thinking about his ex. I'm not saying this to shame him, just to show that his emotions were still raw, almost eight months after the breakup.

In hindsight, that day was the beginning of the end. And not because I think men shouldn't cry—on the contrary, I think it takes a very strong man to cry. I think it signaled a death knell because it was clear that he was most definitely NOT over his ex.

After I confronted him about this, we both agreed that he should not be dating. It wasn't fair to me—or any other women that he might date—because he would essentially be leading us on. At that point, our relationship transformed from dating to a very close friendship. But as a result, *he and I* became codependent, and our lives became enmeshed like a bunch of chain-link necklaces all knotted and tangled together.

It took me almost two more years to unravel myself from that mess. Two more years of consoling him on a daily basis when he wept over his lost love. Two more years of him telling me that he wasn't ready to date, but when he *was* ready, I'd be the one for him and it would be even sweeter because we'd developed such a deep and profound friendship, just like Ross and Rachel from *Friends*.

Two more years of finding his profile on Match and listening to him lie to my face that he wasn't dating other women. Two more years of putting my life on hold for a guy who was unable to see the remarkable woman standing before him—a woman who, for reasons that now baffle me, thought she wanted to be with this man who still relied on his parents for monetary support well into his forties because he insisted on living well beyond his means. To my friends and family who stood by me during this time (and encouraged me to dump him) and to those who are reading this and wondering, *What was she thinking?* I plead temporary insanity and paraphrase the words of an extremely wise man (Bono) who said that every woman dates an idiot at some point in her life. Lord knows, I've dated my fair share.

What finally pushed me over the edge? Well, about a week before Christmas of 2013, Tommy and I were supposed to hang out—at his place, of course. My office wasn't far from his apartment, so I headed there after work. He told me to wait in his apartment, and he'd meet me there after his yoga class. After letting myself in, I wanted to look up something on the Internet and couldn't get a signal on my phone, so I went to his computer. There, I found a young woman's Match.com profile on the screen, and her name, number, and a meeting time scribbled on a piece of paper. With this evidence staring me in the face, something clicked inside me. I wrote him a brief note stating that I was done, said goodbye to his cat, and walked out of the apartment—and his life—for good.

After a few days crying to myself and moping around my childhood home over Christmas break, a switch in me flipped. As I realized that I was free, I danced around the family room with abandon, singing at the top of my lungs to "Stronger" by Kelly Clarkson and "Roar" by Katy Perry. I'm sure my dad thought I was losing it since he didn't even know about Tommy, but I didn't care. I was floating like a butterfly, no longer beholden to a person who couldn't be bothered to travel the short distance to hang out at my place once in a while. Everything had been about him and on his terms: what *he* wanted to do, where *he* wanted to go, hanging out with *his* friends, not mine. And once I was liberated, I decided that I was done with men for a while—at least human ones. I decided it was time to give my love and affection to someone who truly wanted it, deserved it, and appreciated it. I decided it was finally time to get a dog.

Chapter 2

Fortysomething Woman Seeks
Four-Legged Soulmate

In late December 2013, a tingle of excitement ran through my veins as I sat in the recliner in my parents' family room with my legs propped up and my laptop on my belly, opened a new browser tab and a pristine Excel document, and began my dog search. For at least a decade, I knew I wanted a Westie (West Highland terrier)—I even clipped photos of Westies from magazines and posted them on my fridge like a makeshift vision board. But I also wanted a rescue dog, not one from a pet store, puppy mill, or breeder, so I kept an open mind. I navigated to Petfinder.com—which is basically Match.com for finding a furry soulmate—because most rescue groups were also advertising there, so it was like one-stop shopping.

Within a few days, I sent out my first applications, then I eagerly waited to hear back. While I was still at my dad's house, I got the exultant news that I was approved to adopt a dog named Max, who was being fostered in the Chicago suburbs. I was abuzz with anticipation as I made plans to bring home a new furry friend. But just twelve hours before I was scheduled to pick up Max, the adoption coordinator or foster parents changed their minds, stating that he had separation anxiety (SA) and needed to be placed in a home with a stay-at-home parent. Tears welled in my eyes and a sense of despondency filled my entire being as those old feelings of rejection surfaced inside me again. But I persisted.

Long before I'd decided to adopt another dog, I'd read *The Loved Dog*—a book by Tamar Geller, Oprah Winfrey's dog trainer—which is all about using nonaggressive methods to teach your dog to be well-behaved. Once I returned to Chicago, I pulled out my dog-eared copy of the book and reacquainted myself with those techniques. I also contacted a local dog trainer to discuss how to treat separation anxiety through behavior modification and positive reinforcement. After speaking with Sean at Found Chicago, a dog boarding and training facility in my neighborhood, I felt confident that I could help my future dog deal with separation anxiety issues should they arise.

After the first of the year, I opened up my search parameters on Petfinder to anywhere within driving distance of Chicago. Although most of the dogs I inquired about were in Illinois, Indiana, Michigan, and Wisconsin, others were in Tennessee, Arkansas, Connecticut, Texas, and Florida—more than a thousand miles away. On the rare occasion that an out-of-state rescue did respond to me, they always had an excuse why I didn't want the dog I had asked about. One, a Maltese named Cooper from Chattanooga, Tennessee, was referred to on the website as a "little gentleman," "affectionate with people," and "good with other dogs." Yet, the response I received said they had "no 'normal' dogs" (their words, not mine) and that they were all puppy mill dogs who needed "another well-socialized dog in residence and a fenced-in yard because they don't know how to walk on a leash." As consolation, they suggested I look on Craigslist.

Facing the reality of how puppy mill dogs are treated broke my heart, but it didn't deter me from pursuing Cooper. I replied that I did have a fenced-in backyard, was willing to work with Cooper at home and in obedience classes, and that he would be spending a lot of time with my landlord's well-socialized dog. My message went unanswered.

I also applied for a Westie-Maltese mix named Brady, who was living in Madison, Wisconsin. However, the organization told me he was currently being fostered by a retired couple, and they hoped to place him in a similar environment so he wouldn't be left alone during the day.

Finally, on January 24, a rescue group in Chicago approved me to adopt a Maltipoo named Desi. The adoption coordinator said the next step was a meet-and-greet to see if Desi and I were a good match. She said Brian, the foster dad, would be contacting me to set up a meeting. A week passed with no word from Brian, so I wrote back to the adoption coordinator, who said she'd reach out to him again. Two more weeks passed before Brian finally emailed me with his phone number to schedule a meet-and-greet. When I called the number, nobody answered, so I left a voice mail and then another. After a couple days with no reply, I emailed Brian again. "Oops," he said. "I mistyped my phone number." [Insert eye roll here.]

When I asked about setting up a meeting for that weekend, Brian said he could accommodate that, however Desi, who he described as "an awesome little guy," had been staying out in the suburbs with a friend for a few weeks because he was too busy with work to take care of him. My thought was, *Why would you sign up to foster dogs if you're too busy to take care of them yourself?* But I didn't say anything because that was between him and the rescue organization.

Finally, on Sunday, February 16, Brian brought Desi to my apartment. He was a curious little bundle of energy—Desi, not Brian—and we hit it off immediately. My landlords, Edwin and Eva, also brought their toy poodle, Bella, to my apartment to see how she and Desi would get along with each other because they'd be spending a lot of time together. Edwin would take them potty when he got home from work around two, then watch them both in his apartment. Desi and Bella became fast friends, and since the visit had gone so well and I was already approved to adopt Desi, I figured I would soon become his mommy.

After waiting on pins and needles to hear back from Brian, he finally emailed me four days later to inform me that the rescue group had decided that due to Desi's "really bad separation anxiety," they didn't think he'd be a good fit for me, stating that "the main concern was that he'd be alone for up to six hours a day and he's really going to need someone to be home with him most of the time."

This was the first I'd heard of Desi's separation anxiety, so after a good cry over having the rug ripped out from under me again, I pushed back. I replied to Brian and the adoption coordinator and respectfully disagreed, saying: "As I mentioned when we met, I've done quite a bit of research on separation anxiety (SA) and behavioral modification techniques used to treat it. While I realize that your heart breaks to hear Desi cry when he's left alone (and believe me, mine would too), everything I've read says that having someone with him 24/7 or as much as possible will only exacerbate his neediness and his anxiety during those inevitable times when it's necessary for him to be left alone.

"I know firsthand what it's like to have a dog with SA. Arnold, my childhood dog, lived to be twenty-one and I got him when I was seven. For the first fourteen years of his life, he was hardly ever left alone because he was at home with my mom during the day. But when we had to leave him alone, he became very anxious and destructive. By the time he and I moved into our own place, his SA was out of control, with howling, destructive behavior, and going potty on the floor or in his crate. Knowing what I know now, I see how being with my mom all day only made his anxiety worse and did nothing to get at the root of the issue or help him overcome it.

"As I stressed during our meeting, I'm not concerned about Desi's separation anxiety because I know there are many ways to treat it. As I said, I'm willing to do whatever I can as Desi's dog mom to get him the help he needs to face his fears, whether that be taking him to day care while I'm at work, hiring a dog trainer to treat his anxiety through behavioral modification techniques and working with him myself, and, as a last resort, antianxiety medication. Quite honestly, when he and my landlord's dog, Bella, warmed up to each other, he was completely oblivious that we were even there.

"I've also contacted a dog behaviorist here in Chicago who agreed that placing a dog with separation anxiety in a home where he's seldom left alone is only going to worsen his anxiety. He's willing to meet with you, me, and Desi for a free thirty-minute consultation, during which time he should be able to assess the likelihood that Desi could overcome his fears through behavioral modification techniques. I would like you to at least consider taking Desi to meet with the dog trainer for an assessment. If he determines that Desi is a good candidate for behavioral modifica-tion, I'd gladly pay for his treatment if you were to reconsider and let me adopt him. Between that and my willingness to do whatever it takes to get Desi the help he needs to overcome his fears, I hope you can see that I would be a good fit for him and would give him the best life possible. As fellow dog lovers, I would hope that you'd want what's best for him in the long run, i.e., treating his anxiety rather than suppressing it."

Much to my surprise, I heard back from the adoption coordinator. But ultimately she said, "We feel it's in Desi's best interest to not put him through that (behavioral modification) if he doesn't have to." What they didn't realize was that they'd inadvertently forwarded an email Brian had sent to them saying that he felt a retired woman who lived in the far north suburbs and had another dog would be a better fit for Desi—despite the fact that I'd already been approved to adopt him. He also questioned whether they should even respond to my email or just ignore it. Very professional.

At that point, I began to wonder: *Are single people like me who work outside the home not allowed to adopt dogs because they have separation anxiety, even if we're willing to do whatever it takes to help them overcome it?* Fired up, I wrote back and did not sugarcoat my feelings: "As I explained in my application and to Brian, although I myself do not have another dog, my landlords have a toy poodle (Bella, whom Desi met and adored), and, if necessary, we will keep them together while we're all at work. Aside from my landlords and their children, I'm the only other tenant in the building, so they would be the only ones to register a complaint if he cried while I was away. Plus, if he did cry, they've gladly agreed to watch him when I'm out. Basically, those reasons—which Brian was fully aware of—negate what you've told me as to why my application was revoked and Desi was placed with someone else. Brian told me Desi needs to go to a home where someone is home with him during the day. Then you said he just needs another companion animal with him during the day, which, as stated, I could provide.

"I'm very unhappy with the way your organization handled this situation. I was approved to adopt Desi *a month ago* and strung along while it was known to everyone (except me) that he has separation anxiety and would not be placed with someone who works outside the home. It was clearly stated on my application that I work during the day and do not have any other pets. Therefore, I never should've been approved to adopt him if it was your intention all along that he not be left alone during the day, even though—as mentioned to you, to Brian, and on my application—I have the means to resolve the matter according to your stated criteria. In addition, Desi's anxiety issues should've been noted on his profile. Not to mention Brian waiting three weeks to finally contact me after I was approved. That's simply unacceptable and unprofessional."

I received a nice response back from the director, owning up to their mistakes and suggesting a couple other available dogs that I might be interested in, but by then, I was done with that organization. And quite honestly, after my two experiences being approved to adopt a specific dog and then ultimately being told I couldn't, I was completely soured on the whole rescue process. *It seems like it might be easier to adopt a kid,* I thought to myself sarcastically.

That weekend, I stewed over the whole Desi Debacle. Practically on the verge of tears, I grumbled to my friend and coworker Karen over brunch, "Do I have to quit my job in order to adopt a dog?"

"You wouldn't think so," Karen replied. "Oy vey ... There are so many dogs out there who need good homes. You can provide that and would be a great dog mom."

"Thanks," I mumbled dejectedly. "But I am this close to giving up or at least putting my dog search on hold. You know I don't handle rejection well. But to be that close to adopting a dog—not once but twice—and have it ripped away has been agonizing."

On Monday, I saw my therapist and told her what had happened. She sympathized but urged me not to give up hope. In fact, she told me about another local rescue group, called One Tail at a Time, where a friend of hers volunteered. "Just take a look at their website and see if you like any of their available dogs," she encouraged. "If not, then take a break."

I begrudgingly agreed, thinking, *I'll do it just to humor you, but I'm not getting my hopes up.* The next day, I sat at my desk during my lunch break and viewed the dogs available through One Tail at a Time (OTAT). Only one dog caught my eye: a scruffy little white dog named Boo. When I clicked on his photo to learn more, there wasn't much information about him, other than that he was listed as a Westie-bichon mix. So I decided to reach out for more information.

The previous emails I'd sent inquiring about dogs were full of spunk and excitement, but in my first email to OTAT, all that was stripped from my voice. Clearly, I was playing it close to the vest, saying simply: "I'm inquiring about Boo, a Westie-bichon mix. How old he is? What's his story? Why is he up for adoption? Does he have any anxiety issues that would inhibit him from being left alone during the day while I'm at work?" I nervously hit "send," completely unaware how much that email would change my life.

About forty-five minutes later, I received a reply from Anna at OTAT: "Boo is seven years old and we rescued him from animal control because he had a skin infection. Thankfully, with medication, it has cleared up and he's looking great! He's a mellow guy that does have a midday dog walker, but he's then fine being left alone."

Okay. That sounds promising, I thought to myself. I wrote back a few minutes later, thanking her for her quick response, and replied: "I forgot to ask, how is he around other dogs, cats, and kids? I don't have any of those things, but it's just nice to know since I'm sure he's bound to encounter them at some point."

"He's good around other dogs (though he prefers ones that aren't super in-his-face), great with kids, and hasn't had any known exposure to cats, but my guess is that as long as they don't pick on him, he'd be just fine. He really is a sweet, kindhearted guy."

Obviously, I was gun-shy and guarded about putting my heart back out there because it took me nine days—*NINE DAYS*—to fill out an application for Boo. And when I did, I looked it over no less than three times and had Karen review it as well. My hands trembled as I hit "send" to submit the application. I don't know what I was thinking waiting so long; I'm lucky he was still available!

When an email popped into my inbox later that evening, my heart began to race. I was literally scared to open it for fear of another rejection. When I finally summoned the courage to read it, I relaxed as Anna's words sank in: "Thanks so much for your application for Boo. It looks great! He'll be at our adoption event at Ruff Haus this Saturday (3/8) from 12–3. If you're able to come by and visit him, that would be wonderful. Then, if you think he's a good match, we'd love to arrange a time for him to join your home for the foster-to-adopt (or direct adoption, if you prefer)."

I was floored. *That was SO easy*, I thought. *Why did I wait so long to put in my application?* As my heart began to thrum rapidly—this time with hopeful anticipation that Boo could be mine—I let Anna know I'd be at the adoption event.

Chapter 3

Boo Meets Girl

I woke up Saturday morning filled with nervous excitement, as if I were getting ready for a first date. Butterflies flitted in my stomach, my heart was dancing a jig, and my hands were shaking so vigorously that it took me multiple attempts to insert my contact lenses. Everything seemed to be going well with my *potential* adoption of Boo, but because of my previous disappointments, I was afraid to get my hopes up.

Around noon, I hopped in my car and drove to Ruff Haus, the pet store where the adoption event was being held. I parked on the street nearby, and as I walked toward the store, I took a deep breath and said a quick prayer to God, the universe, my mom, and all my guardian angels, "If Boo is meant to be mine, please let this meeting go well and let the adoption go through."

As I pulled open the glass shop door, a string of overhead bells jingled, almost drowning out the clatter of an El train rumbling by. I stepped inside and turned to my left, where my eyes fell upon the shaggy little guy I'd seen in photos online. "Is this Boo?" I asked the volunteer standing next to him.

When she said yes, I introduced myself and explained that I'd been approved to adopt him. Then I crouched down so I could be more at his level, offered my hand for him to sniff, and said, "Hi, Boo." As he placed his snow-white paws on my knees, relaxed his ears behind his head, and looked up at me with eyes like pools of melted dark chocolate, he seemed to say, "Hi. I've been waiting for you. You're gonna be my mommy." In that moment, the wall of frost built up around my heart instantly thawed. To say that it was love at first sight sounds cliché, but it truly was.

I sat on the floor and played with Boo for a few minutes until the volunteer said, "He might need to potty. Would you like to take him for a walk?"

"Sure," I said. She handed me a leash, and Boo and I were off.

We stepped outside on the cloudy, crisp late winter day and headed down the street. As we made our way around the block, Boo was a perfect little gentleman on the leash. He didn't pull or put on the brakes; he just trotted around with curiosity and spunk. I was a bit surprised by the extent of his skin infection, though. His belly, butt, and armpits were all bald. I'd never seen a dog with alopecia before, but that didn't dissuade me. As we sat next to each other on a park bench on the way back, I said, "Whaddaya think, Boo? You wanna come home with me?" He returned my gaze with a look that said, "I thought you'd never ask."

When we got back to the pet store, I told the volunteer that I did, indeed, want to adopt Boo. But I decided to do a foster-to-adopt, which means that you take the dog home for a few days, maybe a week, essentially for a trial run before actually signing the adoption papers. Given what I'd already been through with Max and Desi, I thought this was the way to go. Plus, my sister Denise, who'd already adopted two dogs through a rescue group in Indiana, had told me that each time an animal is adopted and is then returned to the shelter or rescue, the pet gets a ding on its record, which makes it even more difficult for it to find a forever home. I didn't want that to happen to Boo, and even though I instinctively felt it was going to work out between us, I wanted to proceed with caution.

I thought I'd be able to take Boo home right then, but I was told that the foster mom wasn't at the event, and she had his meds and other stuff, so I'd have to wait. The volunteer told me to email Anna, the adoption coordinator, when I got home to let her know that I wanted to move forward, and she would work out the details.

"Oh. .... Okay," I said, my smile turning to a disappointed frown. It hurt to leave Boo there, and I could tell he didn't want me to go. He had a look of sadness in his eyes that betrayed his fears, "Why are you leaving without me? Don't you wanna be my mommy? What did I do wrong?" I tried to reassure him that he'd be coming home with me as soon as they'd allow it. I hope he understood.

The moment I got home, I emailed Anna. "I met Boo today at the adoption event. He sure is a sweetie. We took a walk and he did his business and was great on a leash. He seemed to really like me too and didn't seem to want me to leave. I would like to proceed with the adoption or foster-to-adopt process. Please let me know when we can make that happen."

Seven agonizing hours later, Anna replied: "So glad that you found Boo to be a great match; he sure is a sweetheart. I've copied Boo's foster mom on this email so you two can coordinate a time to pick up Boo (and his supplies) from her home and start the foster-to-adopt. Once he's been in your home for a few days, we can line up a time to finalize his adoption!"

My friend Karen and I had already made plans to do hot yoga the next morning, so I arranged to pick up Boo around noon, after the class. The foster mom sent me her phone number and address, and surprisingly, she (and therefore, Boo) only lived a few blocks from me. Had I dared to brave the bitter cold of the Chicago winter to take a walk, I might've actually run into them.

The next day, Sunday, March 9, 2014, I picked up Karen for hot yoga as planned. Quivering with excitement, it was difficult for me to relax during the class. I was like a kid on Christmas morning— literally, I was like my gleeful seven-year-old self when Santa brought Arnold to me.

After yoga class, Karen and I parked in front of the foster mom's building then rang the bell for her unit. She buzzed us in, then we made our way up a short flight of stairs to her apartment. As we stood outside her door, a large dog began barking, jumping, and making quite a ruckus on the other side of the wooden barrier. My pounding heart momentarily stopped as I gave Karen a wide-eyed, panic-stricken look and muttered, "I hope there hasn't been a mix-up and Anna sent me to pick up Cujo instead of Boo."

Finally, the foster mom called out, "I'll be right there. Let me just put this guy in another room."

Whew. Once Cujo was safely tucked away, she let us in, offered us a seat, and went to get Boo. I was bouncing with nervous energy as Karen and I sat patiently (or impatiently, in my case) on the couch.

As soon as Boo skittered into the room, he recognized me, jumped into my lap, and smothered my face with kisses. He knew right away that I was there for him and that I was his mommy, not Karen. The foster mom had already packed up Boo's supplies, and once the leash was clipped onto his collar, he was playfully nudging me toward the door as if to say, "Let's blow this joint!" But the foster mom needed to go over a few things with me first.

She said Boo had just been neutered a few days prior, so he was on antibiotics and needed to wear an Elizabethan collar, aka a "cone of shame," to avoid licking or biting that area. He also had the aforementioned skin infection and an ear infection, so there were drops and other meds to treat those.

She also divulged a little more about his backstory: "In early January, animal control picked up Boo in the far western suburbs. He was found wandering the streets with another small dog, a poodle mix we named Cody. The two of them were taken to the humane society, and when their owners hadn't claimed them after the mandatory seven-day hold, we (meaning One Tail at a Time) scooped them both up. We believe both dogs are around seven years old and had been living on the streets for several weeks at that point."

My heart ached thinking about Boo—or any dogs or cats—living on the streets, especially during the harsh winter conditions in the Midwest.

"Because Boo and Cody were picked up together," the foster mom continued, "we thought they were a bonded pair, so they were placed in the same foster home. But when Cody began taunting and bullying Boo, they were separated, and, after that, both boys were much happier."

Once we had all of Boo's supplies and were filled in on his story and treatment protocol, it was time to go. As much as I love dogs, I can't imagine fostering them because it would be so hard to say goodbye. I'd heard that the dogs are usually reluctant to leave the safety of the foster home they likely thought was their forever home. It can also be difficult for the foster families to say goodbye. However, in this case, it seemed like the foster mom and Boo hadn't really bonded because she seemed rather aloof when it was time for us to go. But about a year later, when my sister Denise started fostering dogs, I asked her how she could give them up. Denise, who doesn't often show her emotions, said it's not easy, but she's just happy to see the dogs go to a good home. So that was probably the case with Boo's foster mom—or maybe she was just putting on a happy face for us. Either way, one thing was clear: Boo was ready to get out of there and get to his new home.

Before going to my place, Karen and I decided to take Boo on a shopping spree. We headed to a nearby pet store and picked up a few things for him, including a new collar and leash, some toys, treats, and a bag of food. (I'd already purchased bowls and a bed for him.) Back at my apartment, I gave Little Boy Boo, as I called him, the run of the place. He joyfully romped around, exploring his new digs, and instinctively knew it was home. He was bursting with exuberant energy and had a huge grin on his face as if saying, "Yay! I've finally found my forever home and have a mommy again!" I giggled with glee at his playful antics, amazed at how he instantly warmed my heart and my home.

As Karen and I sat on the floor and played with Boo, I removed the cone. It quickly became apparent to me that they might've misjudged his age. I'm no expert, but the little guy had a LOT of energy. The foster mom said he liked his naps, but I had a difficult time believing he was seven. His age didn't matter to me, but he seemed like he was definitely under four, perhaps only one or two. In addition to gleaming white teeth, he had quick reflexes and loved to play with toys, particularly plush ones with squeakers. As much as he liked to make them squeal, it was his mission to tear apart the toy, remove all the batting, and rip out the squeaker. By the end of the day, he'd already destroyed one of the toys I'd bought him, a little blue monkey. With his goal accomplished, he cuddled up next to me on the couch, lying on his back with his arms limply bent at the wrists, in what soon became known as "rub-my-belly position," and quickly fell asleep.

Karen—or Auntie Karen as she was soon dubbed—spent an hour or so at my place, playing with my new bundle of joy. During that time, we discussed names for him. For years, I'd planned to name my next dog Wrigley. But about half of all male dogs in Chicago (at least on the North Side) are named Wrigley, so that was starting to lose its appeal. Although it was certainly fitting because he was a *wriggly* (and wiggly) little guy—another sign that he was most likely younger than seven.

I considered a handful of other names, including Albert, for his plume of fluffy white hair à la Einstein; Ronnie, for Cubs legend Ron Santo; Benny, for Benny Goodman, aka the "King of Swing" (I love swing dancing and big band music); George because he had a little swagger when he walked, like George Jefferson; and Scooter because he did a "Boot Scoot Boogie" on the rug when I first brought him home. I'd also considered calling him Freddie after my Uncle Mike (whose real first name was Frederick), who had recently passed away.

As Karen and I played with Boo in my dining room, we tried to gauge which name he liked best. I almost went with Freddie because when I called him that, he stood up on his hind legs and did a little cha-cha, like he was performing on *Dancing with the Stars*, which made me think of Fred Astaire. Over the next few days, I even conducted a poll on Facebook for my friends to help me choose a name, and as expected, Wrigley won (by a single vote). But ultimately, the deciding vote was mine. A few days after bringing him home, I looked at that adorable little face and gazed into those deep, soulful brown eyes at the sweet gentleman who had already captured my heart and said, "You are a good man." Right then, I knew he was a Benny. He looks like a Benny, don't you think?

But on that first day, he was still Boo. After Karen went home, he and I snuggled on the couch while I posted photos of him on Facebook and emailed friends and family members to introduce them to "the new man in my life." With the guys I'd dated, I often waited months to let my family and friends know about them because I wanted to make sure they were keepers. (Spoiler alert: They generally weren't.) But with Benny/Boo, never once did it cross my mind that I was being presumptuous—that maybe it wouldn't work out. Just as he seemed to know that I was his mommy, I knew that he was my little boy. We were simply meant to be.

In fact, until Benny came into my life, I didn't realize how sad and lonely I was. From day one, he filled my world with so much unconditional love and joy and happiness that I wondered how I'd ever survived before him. He ignited a spark in my heart that had been dormant for years, and he brought so much light into my life that I felt like I was Dorothy Gale, stepping from the black-and-white of Kansas into the vibrant technicolor world of Oz.

On our first night together, when I took Boo out for bedtime potties, I quickly learned a secret he'd been harboring. As we crept down the sidewalk in the dark, all of a sudden, he yanked on the leash and took off running, scraping his cone of shame on the ground and dragging me behind him as I desperately stumbled to keep up. I didn't want to let go of his leash, lest he get lost or run into the street, but he was choking himself and gasping like a smoker with a three-pack-a-day habit. After a few seconds, it dawned on me that he was in hot pursuit of a bunny who'd emerged from the bushes when we walked by.

"Slow down, buddy!" I hollered. But he was unable to reel in his primal instincts, and I worried that he'd break his neck or asphyxiate himself. When he finally settled down, I announced, "We're getting you a harness tomorrow."

The next morning, I awoke with a furry little cuddle bug nestled by my feet. It had been my intention to have Boo sleep in his bed on the floor, but he had other ideas. As soon as I'd turned off the light, he started whimpering, so I lifted him into my bed and said, "Oh, all right. You can sleep up here."

I had wanted to let him sleep in my bed all along, but I'd read that it could be disruptive for romantic relationships, so I thought I'd try forcing him to sleep on the floor. But when he cried, I thought to myself, *Screw it. I have no romantic prospects on the horizon, so any guy who wants to be with me is just going to have to accept that this little one sleeps in the bed too.*

Fortunately, the stars aligned in a way that enabled me to work from home my first week with my baby boy. At the time, the publishing company where I worked didn't allow employees to work from home on a regular basis. We all had laptops, though, so if we were feeling under the weather but well enough to work, we could do so from home rather than take a sick day or infect others at the office. But in this case, I'd asked my boss to let me work from home for the full week. Such a request was a bit unprecedented, but it was perfect timing because in addition to my regular editorial duties, I was also writing a children's book for the company on my favorite band, U2. I consider myself somewhat of an expert on the history of the band, so the company was basically saving money by having me write it, rather than hiring someone to do it. The least they could do was let me work on it from the comfort of my home so I didn't have to schlep all my reference materials (books, magazines, CDs, and DVDs) on the El train and into the office.

To help Benny socialize with Bella, Edwin and Eva brought her up to my apartment and I watched her during the day while they were at work. Benny and Bella got along like peanut butter and chocolate, although Benny was a bit shy. Whereas Bella wanted to play with him, he seemed content to play with his toys.

Having that first week at home with Benny was a godsend. As I worked on the first draft of the U2 manuscript, I stretched out on the couch, sandwiched between Benny and Bella, which strengthened the bond between mother and son. I also got Benny into a routine with his meals and walks, and, putting my newfound knowledge of how to nip separation anxiety in the bud, I spent a little time each day leaving him at home alone for increasingly longer periods of time to get him used to me being gone and reassuring him that I'd always return.

During the week, Anna from OTAT reached out to see how things were going with Benny and me. I told her that we were doing great, that he was such a sweet little guy, and that he'd made himself right at home. We made plans to meet on March 17, to finalize the adoption.

The night before we made it official, I decided it was time to give Benny his first bath. I didn't know how he'd react, though. Despite being a "water dog" and loving the swimming pool, Arnold hated getting a bath. He'd shake and spray me with water and try to jump out of the tub any chance he got. But with Benny, I needn't have worried. As usual, he was a perfect little gentleman. After filling the tub with a couple inches of warm water, I placed him in it without incident. He stood stone-still and let me lather him up and pour large cups of warm water over him to rinse. When he was all clean, I wrapped him in a towel and cradled him in my arms like a baby. When he started to shiver, I blow-dried his long locks to warm him up.

On Monday evening, we met Anna at the veterinary clinic where Benny was due for a follow-up visit. There, we saw the doctor who'd originally estimated that Benny was seven years old. He also gave me some shocking news.

"Benny has a slight heart murmur," he said.

"Oh my God! Is that serious? Do I need to make sure he doesn't run or get too excited?"

"No," the doctor replied nonchalantly. "It's just something you should be aware of, particularly if he needs anesthesia at some point."

After the exam, I signed the adoption papers, paid the $150 fee, and Benny was officially mine. It was the best $150 I ever spent!

Anna also turned over all the paperwork OTAT had on Benny Boo. I'd suspected all along that he wasn't Westie-bichon but perhaps Westie-Maltese. To my knowledge, bichons have tight, curly hair, whereas Maltese have more straight or wavy hair. At the time, Benny's hair was about four inches long and stick-straight. Plus, a couple other dogs that I'd inquired about on Petfinder bore a striking resemblance to Benny, and they were both Westie-Maltese. And when I started looking through the paperwork Anna gave me, I noticed that the suburban animal control that had initially found Benny noted him as Maltese. That he was part Westie was obvious from his barrel chest, the shape of his face, and his perky pointed ears, so from that point forward, whenever someone asked his breed, I told them he was Westie-Maltese.

I also found out that he'd been neutered back on January 29, not in early March as the foster mom had told me, which I found strange. He didn't seem at all interested in licking or biting the surgery zone whenever I gave him some cone-free time, so I stopped making him wear it, which he seemed to appreciate.

After that first week at home with Benny, I had to go back into the office. My heart ached when I had to leave him, and I know he wasn't thrilled with the arrangement either. But I hoped that due to our practice runs with me going away for a little bit each day, he'd feel confident that I'd come back.

Each weekday morning, I cordoned off the kitchen with a baby gate and placed Benny's bed, food, water, and some toys inside, giving him a ten-by-ten-foot space to himself. Even so, whenever I'd leave, he'd start whimpering and then crying within moments of me closing the door. It broke my heart to leave for work, but what choice did I have? I would wait downstairs for a few minutes and then go back up and linger outside the doorway to see if he was still crying, and usually by then, he'd settled down.

Edwin, who got home from work around two or so, was gracious enough to take Benny outside to do his business and then keep him in his and Eva's apartment until I got home. They were the best neighbors/landlords I could've asked for.

It wasn't long before Benny and I settled into a routine. I'd rush home from work, eager to be reunited with him after a long day at the office. Just like my childhood self would run up the driveway, antsy to see Arnold after getting off the school bus, I'd practically sprint home from the El. Knowing that Benny was waiting for me and would be bursting with joy when he saw me made me feel so special and loved, something I hadn't felt in the longest time.

After picking up Benny from Edwin and Eva's apartment, we'd go for a stroll then head back to our place and play fetch. Our apartment was what's known as "shotgun" style, where you can see straight from the kitchen at the back of the unit out the living room windows at the front. Altogether, the distance from the back door to the front window was probably over fifty feet, so I'd grab a toy and chuck it down the long hallway. I loved watching Benny's adorable little "wigglebutt" gallop across the hardwood floors in pursuit of a toy. Unfortunately, he didn't quite grasp the concept of returning the ball to me, so I'd invariably end up walking the length of the building to fetch the toy myself then toss it back down the hallway for him to, once again, chase after. (In his defense, he was a terrier, not a retriever, so he was probably thinking, *Why does she keep taking the toy away from me and throwing it back down the hall?*) We'd spend twenty to thirty minutes doing this every day until both of us were panting, worn out, and ready for dinner. It was a nice workout for me, which was good because I never went back to hot yoga—or any gym for that matter—after adopting Benny because I wanted to be with him as much as possible.

From the get-go, I treated Benny as if he were my child rather than merely a pet, and I didn't care what anyone thought. Perhaps this was due to the innate nurturer in me or the fact that I had no prospects for a husband and couldn't afford to adopt a child on my own (or freeze my eggs, which I'd researched). But I also treated Arnold like my son, particularly after he and I moved away for college, so maybe that's just my nature.

A week after his adoption was finalized, Benny got his first haircut. The veterinary clinic also offered grooming services, so we made an appointment there for late March. I wasn't really sure what to ask for, but after consulting with Felipe, the groomer we were assigned to, we decided to go with a puppy cut. I was floored when I first saw him. Not that Benny wasn't cute before, but he looked so handsome with his new do! Felipe had done an amazing job transforming Benny from a little ragamuffin to an adorable pup who could've graced the cover of magazines. After that, the puppy cut became Benny's signature style.

As the temperatures warmed up and winter thawed into spring, two things became crystal clear: Chicago has a lot of squirrels, and Benny had a love-hate relationship with the little critters. After our initial foray going outside after dark, when Benny nearly broke his neck—and almost dislocated my shoulder—I did, indeed, buy him a harness. It was a lifesaver because whenever he saw a squirrel, which was pretty much every day, he'd take off chugging down the sidewalk, chasing after it with me in tow. He'd let out a shrill, ear-piercing shriek to announce that the chase was on, then he'd track the bushy-tailed rodent up a tree, sometimes attempting to climb the tree in his manic pursuit, all the while rapidly whipping his tail back and forth like a flag in a hurricane. I often wondered what he'd do if he actually caught a squirrel (or a bunny or chipmunk) but, then again, I probably didn't want to know.

Chapter 4

Benny's Bottomless Belly

From the outset, Benny was a really good boy, which made me wonder why his previous owner hadn't claimed him during his week at the humane society. I didn't dwell on it too much, though, because I felt it was God's and the universe's way of bringing Benny and me together.

Other than when he was chasing squirrels, he walked very well on a leash, although he was extremely curious and stopped about every five feet to sniff out things and pee, marking and claiming territory like he was buying up property in a game of Monopoly. Whenever he'd spend too much time scrutinizing a specific spot, I'd give him a gentle tug on the leash and say, "Lift it or leave, buddy"—a cleaner version of the phrase my grandmother used to say, which was "Shit or get off the pot."

He very rarely had an accident in the house and seemed to know some basic commands. He also never barked. He was just a happy-go-lucky little guy who wanted to eat, sleep, play with his toys, and cuddle with Mommy.

It was also clear that Benny was very food motivated. There's almost nothing he wouldn't do for a treat. I had decided before I even adopted him that I was going to feed him a better diet than Arnold ever ate. Back in the 1980s and '90s, at least where I grew up near South Bend, Indiana, we didn't have big box pet stores, so we bought all of Arnold's food and treats at the grocery store. As a result, Arnold didn't eat the highest quality food. Not to mention all the people food and table scraps he consumed, including Fritos, bologna, and pork rinds that my dad would share with him. Arnold was sixteen years old when he started eating fancier food due to some health issues, and it had to be purchased from the vet. Despite his "junk-food" diet, he lived to be twenty-one, so I figured with Benny, if I fed him healthier foods, he'd live at least as long as Arnold did.

So, no matter how difficult it was to resist Benny's captivating, chocolate-brown, puppy-dog eyes when he wanted something that I was eating, I remained strong—for the most part. When I accidentally dropped a piece of broccoli on the floor and he Hoovered it up before I could even bend over, he looked at me as if saying, "Yum! Can I have some more?" After that, I started giving him broccoli as a treat. And he loved it! I printed a list of fruits and vegetables that were harmful to dogs so I knew what to avoid, and little by little, I offered him a variety of healthy snacks, including sweet potato chunks, green beans, peas, lettuce, carrots, peeled apple, and blueberries. My friends couldn't believe it when Benny and I would show up to hang out and I'd come toting a container of broccoli and sweet potatoes for him instead of "treats."

The only downside of this was that all those fiber-rich foods would cause Benny to pass gas. We'd be sitting on the couch, relaxing, when suddenly I'd hear *pffft*, the telltale sign of a toot slipping out. In a flash, Benny would be on his feet, glance at his rear end, and, looking quite embarrassed, jump off the couch to get away from the stink bomb wafting through the air. I'd later hear this referred to as crop-dusting. Whatever you call it, I found it hilarious, but I tried not to laugh so I wouldn't cause him further humiliation.

I think Benny's willingness to eat almost anything stemmed from his time living on the streets, when he didn't know what his next meal would be or where it would come from. The vet agreed that it was probably psychological, like a form of PTSD, so he encouraged me not to overfeed Benny, no matter how hungry he acted. Even so, Benny was slightly underweight at fourteen pounds when I adopted him, and the vet wanted him to get up to around sixteen.

Benny must've heard the vet say that he needed to gain weight, so he took matters into his own paws. We went to the South Bend area at the end of March so he could meet his grandpa, his Aunt Denise and Uncle Bernie and their dogs—his cousins, Angel and

Binky—and my closest friends, Margaret and Scott. While I was there visiting, I picked up some groceries since I was unable to do my shopping in Chicago that weekend.

By the time we got home on Sunday, it was after 9:00 p.m., so I couldn't find a parking spot on my block. Because I had groceries, Benny, and all our stuff to unload, I pulled down the alley, squeezed my Ford Taurus in front of Edwin and Eva's garage, put on my hazard lights, then took Benny and a few bags of groceries inside. After dropping them off, I went to find a parking spot. I couldn't have been gone more than five minutes, but when I returned to the kitchen and saw Benny licking his chops, I immediately realized my mistake. Apparently Benny hadn't trained me well enough yet (or perhaps he had in *his* mind) because I'd left a bag of groceries on the floor while I was gone, and that bag just happened to contain a pound of turkey breast, freshly sliced from the deli.

"OMG, Benny!" I scolded. "Did you just gobble up an entire pound of turkey?"

He looked up at me with those innocent eyes. And despite the plastic packaging stuck to his lips, his eyes were saying, "No, not me, Mommy. I didn't do it."

I pursed my lips, shook my head, and let out a deep sigh. Despite my frustration, I wasn't about to spank Benny. I couldn't bear to do that even if I wanted to. Besides, I knew from reading *The Loved Dog* that negative reinforcement—in other words, not rewarding bad behavior—was the key to successful training. Shaming, spanking, and causing physical harm will only hurt a dog's psyche, and I certainly didn't want to do that.

"No treats for the rest of the night, Benny. That's your punishment," I proclaimed. "Besides, your tummy's gonna punish you enough."

Benny's tummy did, indeed, punish him because he had an upset stomach for the next couple days. I definitely learned my lesson about not leaving food unattended around him and tried to convince him that he was no longer a homeless pup who had to scavenge for scraps and eat anything he found.

I'd like to say he learned his lesson too, but we did have another incident later on where he managed to pull a container of white chocolate chip cookies down from a height of about three feet off the ground. When I heard the crash and found him noshing on them, I quickly learned that the darker the chocolate, the more

dangerous it is for dogs. Fortunately, with this being white chocolate, the risk was minimal, but he still suffered from diarrhea for
a few days.

Another time, a few years later, he purloined a pistachio muffin.
While I went back to the kitchen to get a glass of milk, I left it on
a plate in the middle of the coffee table, thinking it was safely out
of his reach. But Benny, performing a feat of acrobatics, stretched
out his little body, snatched that muffin off my plate, and inhaled
it in a matter of seconds. When I returned to the living room, saw
my empty plate, and noticed neon green crumbs in his beard, I
groaned, "Benny, what am I gonna do with you?"

Once again, his tummy punished him, this time with diarrhea
that looked like he'd swallowed a glow stick. After that, whenever
the U2 song "Neon Lights" came on in the car, I would sing the
tune with lyrics I'd altered especially for him:

> *Neon poops.*
> *Benny made neon poops.*
> *After he ate Mommy's*
> *Pistachio muffin.*

Bono, I don't mind if you use my lyrics as long as it's at a show
in Chicago so I can witness it. And if you want to leave me some
front-row tickets and meet-and-greet passes, I won't say no.

After that little episode, my training was complete, and I learned
to never EVER leave Benny unattended with any food unless it's
his, even if you think he can't reach it. Like I said, he was very food
motivated.

Chapter 5

Benny the Bully

True to what I'd been told, Benny was good with other dogs as long as they didn't pick on him. We had several small dogs in our neighborhood, so he easily made friends, with the aforementioned Bella and Bobo, a Westie who lived a couple doors down, becoming his besties. After a while, Benny even found a girlfriend, a petite Maltese named Lily. Whenever Benny would see Lily, it was like an angel had descended from heaven, plucking the strings of a harp. He'd pick up his pace and suddenly begin walking with a little swagger but would always maintain his cool. Lily remained poised too, but you could see a sparkle in her eyes and a coy smile on her face whenever she'd see Benny moseying down the sidewalk. Her sister, a miniature Schnauzer named Roxie, was not so demure. She would bark and yell and lunge at Benny as if she were playing hard to get, but he found that kind of behavior off-putting and unattractive. He much preferred a quiet, well-mannered lady who mirrored his calm self.

While it was true that Benny was quite mellow and good around other dogs, he definitely preferred the company of humans. He also seemed to have a bit of a Napoleon complex, which, by definition, means that in an effort to compensate for his diminutive stature, he'd become aggressive around larger dogs. It also could've been that he'd been bullied by a big dog at some point in his life, so before they could torment him, he'd become the aggressor and taunt them. Another theory is that he suffered from "testicle envy," which is when neutered dogs become unhinged around intact male dogs. Honestly, it might've been all of the above.

The first time I witnessed Benny exhibit this behavior was over Memorial Day weekend in 2014, when my best friend Margaret invited a group of people over for a cookout at her new house in South Bend. Benny was on his best behavior, just chilling on my lap and playing the shy guy when people would come up and say how cute he was or ask to pet him. A couple larger dogs were also in attendance; however, Benny seemed uninterested in the other canines. That changed when Nikolai arrived.

Nikolai was young—one or two, I think—but he was pretty calm. As a Siberian husky, he was also enormous! At eighty-plus pounds, he was over five times Benny's size. Nikolai was just quietly minding his own business, sitting on the patio across from us, when Benny went ballistic. He jumped off my lap, bared his teeth in a snarl, and started growling and lunging at Nikolai. I'd never seen Benny act that way, and for him to do so unprovoked seemed completely out of character.

My cheeks reddened with embarrassment as I tried to wrangle Benny away from Nikolai. "Benny, calm down! What has gotten into you?" I scolded.

Mortified by Benny's behavior, I apologized to Nikolai's parents, but I couldn't help but chuckle internally at the absurdity of the scene playing out before me. Nikolai just looked at Benny as if saying, "Seriously, little dude? My *head* is bigger than you. I could eat you for lunch."

When my attempts to rein in Benny failed, we took a time-out and I carried him around the backyard, trying to get him to settle down. With his front paws straddling my shoulders and his legs wrapped around my waist, Benny continued to bark and snarl at Nikolai, but eventually, he simmered down. Even so, for the rest of the evening, we kept our distance from Nikolai and his parents.

In July, my friend Josh came to visit from Detroit and brought his boxer, Hector, with him. Benny and Hector didn't become best buds, but Benny also didn't want to attack Hector like he did Nikolai. However, when Josh and I took our boys to the dog beach, Benny the Bully surfaced again, although he seemed selective about where he directed his ire. He sniffed a giant German shepherd but, rather wisely, decided to leave him alone. Later on, he befriended a Maltipoo, and, together, they ganged up against a black-and-white spotted Lab mix. Benny waded into Lake Michigan until it was about chest-high for him, but he clearly didn't like the waves crashing into him, so he quickly got out and shook his entire body from bow to stern. Then he started shouting at Hector and the Lab as they frolicked in the water. It was the first time I'd ever heard him bark! When I heard him utter, "WOOF! WOOF!" I was shocked at the timbre of his voice, which was much deeper than I'd expected from such a little guy and quite different from his screeching squirrel call and the mournful cries he emitted when I left for work each day.

As Hector and the other dog bounded through the water, Benny bellowed at them from the shore. Eventually, Benny started walking away, but when the Lab chased after him, Benny wasn't about to give in. As the Lab ran by, Benny took off sprinting toward him. "I had no idea he could move that fast!" I said through peals of laughter.

When the Lab gamboled back into the lake, Benny and his Maltipoo accomplice stood along the shore as if setting up a block-ade to prevent him from getting out of the water. Benny continued to hound him and bark at him, but I don't know if he was saying, "You stay there!" or "Get out of the water! It's dangerous!" After a while, the Maltipoo gave up, but Benny sat on the beach and had a showdown with the Lab, the two of them staring at each other, just waiting for the other to make a move.

When the Lab finally emerged from the water, he galloped toward Benny, then quickly pivoted and darted off in the opposite direction. Benny once again gave chase, kicking up rooster tails of sand in his wake. As they made erratic loops around the beach, Benny zigzagged between a guy's legs. To avoid getting knocked over, the guy hopped in the air like he was skipping rope. Soon, a pack of dogs of various sizes joined the action, including a massive jet-black Newfoundland, all of them following Benny's lead and chasing the Lab. Several of the dog parents cheered Benny on as they enjoyed the slapstick antics. This time, Benny didn't snarl or growl at his nemesis like he did with Nikolai, but for whatever reason, he clearly had a beef with some big dogs.

About a month later, Benny and I were taking a walk when we discovered a female shih tzu mix wandering through the neighbor-hood. When she came over to say hi to Benny, I was able to scoop her up. She wasn't wearing a collar, just like Benny when he'd been found on the streets back in January. We went inside so I could grab my car keys and a spare collar and leash for her, then the three of us drove around the neighborhood to see if anyone was out looking for her. Satisfied that they weren't, we went to the nearest vet so I could see if she was microchipped. Again, like Benny when they found him, she wasn't chipped.

I don't mean to sound judgmental, but please keep a collar and tags on your pets or at least get them microchipped. It's relatively inexpensive and doesn't harm the pet. This little girl was a "designer dog," so she probably cost hundreds, if not thousands, of dollars. Therefore, I don't understand why her owners wouldn't pay an extra thirty bucks to get her chipped. I realize if she gets lost, there's no guarantee that the person who finds her will see if she's chipped to locate her owners. There's always the possibility that they'll just keep her for themselves. But if she *is* chipped, there's a much greater chance that she'll be returned to her rightful owner. Stepping off my soapbox now.

Not knowing what else to do, the three of us headed back to my apartment. My plan was to take her picture and plaster "Found Dog" signs around the neighborhood. She was adorable and clearly just a puppy, so I couldn't bear to take her to a shelter. I decided that if no one had claimed her within a week or two, we'd either keep her or contact OTAT to find her a home.

Benny didn't seem too thrilled about the idea of having a little sister—or any sibling for that matter. He wasn't mean or aggressive toward her, but by the way he pouted and moaned from the back seat while we were driving to the vet, I could tell he was none too pleased with the situation or the interloper next to his mommy.

After we returned from the vet, we took a walk around the block, once more looking to see if anyone was searching for the shih tzu. As we rounded the corner, heading back to our apartment, a little girl and her dad were coming toward us, and when the girl saw the puppy with Benny and me, she started dashing down the sidewalk, calling the dog's name. The pup was just as excited to see her, so I knew we'd found her family. I didn't scold them or tell them what to do, but I made it known that we had no idea who she belonged to because she had no tags and no microchip. Hopefully they remedied that. We were all grateful when they were reunited, particularly Benny, who definitely liked being an only child.

In September, my sister Denise had a procedure called radioactive iodine therapy done to treat hyperthyroidism. She simply had to take a pill, but it actually made her temporarily radioactive, so she couldn't be around adults for three days or children or pets for a week. During that time, her husband, Bernie, and their dogs, Angel and Binky, came to stay with me. Benny had spent a fair amount of time with his cousins by then, and they got along well. He and Binky were about the same size and age (if I was right about Benny's age), so they'd often playfully tussle on the floor. But trying to walk the two of them at the same time was a comedy of errors.

I'd always take Angel out separately because she was born with her right front arm bent toward her chest, so she basically walked on three limbs. Even so, walking her was easy compared to taking Benny and Binky out together to do their business, which always went something like this: As soon as we'd hit the sidewalk, they'd scamper off in two different directions, yanking my arms out to either side as if I were a Stretch Armstrong doll. Then, as if it were a well-choreographed dance routine they'd been rehearsing, they'd switch sides, forcing me to cross my arms in front of me. Then the one on the left would continue moving counterclockwise toward my backside, obligating me to pirouette to prevent their leashes from wrapping me up like a mummy. Lather, rinse, repeat.

Luckily, before Angel and Binky came to stay with me, Denise had purchased a lifesaver known as a coupler, which essentially turns two leashes into one. It's shaped like a Y, with the two end straps clipping to their harnesses and the single strap connecting to the leash. They could still crisscross each other, but they couldn't take me on the ride with them and spin me in circles.

The first time I walked them around the neighborhood with the coupler was divine. They had to work in tandem, though, because if one stopped to sniff something or do his business, the other had to stop too. As we pleasantly strolled down the sidewalk, the song "Ebony and Ivory" by Paul McCartney and Stevie Wonder popped into my head. I giggled to myself as I looked at Binky with his smooth black coat and Benny with his wiry white fur, Ebony and Ivory walking together in perfect harmony. Mostly perfect anyway. There were still moments when one would have to whiz while hopping on three legs because the other had caught sight of something and decided it was time for the pee-pee train to chug along.

During their stay with me, Angel and Binky got into a rumble on the living room floor. I'm not sure if it started over rights to a toy, but they got in each other's faces, like siblings often do. As they wrestled on the floor, snarling and play-biting each other, Benny just stood back, like a referee, debating whether he should join them or try to break up the brawl. Eventually, Benny walked away and stood by me as if saying, "Count me out, guys. I'm a lover, not a fighter."

Even when Binky grabbed one of Benny's favorite toys and started shaking it viciously, clearly pleased with his contraband coup, Benny didn't put up a fight. Instead, he just sat calmly on the floor and looked up at me as if to say, "Mom ... Binky took my toy! Will you please get it back for me? He's cray-cray."

Later that week, Benny found his voice. He and Binky were standing guard with their front paws perched on the arm of the couch, keeping an eye out for trespassers, i.e., people walking down the sidewalk, minding their own business. Binky would bark at anything that moved, but up to that point, the only time I'd ever heard Benny bark was at the dog beach with Josh and Hector. However, when Binky started in, so did Benny. His voice was literally hoarse because it had been over two months since he'd last barked. I don't think he even knew what he was barking at, he just did it because Binky was. In fact, he looked back at me like he was asking permission. "Is it okay if I bark too, Mom?"

I gave him a nod and said, "It's fine ... just don't make a habit of it."

And he didn't. Other than when Binky would get him riled up, Benny never met a stranger—at least not a two-legged one.

Chapter 6

Paint Chips, Possibilities, and Retirement

Although Benny enriched my life in countless ways and filled me with more joy and happiness than I'd ever experienced, I still longed to get married and have a family. In fact, in the yearbook during my senior year of high school, I'd predicted that I'd be married by twenty-three and have four children—including twins—by age thirty. But somewhere along the way, I realized that I wasn't totally in control of my destiny.

When I turned forty-two in the summer of 2014, I realized my opportunity to have children of my own was winding down. When I was in my twenties and even my thirties, the door seemed wide open—there was plenty of time to have kids. But now I felt trapped in a dark room with only a sliver of light peeking through the door, which was inching closed, little by little, day by day. So, in a last-ditch attempt, I reactivated my profile on Match.

In early August, I started dating Nick, a guy I met through the site. Although he wasn't necessarily my type, he was funny and super nice, so I decided to give it a shot. Besides, considering my lousy luck with men and the whole Tommy time-suck, I started wondering if my innate ability to pick men was just off. So, like George Castanza from *Seinfeld*, I decided to do the opposite of what I'd normally do—and it seemed to work. Nick and I immediately hit it off, and within a few weeks, we were having the exclusivity talk. Over Labor Day weekend, he invited me to a party at his friends' house. Being a relatively shy person, I was nervous, but when they said Benny could come, I instantly relaxed. Already, Benny had become my security blanket, a life raft that I clung to in order to ease my anxiety and shroud my shyness.

While I was dating Nick, I found a growth on Benny's left armpit. In a panic, I took him to the vet who performed a needle aspirate and ran a cytology report, which deemed that it was likely a plasma cell tumor. They said it was probably benign, but they wouldn't know for sure unless they took a biopsy. If it was benign and they did nothing, it would likely recur, but if they removed it surgically, it would cure it. However, their surgical estimate was around a thousand dollars.

Nick lived in the West Loop neighborhood, just a couple blocks from the Animal Care Center of Chicago (ACCC), so I decided to go there for a second opinion. The ACCC also accepted Pet Assure, a program that offers discounted veterinary services to those who purchase a subscription. However, only certain vets accept it. With Pet Assure, the ACCC's estimate was less than four hundred dollars. After doing my due diligence and discovering that the ACCC was highly rated, I decided to go with them.

Benny's surgery was scheduled for the morning of October 6. As we waited in the lobby, he became curious about a kitten sitting nearby in a crate. To my knowledge, this was his first exposure to a feline friend. He relaxed his ears and lowered them behind his head like a bunny as he and the kitty sniffed one another and touched noses through the bars as if giving each other Eskimo kisses. *God, please let my sweet baby boy make it through this surgery,* I prayed.

While Benny was in surgery, I was a restless, nervous wreck, unable to concentrate on anything except my little boy. At Nick's condo, I vacillated between sitting and pacing as I prayed and took deep breaths to calm my fears and anxiety. When the ACCC called later that afternoon to say the surgery had gone well and Benny was ready to go home, I felt like a deflating balloon as I breathed a sigh of relief.

Nick and I drove the two blocks to pick up Benny so he wouldn't have to walk while he was still groggy from the anesthesia. When we got back to Nick's place, I gave Benny a plush squirrel as a gift for being such a brave boy during the surgery. Mr. Squirrel immediately became Benny's favorite toy, and even after the squeaker was punctured, he still liked to chomp, lick, and cuddle with it.

A month after Benny's surgery, I came home from a long, stressful day at work to find a mess. By this time, we had a well-established routine with Edwin walking Benny in the afternoon and then returning him to my apartment. But on this particular day, something in Benny had snapped. Whether he had to potty after Edwin took him out and didn't want to do it on the kitchen floor or whether it was separation anxiety or both, I can't say for sure. But as I entered the kitchen, the evidence that Benny had had some sort of panic attack was undeniable. Deep scratches lined the wooden back door, a three-by-three-inch chunk of paint had been chewed off the wall, just above the baseboard, and a three-foot-tall wicker basket where I stored shoes had been shredded to smithereens. It looked like a wolverine had been let loose in the apartment.

"Oh . . . My . . . God, Benny! . . . What have you done?" I uttered with shock as I combed my fingers through my hair and grabbed a fistful of blonde locks on either side of my head. I surveyed the damage, relieved that my stash of shoes had escaped unscathed.

Despite ingesting paint chips, Benny seemed fine. In fact, he was bouncing around, clawing at my legs with a combination of jubilance and relief that I was home because 1) he missed me and 2) he needed to potty. Exasperated, I clipped on his leash and took him for a walk.

As we stepped outside, the November air nipped at my cheeks, and since daylight savings time had already kicked in, the sky was as black as coal. As we strolled around the block, fallen leaves crunched under our feet and the only light came from the glow of the streetlamps looming above. While Benny casually sniffed and checked his "pee-mail," i.e., messages left by other dogs, I began to worry. I'd painted the wall myself, so I knew the top coat was lead-free, but he had gnawed off several layers. And even if none of those layers contained lead, I surmised that eating paint couldn't be good for him.

When we got back to the apartment, I tried to find some information online and even called poison control, but they were of no help. Eventually, I called Nick and we decided to take Benny to the vet. By this time, it was after 9 p.m., so our only option was an emergency animal hospital.

The vet working that night examined Benny, ran some blood work, and gave him fluids. They also wanted a urine sample, but Benny wouldn't produce for them, so they sent us outside under the inky sky with a cup attached to a long pole. I'm not sure if you've ever tried this, but getting a dog to pee in a cup is no easy feat. Every time Benny would lift his leg, I would wave the pole to position the cup underneath him, but as soon as I did, he'd either lower his leg, kicking the cup to the ground in the process, or he'd stop peeing and move away from the contraption. I'm sure we looked like we were performing some sort of vaudevillian pratfalls. After about twenty minutes of this, we'd only collected a few drops, but fortunately that was enough for them to run the test. Once it was determined that Benny was fine, they sent us home with antidiarrheal meds.

With things going well with Nick, it wasn't long before I met his parents, who had emigrated from Greece before Nick was born. He said they really liked me, but I didn't think the meeting went so well. I had a difficult time understanding what they were saying through their thick Greek accents, and sometimes they even spoke Greek around the dinner table. So, in my insecure mind, I was sure they were judging me. Nevertheless, Nick was soon hinting at us moving in together and even brought up the subject of marriage. But he and his family were Greek Orthodox, and he insisted that I would have to convert. I wasn't sure about that and felt everything was moving too quickly. At that point, we'd only known each other three months!

Benny seemed to like having a male figure in his life, and he got along well with Nick. However, Nick was adamant that he didn't want Benny in the bed when I stayed over. But Benny didn't like sleeping on the floor, even in his own comfy bed, and he didn't understand why he couldn't snuggle with Mommy at bedtime like he did at home. I also had a difficult time sleeping at Nick's place because he snored like a locomotive. Since Benny had been relegated to the floor, he would whimper and cry, so I would wait until the train whistle began to blow, then I'd put Benny in the bed next to me. In the morning when Nick would notice Benny in the bed, I'd play dumb and say that he must've jumped up there in the middle of the night.

Nick worked as a commercial real-estate appraiser, so he spent a lot of time on the road, traveling around the Chicagoland area and sometimes even farther, but he was generally home every night. On a Saturday in early December, he had to travel to a site in the Quad Cities area, on the Illinois-Iowa border, so he asked Benny and me to come along for the ride. Throughout our relationship, the conversation had always flowed freely, but during the ride, he was especially quiet, which I thought was odd. However, when I asked him if something was wrong, he said no. My women's intuition told me otherwise, but I took his word for it.

A few days later, Nick was supposed to come to my apartment for dinner. Because his family owned a restaurant, he was an excellent chef, so he did most of the cooking in our relationship. But this time, I wanted to make a special dinner for him. I'd researched new recipes and had everything planned out. While I was at work, he called and said he was outside my office building and asked if he could come up. I went downstairs to greet him and brought him up to my office, which I shared with my friend and coworker Karen (Benny's Aunt Karen). It was a nice treat having him stop by the office, and when he got ready to leave, he kissed me goodbye and said he was looking forward to seeing me in a couple hours for dinner at my place.

I was flitting around the kitchen, preparing dinner, when he called just before he was set to arrive at my apartment. My doorbell didn't work, so I figured he was downstairs and needed to be let into the building. But much to my surprise, not only did he cancel, he broke up with me!

I was so floored that I couldn't speak, so in my silence, he continued, "I just feel like things are moving too fast."

"*You're* the one who's been rushing things by insisting I meet your parents and talking about moving in together and getting married!" I retorted.

He agreed, but essentially, he'd scared himself by jumping the gun.

"Is there someone else? Please tell me the truth," I begged.

"No! There's nobody else. I just don't deserve a girl like you," he patronized. "You're such a wonderful person—so kind and sweet and caring and beautiful."

Whatever.

After hanging up with Nick, I called Karen to tell her what had happened. She was almost as stunned as I was. "What??? He was just at the office. He seemed fine. He said he was looking forward to going to your place for dinner tonight! What happened?"

"I have absolutely no idea," I told her. And I honestly didn't. I was completely baffled.

After ending the call with Karen, I threw away the dinner I'd made and cried on the couch while Benny straddled my chest and licked away my tears. I couldn't help but question if something was inherently wrong with me. Maybe I wasn't meant to get married and have children like I'd always dreamed of. Perhaps I was supposed to be content with the status quo: just me and Benny. He was the best dog I could've ever imagined and was more like a child to me than a mere pet. I was blessed to have him and considered him my doggie soulmate. Even so, I couldn't help but think of the old saying, "Every pot has a lid." *Maybe I don't have a lid,* I wondered. *Maybe God forgot to assign me a* human *soulmate.*

I told Benny that night and in the weeks to come that I knew he wanted a daddy, but Nick wasn't the one. "It's not your fault or because of anything you did," I assured him. "It's because of me."

But then I realized that I hadn't done anything wrong this time. All my life, I'd blamed myself for relationships ending, even if I hadn't done anything wrong and it just wasn't a good match or the timing was off.

"No, actually," I told Benny, "it's not my fault either. It's Nick's fault. He got ahead of himself, talking about the future, and now he's scared."

A week later, we left for my dad's for Christmas break. On the way, we stopped at Nick's place to pick up some things I'd left there. He met us at the door and handed me a box. He didn't even acknowledge Benny, which seemed rude and hurt Benny's feelings. Once we were back in the car, I noticed that none of the stuff Nick had purchased for Benny was in the box. He didn't even have a pet, yet he purposely kept two dog bowls and the toys he'd bought for Benny. I thought it was extremely selfish to keep the toys he'd given Benny, but Benny didn't seem to care and I just wanted to be done with Nick. This was my first Christmas with Benny, and I wasn't about to let some idiot dumping me or stealing Benny's toys ruin it for us.

And I didn't. Despite getting dumped right before Christmas— again—Benny filled my heart with so much joy and light that for the first time since my mom had passed in 2005, I didn't just go through the motions of celebrating the holidays. Benny and I started an annual tradition of having his picture taken with Santa, and we had a wonderful Christmas together, spending time with family and friends.

On Christmas morning, Benny revealed another secret to me: He was an excellent present opener. Any gift that was in front of him—whether it was his or not—he instinctively knew how to open it. He'd place one paw on it and rip the paper off with his teeth. If it was in a bag with tissue paper, he'd ram his head in the bag and pull out the loot. If it was a toy, he'd parade around the room with his head held high, squeaking it nonstop. If it was a treat, he'd immediately want to do a taste test and would tear into the bag himself. His excitement was contagious. It was like watching a child on Christmas morning.

Given that I'm a sensitive person who feels things very deeply, especially heartache and grief, and doesn't bounce back from hurt quickly, I thought I'd be more upset over the breakup with Nick than I was. But my sadness soon dissipated and turned into anger. *I am sick and tired of dating men who can't commit,* I thought to myself. *And I'm fed up with feeling like there's something wrong with me because these guys don't want me. I've had it! I'm done! I'm officially declaring my retirement from dating.*

It was actually a relief. I no longer had to go on pointless dates, where I couldn't wait to leave so I could get home to Benny. I was perfectly content with it being just Benny and me, and as I'd warned my friends who had encouraged me to get a dog four years earlier, I didn't feel the desire to go out and socialize as much. Snuggling on the couch with my little cuddle bug had become my preferred pastime. Told you so!

Chapter 7

A Most Extravagant Birthday Gift

"I'm sorry to have wasted your time," I told my realtor, Suzy, as I kicked snow off my boots before ducking into the passenger seat of her car. We'd looked at five different condos or townhomes on a Saturday afternoon, and none of them struck my fancy. I was starting to feel like Goldilocks, i.e., never satisfied.

"That's okay," Suzy assured me. "We'll find something for you."

But as she drove back to my apartment, gripping the steering wheel as snow fell in heavy clumps, I couldn't hide my frustration. "Every place we saw looked smaller than it did in the photos! What gives?"

"Some realtors or real-estate photographers use special filters or lenses to make rooms appear brighter, larger, and more appealing," Suzy explained.

"Well that's misleading," I grumbled as I gazed out the window at passing cars trying not to skid off the road. "I know I have very specific criteria for what I'm looking for, but every time we find something that seems promising online, it ends up being a huge disappointment."

"I know. But we'll find the right one for you. It just takes time."

Where have I heard that before? I groaned to myself. *Finding the right home is proving to be just as elusive as finding the right guy.*

During the summer of 2014, even before I started dating Nick, I'd been looking for a condo in Chicago. I loved my apartment and my landlords, but I wanted to own something rather than throw away money on rent every month. But it was difficult to find something even remotely comparable to my spacious apartment in my price range. And when Nick started talking about us potentially moving in together, I didn't see the point in buying my own place.

But with him out of the picture, I decided to renew my home search. Just like I had the year before when I began looking for dogs, I sat in the family room of my dad's house over Christmas vacation and started doing some online research. Only this time, Benny was squeezed in the recliner with me. But I soon realized that in order to find a place I could afford that checked all the boxes, I was going to have to make a drastic change. "Benny," I said, "I think we're gonna have to move to the burbs."

I focused my search on the northern suburbs, specifically Schaumburg, Hoffman Estates, Arlington Heights, and Evanston, if I could afford it. I found Suzy through Redfin, and in early January 2015, she and I started trekking out to the burbs on the weekends to look at places.

By late January, I'd widened my search to the southwest suburbs near where some of my friends lived. Suzy wasn't familiar with the area, so she asked her colleague Mark to accompany us. We toured five more places in one blustery, snowy afternoon, but I still hadn't found what I was looking for.

The following Thursday, I vented to my friend Sharon and told her that I was considering taking a break from the search until spring.

"Before you do that, have you looked in Hanover Park?" she asked.

"Where's that?" I'd never even heard of it.

"It's just south of the west side of Schaumburg," Sharon replied. She and her husband, Henry, lived in Elk Grove Village, the town just east of Schaumburg, and I remembered how long the drive felt whenever I'd go visit them from Chicago.

"I'll take a look," I promised, not getting my hopes up.

After Sharon and I hung up, I grabbed my laptop and started searching for places in Hanover Park. One stood out to me. It was a two-story town house with two bedrooms plus a loft that could be used as an office, two and a half bathrooms, beautiful dark hardwood floors, a gas fireplace, a deck, a two-car garage, and a walkout basement. *And* it was in my price range. Check. Check. Check. Check. Check.

I emailed Suzy right away, told her I was highly interested in seeing the place, and asked her to set up a tour for the following evening, if possible. Knowing that it was priced to sell, I had a hunch it would be under contract by the weekend.

Confident that this place was going to be Goldilocks's favorite, I emailed my mortgage broker to get a couple loan scenarios and make sure my preapproval letter was still good. I also reached out to my insurance agent for a homeowner's quote.

Suzy couldn't get me in on Friday, so she set up an appointment for the town house in Hanover Park, along with a couple others, on Saturday. But when her son unexpectedly ended up in the hospital, Mark filled in at the last minute.

My friend Sharon came along for the ride. As soon as we stepped inside the town house in Hanover Park, I knew it was the one. Unlike the other places I'd seen, the pictures actually did this one justice. In fact, the rooms seemed larger in person than they had online! However, there was one *significant* drawback. The current owner was a smoker, and the place—even the garage—reeked of cigarette smoke. I grew up with parents who smoked, and I always hated it—smoking, not my parents—likely because I had a difficult time breathing the smoke-infested air.

Nevertheless, both Mark and Sharon assured me there were products that could remove the stench, so I decided to take the plunge. The three of us sat around the homeowner's kitchen table, while Mark wrote up a full-price offer with a 3 percent credit at closing. Then I signed my name and initials about fifty times.

I was on pins and needles until the seller accepted my offer the following evening. On Monday, a five-week-long flurry of emails began between me, Mark, my mortgage guy, the inspector, my insurance agent, and my real-estate attorney (which is required in Illinois). My heart rate was in a constant state of elevation, but every time I thought about owning the place, my body tingled with excitement.

The only real stumbling block with the home purchase was when the place didn't appraise for the price I'd offered. This is a true testament to how much the real-estate bubble was still affecting housing prices in 2015. The seller had priced this gorgeous town house about fifty thousand dollars *less* than he'd paid for it in 2007, and the appraisal still came in ten grand lower.

But it all worked out in the end. We pivoted and amended the contract to drop the closing credit and lowered the offer price to match the appraised amount. It was all good in the neighborhood.

The hardest part was letting Edwin and Eva know that Benny and I were moving out. I'd lived there for almost six years, and they and their children were like family to me. They were also sad to see us go and said I was the best tenant they'd ever had.

It was also difficult for Benny and me to move away from our friends and to give up the perk of having Edwin take Benny potty when he got home from work. We'd also taken turns watching each other's dogs while we were on vacation. Not that I traveled very often, but when my niece graduated from high school in California in June 2014, Edwin and Eva had taken care of Benny for me. And when they went to Puerto Rico, I watched Bella.

Just like when I'd first moved to Chicago in 2003, leaving everyone behind wasn't going to be easy, but I felt that it was something I *had* to do. And I never really thought I'd be able to afford to own a place in the Chicago area, so this was a proud moment for me. I felt like I'd finally made it. Cue Kelly Clarkson's "Breakaway" and Mary Tyler Moore tossing her beret in the air.

For the most part, once the contract was amended, it was smooth sailing. A closing date was set for late morning on March 10—a year and a day after I brought Benny home. I'd taken the week off work to move, but as of five thirty on March 9, the title company was still waiting for the required paperwork, and the next morning, the attorney was questioning whether we were actually going to close that day. *My nerves are frazzled from all this drama,* I grumbled to myself. But ultimately, we were able to close on time.

Afterward, I picked up Benny and a load of stuff from our apartment. As we made the forty-five-minute trip to our new place in the burbs, the car was so packed to the gills that Benny had to sit under a faux ficus. He looked like he was skulking through the jungle.

As he curiously explored the new digs after we arrived, I explained to him that this was our new home and quipped, "Don't expect such an extravagant birthday gift every year."

I hired movers to load, transport, and unload the furniture and heavier boxes, but my dad and I planned to do the rest to save money. He and his fur baby, Sweetie, a miniature American Eskimo dog, arrived in his teal '94 Chevy pickup the next morning. My dad has always been hale, hearty, and handy, but on this particular day, he was dealing with some back issues, so I carried all the remaining boxes—and there were still a LOT of boxes—down the two flights of stairs and to the alley then arranged them in the covered bed of the truck while Dad supervised. After filling up a truckful and packing my car with a load, we caravanned out to the burbs. Once there, I unloaded everything while Dad wrangled Benny and Sweetie, then we headed back to the city to do it all over again two more times. By the end of the day, every part of my body ached.

Dad and Sweetie spent the next couple days with us before heading home on Friday. On Saturday morning, Benny and I made one final trip to our old apartment to clean and pick up the last of our stuff. We made it back to our new place just in time for Denise, Bernie, Angel, and Binky to arrive. Denise helped me unpack the kitchen, then we ordered pizza and had a belated birthday party for Benny.

Denise had purchased three of the same steak-shaped plush squeaky toys so each of the dogs could have one, but Benny hadn't trained her well enough yet, so she'd put them all in the same bag. Benny, the expert present opener, pulled them out of the bag one by one, and being the birthday boy, he assumed they were all for him. Denise, Bernie, and I each took one, but Benny, whirling his tail like a pinwheel blowing in the wind, hopped from cushion to cushion across the couch, collecting his cache of toys and protecting them with his paws. Eventually, he did share them with his cousins.

Benny and I quickly settled in at our new place, but by moving to the burbs, I'd added about thirty minutes each way to my commute, and I hated being away from him that long. I didn't expect him to hold it while I was gone for nine hours a day, but I couldn't afford a dog walker and we didn't know anyone who lived nearby. So after a few days of him holding it until I got home, I came up with a solution. I figured if cats could be litter box trained, so could

Benny ... sort of. I bought a plastic twelve-by-twelve-inch case intended to hold scrapbook paper, split the top from the bottom, put them on the floor, and said, "This is to do your potties in while Mommy's away." (And yes, as my dad asked, I even demonstrated to him how to use them. But I just went through the motions, I didn't actually *go* in them.) A couple days later, I came home from work to a surprise: Benny had peed in his "potty bucket." A few days after that, he pooped in the other one. *My boy is a genius!*

Even so, I put up a baby gate in the eat-in kitchen and sequestered him there. On the chance that he became frustrated, bored, or escaped and decided to get destructive, I felt there was little in the kitchen that he could actually destroy. (The door to the garage was metal and I prayed his paint-eating days were over.) But after a while, he figured out that if he pushed on the gate enough times, it would fall over. Once he realized that, most days I would come home to find the gate on the floor and Benny snoozing on the couch. For the most part, he wasn't destructive, but a few times he did take out his anger at being left alone in an unusual way.

One day, I came home from work and smelled poop, but I could not find it anywhere. Finally, later that evening, I came upon the source.

"Benny, did you poop in the fireplace?" Even with my hands on my hips and a pinched expression on my face, I had to stifle a laugh.

He gave me that innocent, doe-eyed look that said, "Not me, Mommy. Someone else must've done it."

I wish I had a security camera at the time because I would've loved to have seen him back his little rear end into the fireplace and drop his payload in there.

To keep Benny company during the day, I considered getting a cat, even though I'm allergic to certain breeds. But knowing how much Benny liked being an only child, I figured he'd rather be alone while I was away. My friend Bill suggested leaving the TV turned on and tuned in to the Animal Planet channel, but that only made Benny more anxious. Perhaps scenes of lions and tigers ripping apart their prey in sub-Saharan Africa was too frightening for him. Luckily, I soon learned that he found Steve Harvey's voice comforting, so whenever I'd leave, I'd put on the Game Show

Network so he could listen to the soothing sounds of Steve Harvey on *Family Feud*.

Although this generally appeased Benny, it didn't make leaving him any easier for me. Every morning when I'd hop on the Metra, about five minutes from our house, I'd rest my head on the window of the train car and gaze longingly toward home with tears in my eyes and a tightness in my chest as we pulled out of the station. Wondering if he was lonely and not knowing how he was doing amped up my anxiety, so it wasn't long before I invested in a "Benny cam" with two-way audio, which allowed me to check on him throughout the day. For the most part, whenever I tuned in, he was sleeping or sitting quietly in his bed, but if he was barking or howling, I would speak to him through the app on my phone and say, "Benny, calm down. Mommy will be home soon." He'd often give an aggravated grumble then settle back down, but his ear-piercing outbursts earned him the nickname Howler Monkey.

From the start, Benny was skeptical about the hardwood stairs leading to the second floor of our town house, as well as those going to the basement. In fact, something must've traumatized him early in life because I'm pretty sure he had a fear of heights. When we lived in the city, he'd refused to walk up the stairs to our second-floor abode, and whenever I'd hold him while standing on a balcony or any space high off the ground, he'd quiver and cling to me tightly with his legs wrapped around my waist and his claws digging into the back of my shoulders. At our new place, he tried to get over his fear, but when he took a tumble down the stairs a few weeks after we moved in, he started putting on the brakes whenever he was expected to navigate them on his own. After that incident, I was happy to carry him.

Benny quickly adapted to his new surroundings. He also made friends much easier than I did. On our first walk around the block, we met Salvatori (Sal for short) and Jimmy—a bichon and a bichon-Lhasa apso mix—and their dad, Louie. Later, when I met their mom, Francine, we bonded over our shared love of New Kids on the Block and *Long Island Medium*.

Soon, Benny had befriended a Westie named Baxter; Chewee, a shih tzu; another Baxter, a dachshund; and Bentley, a mixed breed who was slightly taller than Benny, but they still got along.

A long-haired dachshund named Zed lived a couple doors down, but he had a habit of sticking his nose where it didn't belong, and Benny did NOT appreciate the intrusion. Although small dogs were plentiful in our neighborhood, most of them were male. Benny didn't seem to mind, though. Maybe he was lovesick over having to move away from Lily.

Unlike Benny, I did not make friends in the burbs as easily. As a single woman, the only people in our subdivision who would talk to me were our next-door neighbors and other dog parents. Occasionally, children would stop to say how cute Benny was and tell me he looked like the animated dog Bolt. An elementary-school-aged boy named Raj always wanted to pet Benny whenever we'd stroll past his house. He desperately wanted a dog, but his parents wouldn't allow it. One time, he asked me, "How long do dogs live?"

"Well, they used to say that dogs age seven years for every human year," I explained. "But it varies depending on the breed and size of the dog. In fact, I got a dog when I was about your age, and he lived to be twenty-one! But that was highly unusual."

Raj's face lit up when he heard that. "When I grow up, I'm going to invent a serum that helps dogs live to be fifty!"

I hope Raj is working on that now.

After a few months living in the burbs, Chewee and his dad, Jerry, became our walking buddies, and we'd often stop at Baxter the dachshund's house, where Chewee and the B-Boys—Benny, Baxter, and Bentley (who lived next door)—would sniff each other, play, and roll in the grass while the parents chatted.

The other thing we had an abundance of in our new neighborhood was squirrels, which made Benny happy. Every time he'd catch sight of one of the little varmints mindlessly collecting nuts, he'd take off mushing like a sled dog, pulling me behind. After chasing a squirrel up a tree, he'd jump up and down on his hind legs, his front paws digging into the bark, while he hopped sideways, circling the tree. He'd make such a ruckus with his high-pitched squeal that he sounded like he was being tortured or had been injured.

"Benny, calm down," I'd say, my eyes darting around to see if anyone was staring at us with judgment in their eyes. "People are going to think I'm abusing you!"

Ironically, considering his primal disdain for small wild creatures, early on, Benny was dubbed Bunny or Buns for short. It started off innocently enough as I attempted to call him "Benny" and "buddy" at the same time, and the two words blended together. Fortunately, he didn't seem to mind being called Bunny, even though it was the word for one of his nemeses.

In late May, I was coming home from getting groceries when I noticed a garage sale on a side street in our neighborhood. It's rare that I hit up garage sales, but as I was driving by, I noticed a fold-up Snoopy stroller that I thought would be perfect for Benny—if it fit him and he'd sit in it. I stopped and told the owner I was interested and would be right back.

For a while, I'd been considering getting Benny some wheels. We were planning to attend a few festivals that summer, and I knew he wouldn't want to walk the entire time, nor did I want him to on hot pavement. Perhaps it was because I treated him as such, but he really did act more like a human child than a dog, and once he got tuckered out, he wanted to be carried. But fifteen pounds can start to feel heavy after lugging it around for a while, so I figured I'd give the stroller a shot.

Five minutes later, I returned with Benny in tow. When I placed him in the stroller, he sat nicely like the good little boy that he was. I paid the homeowner the five dollars she was asking for it, and we headed home, Benny contentedly riding in the stroller and likely thinking, *Boy, have I trained her well! I've got it made in the shade.*

The Snoopy stroller was a win-win because it enabled us to stay outside longer without Benny stopping every five feet to sniff or pee on a tree. After doing his business, he'd put his front paws on the seat, which was his way of asking for a boost. We got some funny looks, but Benny would ride with pride. And we definitely got our five-bucks worth out of it.

That summer, Benny and I attended the Long Grove Strawberry Festival with Denise, Bernie, Angel, Binky, and Little Lady, their first foster dog. Denise had a wagon for her three little ones, but

Benny preferred the solitude of his Snoopy stroller. He confidently rolled along with a smile on his face, knowing how special he was that he didn't have to walk in the heat and humidity.

Before Benny came into my life, I used to love going for long bike rides. I'd spend a couple hours riding along the river near my neighborhood and occasionally head over to the path that hugs Lake Michigan. For a couple summers, I even rode my bike to work. But as I'd predicted, after adopting Benny, I didn't want to do those things because I didn't want to be away from him, especially after I'd been at work all day. So, in the summer of 2014, when I saw a woman towing her two dogs in a bicycle trailer, I had an epiphany.

Knowing how calm and relaxed Benny was as long as he was with me (people always described him as "chill"), I figured he'd take right to the bike trailer. So while we still lived in Chicago, I purchased a pretty aqua blue one that matched my bicycle. At the time, we lived only two blocks from a park with an awesome bike and walking path, so I had high hopes that Benny and I could take long rides together. Unfortunately, Benny didn't share that vision.

We couldn't even make it the two blocks to the park without him wailing like a banshee. I figured maybe it was because, sitting that close to the ground, the ride was too bumpy, so I placed his four-inch-thick foam bed in the trailer with a plush blanket on top of it, but he still cried. Then it occurred to me that he might be afraid of the cars (which were mostly parked along the curb) as we made our way to the park, so I started riding on the sidewalk, but he still wasn't a happy camper. Considering that perhaps he was claustrophobic, I removed the sun cover so he could get more ventilation and see more of his surroundings. (There was still a mesh cover over him, so he couldn't jump out.) But that didn't work either. I even tried going just short distances to get him acclimated. That seemed to work for a bit, but eventually, he'd start howling again. After trying for a month or so, I gave up.

During the summer of 2015, I decided to give it another go. Although there hadn't been a lot of traffic on the roads leading to the park in Chicago, there had been a lot of parked cars, so I thought maybe that's what had spooked Benny. Our neighborhood in the burbs was much quieter, so we started again with very short distances. At first it seemed to work, but after I'd pick up some speed, he would freak out. I ended up riding by myself and leaving Benny at home, and he seemed okay with that. I never did figure out what his aversion to the trailer was, though, because he loved riding in the car and in his stroller.

In October 2015, for our first Halloween in our new town, Benny and I dressed in complimentary costumes—him as Superdog and me as Supergirl—to hand out candy to trick-or-treaters. We hadn't dressed up the year before because when Denise loaned me some costumes for Benny to try, he looked at me like he was plotting to kill me in my sleep. But he didn't have a problem with the Superdog outfit. And when I entered us in a contest, we won first prize for Best Owner and Dog costume, which garnered us quite a bag of swag.

Over time, Benny actually came to like wearing clothes because he realized they kept him warm and (mostly) prevented him from getting wet in the dreaded rain. For someone who we often joked looked like a baby polar bear, Benny did not like being cold. As a result, over time, he accumulated a substantial wardrobe. Eventually, every day from October to April, he sported some article of clothing, including pajamas and a parka for the wintertime, a bathrobe to keep him warm after his baths, which we called tubbies, and an assortment of T-shirts, sweaters, and sweatshirts, of which his Mommy's Boy hoodie was his favorite.

After Christmas, my dad and Sweetie followed Benny and me home to help with some handyman projects, like assembling the elliptical machine I'd purchased. We had a lot of laughs and it was a nice change of pace having my dad stay at my place, since I was always going back to Michigan to visit him.

Three weeks later, my dad called while I was driving to the grocery store. I could barely understand what he was saying because he was sobbing, but I finally gleaned that Sweetie had passed away. I was in shock. We'd just seen her, and she seemed fine. She'd slowed down a bit in the past couple years, but it was difficult to say whether that was actually her being slower or Benny being younger and running circles around her.

My dad got choked up as he recounted what had happened. "We came back into the garage after being out in the yard," he said. "I saw her come in, so I pressed the button to lower the garage door. But then she must've ran out, and for some reason, the garage door didn't stop when she crossed its path. It continued going down and pinned her to the ground. I didn't know it happened until she started yelping. I pushed the button again and the door went up, but she was in a lot of pain, so I rushed her to the vet."

The vet was only about five minutes away, and they immediately took scans and ran some tests. "The vet said that, physically, Sweetie was fine from the garage door accident," my dad continued, "but the scans showed she was full of cancer." The vet told my dad that it was only a matter of time before the cancer would kill her, and it would likely be a painful death, so my dad made the very difficult decision to let her go.

"Oh my God, Dad! I'm so sorry." My heart broke for him as we cried together over the phone. After losing my mom to cancer in 2005, Sweetie was his constant companion. And although he'd found love again, marrying a kind woman named Waunita in 2011, their romance was cut short when she died of cancer two months before their second wedding anniversary. Sweetie had been there to offer him comfort and solace when he lost two wives, but now she was gone too.

Sweetie had been part of our family for almost thirteen years, so we all felt her loss. For me, it conjured memories of losing Arnold. I clung to Benny a little tighter but refused to even consider that someday I would lose him. I just prayed that somebody was already hard at work on Raj's special serum so Benny would live to be fifty.

Benny and Sweetie were kind of like siblings with an eight-year age difference. They simply tolerated each other and kept to themselves. However, the first time we visited my dad after Sweetie's passing, Benny searched every room in the house looking for her. Although he and Sweetie weren't exactly close, he definitely missed having her around, especially when my dad and I would go somewhere. Benny was used to having Sweetie there to keep him company, but suddenly he found himself all alone, without the watchful eye of his "big sister." But it wouldn't be long before another sister became a prodigious part of our lives.

Chapter 8

Benny Goes to School

"It'll be okay," Lori reassured me. "We'll talk every week, and I'll be home for Christmas before you know it."

"Please don't go," I begged, tears streaming down my face. My young heart was breaking at the thought of my big sister—my second mom—leaving home.

"I have to," Lori said, holding back her own tears. "But I'll be back. I promise."

In June 1980, shortly after she graduated from high school, my sister Lori caught a travel bug—and a bus—and moved to California. I was two months shy of my eighth birthday, and with all my siblings living on their own, I essentially became an only child. I always wished Lori would move back home, but she didn't. And when she got married and started having children in the mid-1990s, I gave up hope.

But her husband began to show his true colors when the children were young. He was immature, selfish, narcissistic, and was often verbally, emotionally, and sometimes physically abusive to my sister. It was a toxic environment for my niece and nephew to grow up in, but whenever Lori would talk about leaving him, he'd threaten her physically and tell her he'd take the kids and she'd never see them again. If Denise, our mom, and I had known how dire the situation was, we would've all driven out there and moved her back. But Lori never let on that it was that bad.

Lori stayed with her husband for way too long, but in early 2016, on their twentieth anniversary, she informed him that she wanted a divorce. This time, he conceded.

When Lori called to tell me she was leaving her husband, she gave me the surprise of a lifetime when she said, "I'm thinking of moving to Chicago. Can the kids and I stay with you until we find our own place?"

I had an extra bedroom and a full but unfinished basement, so I said, "Of course!"

She stuck it out for five more months until her son graduated from high school. In mid-June, Denise flew out to the Bay Area and helped Lori and my niece and nephew load up a U-Haul. Then the four of them made the twenty-one-hundred-mile cross-country trek to my place.

Although Benny had met his Aunt Lori and his cousins before, he still played the shy guy role when they arrived. But when we started unloading boxes, he looked at me like, "Uh … Mom … What the heck is going on?" However, he quickly adapted to our new housemates, especially Aunt Lori, who, as she had been for me, became like a second mom to him.

Lori got home from work before I did, and until they started classes in the fall, my niece and nephew were home all day, so Benny had live-in dog walkers and no longer had to rely on Steve Harvey to babysit. I would simply place Benny in bed with my niece when I left for work, and he and I were no longer filled with anxiety during the day.

During the spring of 2016, shortly before Lori and the kids moved in, I signed Benny up for obedience classes at a local pet store. He was extremely well-behaved, so he didn't really need them, but I'd heard about a program called Paws & Read, where children who are reluctant readers can read to therapy dogs at the local library. Reading to a classroom of their peers often causes children anxiety, but reading to a dog helps them relax and gain confidence in their abilities. I was living proof of the calming effects a dog can have on an anxious human, and because I worked for a children's book publisher, it seemed like a perfect fit for Benny and me to volunteer and help foster a love of reading at the same time. However, the catch was that Benny had to be a licensed therapy dog first, and that required taking a series of three obedience classes and then passing a certification exam.

Attending the classes with Benny was the highlight of my week. He was smart and eager to learn new things, and I enjoyed practicing with him. He especially liked that he got treats for doing what he was told. The level one adult class was easy-peasy—except the night Cathy, Benny's teacher, decided to throw in some agility training just for fun. Benny made it halfway through one of those nylon tunnels, then just decided to sit down and hang out there for a while.

"C'mon, Buns," I coaxed, offering a handful of bite-size training treats. When that didn't work, I used the deep, stern voice I'd learned in class, "Benny, come!" But he still wouldn't budge. So, in order for the other students to give it a try, I had to crawl inside the tunnel and bring him out.

The tunnel incident notwithstanding, Benny passed level one with flying colors at the end of May. He received a certificate and got to pose for photos in a graduation cap. We immediately signed up for the level two class, which began a couple weeks later.

For Benny, the most difficult part of level two was the "stay" command because he really didn't want to let me out of his sight. But in order to pass the class, he had to stay seated with Cathy while I walked out of sight for a full minute. We really had to step up our game and practice at home in order for him to master that one.

"Stay ... Stay ... Stay," I'd say repeatedly, holding up my hand like I was one of the Supremes performing "Stop! In the Name of Love" as I gradually stepped farther away from Benny. But the longest he could hold the position was about thirty seconds or ten steps. We were going through so many training treats that I started offering him some of his favorite veggies instead.

At the end of July, Lori, Benny, and I hopped in my new Ford Escape and headed to the pet store for the level two exam. While we were sitting at a stop sign, waiting to turn out of our subdivision, Benny, who was riding in the back seat, nimbly balanced his front paws on the console and looked eagerly at both of us, radiating excitement with a smile on his face. Just then, a texting teenager rear-ended us. The damage was minimal, but the hit was hard enough that Benny flew from the back seat to the front. As he soared through the air, I grabbed him just before his nose smacked the dashboard. I was livid and let the teenager know that he needed to get off his damn phone and pay attention.

I wanted a police report done, so I called Cathy and told her we'd be late. She was just glad we were all okay and told us to take our time. By the time we arrived at the pet store and began the exam, my hands were still shaking from the adrenaline coursing through my veins following the accident. On top of that, I had butterflies flitting through my stomach, wondering if Benny would be able to sit still and stay with Cathy while I walked away for the seemingly never-ending sixty seconds. Before we began, I inhaled deeply and exhaled slowly several times to calm my nerves. Being the good boy that he was, Benny sat politely with Cathy and just stared up at her while I was gone. He never ceased to amaze me. After passing once again, he got his diploma and I, the proud mommy, posed for photos with my little graduate wearing a mortarboard.

After passing each of his classes, I let Benny pick out a new toy as a graduation gift. But this time, he got a second present: a seat belt. From then on, he always rode in the back seat with his seat belt attached to his harness—never to his collar. Safety first.

Benny still had one more class to take before he could even attempt the AKC Canine Good Citizen test, which was a prerequisite for becoming a licensed therapy dog. Thus far, Benny was able to easily master most of the ten requirements of the AKC test, which includes accepting a friendly stranger, sitting politely for petting, walking through a crowd, behaving politely around other dogs, and walking on a loose leash (i.e., not pulling). The latter was a cinch for him because, fortunately, there were no squirrels scampering around the pet store.

But he definitely needed more practice with "supervised separation" from me, coming when called, and "sit, down, and stay." He'd performed those skills to pass level two, but for level three and the AKC test, he had to master them without being bribed with treats and the supervised separation was extended to three minutes, which, to Benny, might as well have been three hours.

We decided to take off the rest of the summer to work on those subject areas at home. But during our practice sessions when I'd call his name and ask him to come, he seemed to ignore me. And when I stood behind him and called his name, he didn't flinch. Then it dawned on me: *I don't think he can hear me.* He'd somehow learned the hand signals we used in class—perhaps from watching his classmates—but when I used only verbal cues, he remained as still as a statue.

Hearing loss also explained why, despite his many sensitivities, he wasn't afraid of thunder or fireworks and he never barked when the doorbell rang. I just assumed he could hear the doorbell but wasn't much of a barker. After all, he'd accompany me to the door. But maybe that was less about him hearing the doorbell and more about him being my shadow.

We always planned to go back to school and get his certification as a therapy dog, but life got in the way and, sadly, Benny became an obedience school dropout. It's one of my biggest regrets in life because I feel that he really could've made an impact on children and adults alike.

Chapter 9

Accepting My Fate

It was early December 2016, and I was sporting a well-worn gown, sitting on a paper sheet in the cold room of my gynecologist's office. I stared out the window, watching snowflakes gently fall to the ground, and rubbed my arms to keep warm. But it was of no help; I was numb from the earth-shattering news the doctor had just delivered.

Back in September, I began having stomach issues. At first I thought it was just stress and anxiety over my beloved Cubs' run for the postseason, but when it persisted after they won the World Series, I made an appointment with a gastroenterologist. He ran some tests and did an ultrasound of my belly but couldn't find anything that would be causing my issues. Ultimately, it was determined that my tummy troubles were a side effect of a medication I was taking. As soon as I stopped taking the medication, my tummy settled down.

However, when the gastroenterologist reviewed my ultrasound, he noticed something in my uterus and recommended that I follow up with my gynecologist as soon as possible. Her first available appointment was in early December.

After running more tests and performing additional ultrasounds, she concluded that I had a large fibroid tumor in my uterus. She felt it was benign but recommended a hysterectomy. I was forty-four years old, single, and, by my own choosing, hadn't been on a date in two years. But even though I knew my window for having children was closing, I wasn't ready to slam it shut.

"What if I wait and then a couple years down the road, I get pregnant?" My voice cracked as I tried to make sense of what I'd just been told.

"The fibroid is about the size of a six-month fetus, so it's extremely unlikely that you'd be able to carry a baby to full-term," the doctor explained. "With the fibroid, there's just not enough room for it *and* a baby. I'm sorry. . . . I know this isn't what you wanted to hear."

"Can't you just remove the fibroid or break it up with a laser or something without taking out my uterus?" I swallowed deeply to suppress the lump forming in my throat.

"Unfortunately, due to its size and the way it's attached to your uterus, that simply wouldn't work."

I trusted her expertise, so we scheduled the surgery for mid-January 2017. I held it together inside the doctor's office, but as soon as I got in my vehicle, my eyes exploded with tears as my life flashed before my eyes. For as long as I could remember, all I ever wanted out of life was to get married and have children. Between me and my sisters, I was probably the one who wanted children the most. I played with dolls longer than most children—I was eleven when I received a Cabbage Patch Kid for Christmas—and until I began working as a book editor and found my true career calling, I always pictured myself being content as a stay-at-home mom. I know I didn't help my cause by taking a six-year break from dating after my mom was diagnosed with and then passed away from cancer, but I simply wasn't in the right frame of mind to put myself out there to try to find someone. Suddenly, I wished I could turn back the clock and get back all the time I'd wasted.

As I drove home from the doctor's office, I recalled the many conversations I'd had over the years with my dear friend Dr. Bob. Despite a forty-five-year age difference, we became friends in 2000, after meeting at church when I still lived in South Bend. In many ways, he was like a second father to me.

"How will you feel if you don't end up having children?" Dr. Bob often asked during our deep and profound conversations, which is something I never had with my own father. He knew of my desire to marry my soulmate and raise a family, but he also recognized that I wasn't doing much to make that happen and the clock was ticking. If it was true that God helps those who help themselves, I was screwed.

"I guess I would feel like my life would be incomplete."

"But what if it's not in God's plan for you to have children?"

"If I can't be a wife and a mother, then what am I even doing here?" I'd reply, tears welling in my eyes.

At this point in my life, I'd already accepted that I likely wasn't going to have children, but to have someone make that decision for me and for it to happen so unexpectedly sent me into a depressive funk that would take months for me to surface from.

Following the surgery, I spent two nights in the hospital, and even though I knew Benny was in good hands with Lori, it was torture being away from him. It must've been difficult for him too because when I came home, whether I was lying in bed or on the couch, he attached himself to my hip. He was my constant companion and source of emotional support, and I'm convinced he had special healing powers.

The surgery went well, but my recovery was a different story. My entire torso was an inflamed, beet red patch of bumps that I couldn't stop scratching because, despite the fact that I'd informed the surgeon of my allergies to nickel, chromium, and stainless steel—the main components in needles and surgical staples—she still used staples to close my wound. My midsection was angry, painful, and just downright ugly. It looked like I had the measles. And because she used staples, I was left with an inch-wide scar that ran from my belly button to my pubic bone. It was so bad that in the fall, my insurance company agreed to pay for scar revision surgery with a plastic surgeon.

Lucky for me, my sister Lori is a nurse, and she was between jobs when I had my surgery, so I had my own, in-home Florence Nightingale taking care of me. For several weeks, I was unable to lift more than ten pounds, which meant she had to carry Benny up and down the stairs. She also did all the cooking and tended to my nasty wound, but she actually enjoys that gross stuff.

I was off work for several weeks recovering, and through it all, Benny was right by my side. Being at home not only allowed me time to heal physically, it also helped me heal emotionally from the realization that I would never have children. Sure, I experienced regret and moments of anger that I wasn't able to have children, but thanks to Benny's constant presence and long talks with my sisters, a sense of acceptance and gratitude washed over me. I couldn't imagine having a human child who was better behaved than Benny and who loved me unconditionally like he did. He made me laugh and smile and filled my life with joy each and every day, and I knew he'd never outgrow me or become embarrassed to be seen with me as teenagers often do with their parents. Benny wanted to be with me wherever I went, and the feeling was mutual. I got all that for $150, and I didn't have to endure morning sickness, nine months of pregnancy, and hours of excruciating labor. But very soon, my life would take an unexpected twist that would make me wish I'd gotten a second opinion before having the hysterectomy or at least opted to freeze my eggs.

Chapter 10

God Laughs When We Make Plans

While I was at home recovering from my surgery, the publishing company where I worked, which is headquartered in Minnesota, moved the Chicago employees to a coworking space. Within six months, we moved again, this time to a WeWork location a few blocks away. The silver lining of these moves was that we were allowed to work from home if we wanted to, as long as our managers approved. My boss was fine with it as long as we got our work done, but she did request that we go into the office for monthly team meetings. I was overjoyed with the new arrangement because it meant I could do my work with Benny by my side, and even though the coworking spaces weren't as comfy and cozy as our office had been, they were pet-friendly, so whenever I went in for monthly meetings, I'd drive so Benny could come with me. He loved going into the office, and my coworkers all doted on him as if he were the company mascot.

Because I could now work remotely, Benny and I went to visit my dad over Memorial Day weekend, then worked there during the week. I took Friday off and on our way back home, Benny and I stopped to visit Dr. Bob, who was celebrating his ninetieth birthday that day. He was having a birthday bash the next day, but for months I'd had tickets to see U2 at Soldier Field, and—knowing my deep love for the band—Dr. Bob didn't want me missing the concert.

After Benny and I got home, I unpacked, did a quick load of laundry, and repacked my bag. My best friend, Margaret, was coming to town for the U2 concerts that weekend, and she insisted on having a room (and a proper bathroom) within walking distance or a short cab ride from the venue, so she'd made a reservation at a downtown hotel. I planned to stay with her on Saturday night, but I didn't want to leave Benny for more than one sleep, so after meeting her downtown to get numbers scrawled on our hands, I drove back to the burbs and slept in my own bed.

If you're wondering why I drove all the way into the city to have a number penned on my hand, there's an unwritten rule or code of honor among U2 fans who have general admission (GA) tickets. At each show, a line monitor—typically the first person to queue up—comes bearing a notebook and a couple Sharpies. They write their name in the number one slot in the notebook and place a "1" on their hand to denote that they are the first person in line. As other fans arrive, they check in and are assigned a number. This has been accepted policy among the U2 faithful (and probably other bands too) for show after show, tour after tour, so the venue security guards typically go along with it. And so, around four o'clock on the afternoon of Friday, June 2, 2017, Margaret and I checked in and had numbers 129 and 130 inked on our hands. After we ate dinner, I drove home and went to bed early because the first check-in the next day was at 5:00 a.m.

On Saturday morning, I parked my new Ford Escape, affectionately known as Ruby, in a garage near Margaret's hotel, took a ride-share to Soldier Field, and met Margaret a few minutes before attendance was taken. We were given instructions on where the City of Chicago and Soldier Field would allow us to camp out, so we staked our claim, set up our chairs, and made a day of it. Some people might find this boring, but the time flies and it's actually quite fun when you don't get to see your bestie as often as you'd like. We were never at a loss for things to talk about, and, as Margaret always said, I typically made a new friend or two with those camped nearby. My shyness magically disappears when I'm around my U2 brethren.

Our friend Scott arrived later in the afternoon, got his number, and joined us. He couldn't get away from work the day before, so he was content being farther back in the line. He's tall, so he usually has an unobstructed view even if someone shorter, like me, is standing in front of him.

As is typical of any U2 concert, the show was amazing, so I won't go into detail. We had GA tickets for the next night too, so as soon as the show ended, we hustled out of the stadium and queued up to get our numbers for Sunday's show.

Margaret got to the line first, and when I arrived, she said, "Mike's looking for you. I think he's over there." She pointed to a grove of trees outside the tunnel where we had congregated.

"Okay," I said. "I'll find him after I get my number."

Mike is a U2 fan from California that I met in a GA line in Milwaukee in September 2005. We kept in touch, became friends, and saw each other at U2 concerts. Over the years, he became friends with Margaret and Scott too.

After getting some fresh ink on the back of my other hand, I made my way over to the spot Margaret had pointed out, where I found Mike sitting on a large boulder with another guy. Big Mike (his nickname for himself because he's six-four and weighed over 350 pounds at the time) stood up and engulfed my five-foot-four-inch frame in a bear hug. "This is my friend Brad," he said by way of introduction.

After Brad and I greeted each other, I looked at him quizzically and said, "Have we met before?"

"I don't think so," Brad replied.

A few minutes later, Margaret and Scott joined our little group. The three of us had to be back at the GA line for roll call at 5:00 a.m., so Margaret was anxious to return to the hotel and get some rest. But with the sound of the bass still thrumming in my ears and the intense energy from the show reverberating through-out my body, I was too wired to sleep. Plus I wanted to spend some time with Mike, whom I hadn't seen since the U2 concerts in Chicago in 2011, so he convinced me to grab a bite to eat with him and Brad.

As Margaret and Scott headed back to the hotel, Mike, Brad, and I waited in line to board a bus to get us closer to the bars and restaurants along Michigan Avenue. It would've been faster to walk, but Mike was dealing with some health issues, so it was better for him if we rode the bus. While we waited what seemed like an hour to catch a bus, the three of us chatted. I learned that

Brad lived in Indianapolis, so at one point, I casually asked him where he was staying that night. It was a simple question, so when he just stared at me blankly for a few moments of awkward silence, I quipped, "Are you drunk?"

"Uh ... no," he mumbled. "I had a few beers at the show, but I'm not drunk."

I just nodded and smiled skeptically. I've never been much of a drinker because my brother, Steve, struggled with alcoholism, so if Brad was drunk, I wasn't impressed.

Finally, the three of us boarded a "bendy" bus, one of those extra-long buses with an accordion-like bellows in the middle, which enables the vehicle to swiftly navigate turns on city streets. By the time we boarded, the only three seats left together were located inside the bellows, along the joint where the bus bends when turning a corner. Mike and I sat facing forward, while Brad's seat, which was directly in front of us, faced sideways. So every time the bus made a turn, he would move with it, either swiveling toward us or away from us, depending on whether the bus was turning right or left. It was comical every time his seat pivoted, however that, combined with the din of a densely packed city bus full of concertgoers, made conversation difficult, but we tried.

Somewhere along the way, Brad felt inclined to punch up the conversation by saying, "By the way, I hate your city." Then he rotated away from me as the bus made a left turn.

As the bus righted itself and Brad sprang back toward me, I raised my eyebrows, looked at him wide-eyed, and was momentarily speechless. Then I said, "Oh ... uh ... okay. Why do you hate Chicago?"

"I used to date a girl who lives here." End of story.

Between me thinking Brad was drunk and him saying he hated my city, the two of us were getting off to a magnificent start.

After winding through the Museum Campus, along the northern end of Soldier Field, the bus headed north on Lakeshore Drive before making a left onto Roosevelt Road. It didn't stop at Michigan Avenue, so we got off on Wabash, just one block west. We started walking north, but every bar we came to was either packed or no longer serving food, so we kept plodding ahead.

Eventually, we found a spot that wasn't overly crowded. However, they were no longer serving food. Even so, Brad went in to find us a seat. As Mike and I waited outside, I decided to bail.

"I've been up for almost twenty-two hours, and I have to be back at Soldier Field in about four hours, so I'm gonna head back to the hotel," I told Mike.

"I need to get something to eat, and my hotel is on the way, so I'll walk with you," Mike offered.

"Okay, but shouldn't you tell Brad we're leaving?"

"Nah," Mike replied. "He'll figure it out."

"Well, that's kinda rude," I teased.

"Fine. I'll text him," Mike reluctantly agreed.

I still didn't think it was very nice of us to ditch Brad, but Mike knew him better than I did, so off we went. I was too tired to worry about Brad and figured he was a big boy and could find his way back to wherever he was staying.

When I got to Margaret's hotel room, I crawled over Scott, who—being the Southern gentleman that he is—left me the second bed and was snoozing on an air mattress on the floor. When the alarm clock went off a few hours later, my head was throbbing from lack of sleep, but I dragged myself out of bed and got ready for another day in the GA line. Bleary-eyed, the three of us took a ride-share to Soldier Field and arrived in time for the 5:00 a.m. rallying of the troops.

With our position in the queue secured, we were able to come and go as we pleased as long as we were there for the next check-in at four. So when Mike texted and asked if I wanted to meet for lunch, I said yes. Margaret had to check out of the hotel by noon and Mike was staying at my place that night, so he and I met at the parking garage and placed our luggage in Ruby.

While we were meandering down the street, looking for a place to eat, Mike said, "Sooo . . . Brad thinks you're cute."

Despite thinking he was drunk the night before, I also thought Brad was cute. He was tall and slender with dark hair, baby blue eyes, and a sly smile, plus he made me laugh, which was always a plus. "I think he's cute too," I told Mike, feeling a bit like we were in junior high. "But I'm pretty sure I've met him before. Didn't you run into him in Cleveland when you, me, and Margaret went out after the concert in 2005?"

"Oh, yeah. You're right," Mike confirmed. "You two *have* met before."

"I thought so," I said. "And back then, after you introduced us, you told me he thought I was cute and I said he was too, but you told me he was kind of a player, so I didn't want anything to do with him."

"Yeah, I remember that," Mike replied, "but that was almost twelve years ago. Hopefully, he's grown up by now."

"Maybe," I shrugged.

"Well, he texted me a little while ago about getting together after the show," Mike continued. "He said to ask you to come along. I can guarantee he's more interested in seeing you than he is me. You wanna join us?"

"I guess," I begrudgingly agreed, but I wasn't getting my hopes up. With my track record of dating guys who were commitment-phobic, I was reluctant to give my heart to anyone. In fact, I said precisely that a few hours later.

By four o'clock, those of us with GA tickets were back at Soldier Field, ready to move when security mustered us. Due to the scorching temperatures that day, security moved the U2 faithful inside to avoid the heat. Margaret, Scott, and I were sitting on the cold, hard, concrete floor, sequestered in the underbelly of Soldier Field, when Margaret and I delicately brought up a subject with Scott that we were curious about. We didn't want to upset him, but we wanted to ask about his dating life.

In 2013, Scott had gone through a divorce that left him heart-broken and, from our viewpoint, a bit gun-shy about getting back out there. Yes, we were curious, but more importantly, we were concerned for him because he didn't seem to be moving on from his ex. So we carefully broached the subject.

"So, Scott ...," I mumbled hesitantly, having drawn the short straw, "are you dating anyone?"

"Nah ...," he said with a half-hearted laugh, "between work and training for marathons and Ironmans, I don't have time for a relationship." Then, as if we were kids playing a game of hot potato, he tossed the ball to me. "What about you, Jen? Are you dating anyone?"

"Me ... ? Uh ... no," I stammered. "After Tommy and Nick and all the others, I'm tired of guys who can't commit, so I'm offi-cially retired from dating. And I'm completely content with that decision. Relationships just don't seem worth it. I mean, a few weeks or months of happiness aren't worth all the heartache and tears that follow when the relationship ends. Now that it's just me and Benny, I'm much happier and more relaxed. He fills my life with so much joy that I literally have no desire to date."

I'm not sure they believed me, but it was the God's honest truth. However, there's an old saying that goes something like: "If you want to make God laugh, make plans." Surely, he (or she) was looking down at me and having a good chuckle.

Once we were allowed to leave the bowels of Soldier Field and make our way to the GA floor, Margaret, Scott, and I staked our space in the front row, right in front of U2 bassist Adam Clayton. After the show, Margaret and Scott headed home to South Bend, and I met up with Mike and Brad. Since it was after midnight on a Sunday, we didn't bother trying to find a place where we could get something to eat right in the heart of things. Instead, we all hopped into Ruby and I drove us to the Golden Nugget, an all-night, hole-in-the-wall diner in my old stomping grounds.

"Why is there a blanket on the seat?" Brad asked as he crawled into the back seat.

"That's Benny's," I informed him.

"Who's Benny?" Brad inquired.

"My baby boy," I said.

"Oh. ... Do I have to sit on it?"

"Not unless you shed or plan to pee on the seat." Benny had never peed in the car; I was just trying to be funny.

"I'll try to hold it until we get to the restaurant," Brad retorted.

I think Brad thought I had a kid, so I showed him Benny's picture and explained that he was the best little boy in the world.

When we got to the diner, it was a relief to find the place almost empty. I really didn't want to try to have a conversation with my longtime friend or this new guy in a crowded bar. Mike took one side of the booth, and after I scooted into the other side, Brad squeezed in next to me.

We all ordered breakfast and had a ton of fun, sharing U2 stories and just talking. Despite the awkwardness of the previous night, I felt completely at ease around Brad, and we chatted and joked as if we'd known each other for years.

By this time, the U2 children's book I'd been writing when I adopted Benny had been published, so I gave Mike a signed copy. Intrigued and impressed, Brad asked if he could get a signed copy too. I said I could probably arrange that. I also mentioned that Margaret, Scott, and I were contemplating going to the Louisville show on June 16, which had just been added to the tour, and asked if Brad was going since it's much closer to Indy than Chicago. He said he hadn't really thought about it.

Later in the conversation, Mike told a story about a friend of his who'd had a heart attack, so I attempted to ask a simple question, but I was so slaphappy from lack of sleep over the weekend that I flubbed my lines.

"So, did your friend who had the fart attack die?" As soon as the words escaped my mouth, I realized what I'd said and lapsed into a giggle fit that left me laughing and crying nonstop for about five minutes. Brad and Mike laughed along too, but whether they were laughing at my faux pas or just because I was, I don't know.

When it was time to go, I offered to drop off Brad at his hotel, but he insisted on taking a cab. He gave me a brief and slightly awkward hug before he left. I thought we'd hit it off really well, but he didn't ask for my number or suggest we keep in touch. My heart sank a little, but I was determined not to let it bother me. *It's fine. I'm retired from dating and completely content with my solo status,* I reminded myself.

The next day, Mike had an evening flight back to LA, so we drove into the city and took a boat ride on Lake Michigan. Overnight, a cold front had rolled in, so in stark contrast to the sunny skies and sweltering temps the day before, this day was freezing! I'd worn capris and a jean jacket over my top, but I was still shivering. Mike was kind enough to lend me his sweatshirt, but as the boat rocked and keeled through the fog on this cloudy day, I was reminded of what Mark Twain supposedly said: "The coldest winter I ever spent was a summer in San Francisco." *Surely, it must apply to Chicago as well*, I thought as I sipped a hot chocolate—IN JUNE!

After the boat ride, we explored the city a bit before heading up to Evanston. I had a hankering for a turkey burger, onion rings, and a Diet Coke, so I took Mike to the Celtic Knot, one of my favorite Irish pubs in the Chicago area. Throughout the day, Brad kept popping up in the conversation, so whenever Mike would pester me about possibly dating Brad, I'd respond by peppering him with questions: How old is Brad? He seems younger than me. Would he even want another long-distance relationship after what he said the other night? And is he ready for a mature relationship, or is he still a player? Mike didn't really have the answers, so he suggested that I keep the dialogue open should Brad reach out to me.

A little before four, while Mike and I were driving to the airport, I received a notification from Facebook that Brad wanted to be friends.

"Just see where it goes," Mike encouraged. "If nothing else, you'll make a new U2 friend."

I took a deep breath and sighed, "I guess so. . . . Besides, I didn't meet my quota of new U2 friends this weekend."

Chapter 11

Mommy's Secret

After dropping off Mike at the airport, I mulled over what he'd said about corresponding with Brad if he reached out to me. *He friended me on Facebook, but is that really corresponding? Should I just wait to see if he sends me a message, or should I send him one first?*

I hemmed and hawed over it all evening, but I didn't say anything about it to Lori. Finally, a little before midnight, as I was getting into bed, I decided to take the plunge:

> **Jen 6/5/17 11:46 p.m.**
>
> Great hanging out with you this weekend, Brad! I had a lot of fun. I hope I didn't embarrass myself too much during my giggle spurt at the diner last night. Still contemplating going to Louisville. Margaret has a GA for me, but if I go, we won't be camping out all day. We'll probably drive in that day and take our chances at the back of the line and just enjoy the 4K video screen.

Brad played hard to get and waited almost twenty-four hours to reply.

> **Brad 6/6/17 10:39 p.m.**
>
> Hey! Was great meeting you. Ahhh the laughing at the diner was perfect after the long weekend and hot day. I'm still a maybe for Louisville! No plans or tix yet, but it's tempting. Going to DC (as I probably told you) in seats w/ friends, then the Indy show was announced today, which I think you mentioned was a rumor.

I didn't want to seem too eager either, so I waited to reply until I was going to bed the following night:

> **Jen 6/7/17 11:07 p.m.**
>
> You HAVE to come to Louisville. How else am I going to give you a signed copy of my U2 book?

The next day, Brad responded on his lunch break.

> **Brad 6/8/17 12:37 p.m.**
>
> You're right—how would I get a signed copy of your book without going to Louisville?! It's a Friday and only two hours away. Really, how could I NOT go? What time do you think you'll get down there? And you're definitely doing GA toward the back?

> **Jen 6/8/17 5:15 p.m.**
>
> I was thinking the same thing. . . . How could you NOT attend Louisville? That would be like my friends Margaret and Scott from South Bend not going to the Chicago shows. . . . We definitely won't be getting up toward the front because Margaret and I are attending a different concert in Chicago the night before, so no 5:00 a.m. check-ins for us this time.

We chatted the rest of the evening, and every time my phone pinged, my heart fluttered and a jolt of electricity zipped through my body. Just after 12:30 my time (1:30 a.m. for Brad), he signed off by saying:

> **Brad 6/9/17 12:35 a.m.**
>
> Lastly, I'm in for Louisville. Have a good eve.... Dream new dreams tonight.

The last line was a play on a lyric from U2's song "In God's Country," so after that, we began sprinkling song snippets into our conversations. The following afternoon, I mentioned that Margaret, Scott, and I had gotten tickets for the Indianapolis show in September. His response betrayed his excitement:

> **Brad 6/9/17 9:52 p.m.**
>
> Hey! Indy baby!! Funny, I've never actually lived in the same city where U2 has played. You're doing GA, I assume? My buddy from Cincy just let me know he's all in for lining up early for GA, so Indy is ON!
>
> But more importantly, L'ville: Can I meet you on the floor around 7, or are you trying to get a good spot, in which case I should be part of the line? I'm very fun in U2 lines BTW.
>
> Can't wait 'til next Friday!

> **Jen 6/9/17 11:57 p.m.**
>
> Definitely getting excited for L'ville. We'll probably get there around midafternoon, grab some dinner, then head to the show. So as much as I'd love to have you entertain me in the GA line, it'll have to wait for Indy (yes, I got a GA). Unless I can convince you to go to Cleveland over the Fourth of July weekend. And, of course, you're welcome to join us for dinner before the L'ville show.

At that point—possibly even a couple days sooner—I realized Brad and I were flirting. At least in my eyes we were. When I came to that conclusion, I pulled Benny onto my chest and whispered to him, "Can I tell you a secret?"

Benny looked at me with a conspiratorial grin on his face and his chocolate-brown eyes as big as saucers. It was like he was saying, "Oh boy! I'm really good at keeping secrets. Spill it, Mom."

"Mommy met a guy at the U2 concerts last weekend. He's super cute and really smart, and I think I like him. I think he might like me too. I'm going to see him again next week when I go to Louisville with Aunt Margaret and Uncle Scott, so we'll see how it goes. I don't want to get my hopes up, though, so don't tell anyone."

Benny looked at me with eyes so warm they could melt my heart, then he smothered my face with kisses. I knew he loved me with all his heart, but I also knew he longed for a daddy.

The next day, Brad asked about getting a GA ticket. He also added:

> **Brad 6/10/17 3:41 p.m.**
>
> Cleveland!!!!! Possibly. I'm taking it one show at a time. Also, what's the hotel situation like down there? I have a sister who lives in Louisville, but I honestly don't want to bother her arriving super late Friday night. And I'd love to join you before the show for dinner.

> **Jen 6/11/17 1:28 p.m.**
>
> I just talked to Margaret and she says to hold off on getting a ticket for now. She likes the idea of getting a seat and then you can buy her GA. As for the hotel, in true Margaret fashion, she has two booked. Both are within walking distance to the stadium, so let me know if you're interested in the second one.

> **Brad 6/11/17 1:45 p.m.**
>
> I'll hold off on getting a ticket then. If Margaret (she seems so mythical talking about her like I know her before I've even met her) wants a seat, that would be ideal. I'm happy to buy the seat for her and trade for her GA. Tell her whatever she wants, I'll get it!
>
> I'll take the second room, and of course, I'll pay. While Scott seems like an excellent U2 fan, this wouldn't mean I'm sharing a room with him, right?

> **Jen 6/11/17 2:39 p.m.**
>
> I'll let Mythical Margaret know you want the second hotel. I think you and Scott will get along great, but if you'd rather share a room with Margaret, that can be arranged too.

> **Brad 6/11/17, 2:50 p.m.**
>
> So for the hotel, that's just me, right? Unless Margaret and I hit it off. Just want to confirm.

Clearly, we were flirting, but I didn't want him getting any ideas or expectations that anything "physical" was going to happen between us, even if I did end up sharing a room with him. After all, the room had two beds, and this girl doesn't give it up easily, certainly not on the first date—if this even was a date. I had no clue at that point!

The word *clueless* pretty much sums up my relationships with men to that point. I rarely knew where we stood and was too shy and afraid to ask. Heck, I couldn't even really tell when someone was flirting with me. But this time I took a chance. Secure in the knowledge that Brad and I were, indeed, flirting, but not wanting to come off as too forward, I wrote back.

> **Jen 6/11/17 3:09 p.m.**
>
> Well, do you snore? Margaret snores really loud, so I may want to share a room with you so I can get some sleep. If that's okay, of course.

> **Brad 6/11/17 3:17 p.m.**
>
> Nope, no snoring here … at least not that I know of. Yeah, I think that arrangement would work.

Later that evening, I tossed the ball back to him:

> **Jen 6/11/17 10:16 p.m.**
>
> Your mission, should you choose to accept it … Bono comes to you and says, "Brad, for being such a loyal fan for all these years, we're going to let you write the setlist for your dream show." Pick your 25 favorite songs for your dream setlist. I'll do the same, and we can compare.

Just before midnight my time, he responded: "On it." Then about a half hour later, he sent in the first four songs of his dream setlist, complete with a specific intro and precise notes on which exact concert version he would choose for each tune. Then he added:

> **Brad 6/12/17 12:36 a.m.**
>
> To be continued tomorrow AM. You know what's cool?? There's a U2 concert this Friday eve in KY. It's gonna be a good summer.

I had a feeling he was right about that.

Chapter 12

The Summer of Love

Brad was wrong about it being a good summer. It wasn't just good, it was FANTASTIC! After spending time together before, during, and after the U2 concert in Louisville, it was clear that we had chemistry and smooches were exchanged. We started texting each other daily and agreed to meet up for the U2 concert in Cleveland on July 1.

I really didn't want to tell anyone about this flirtation with Brad until I knew if something more substantial would materialize. Obviously, Margaret and Scott knew, but that was the extent of it. Why didn't I want anyone to know? First, as a Cubs fan, I believed in the power of jinxing things. Plus, given my track record with relationships, I didn't want to get ahead of myself and then look like a fool in front of my friends and family like I had many times before. But after Louisville, things seemed to be getting real with Brad, so I decided to involve an expert: I told my sister Lori because I wanted her advice on what to wear in Cleveland.

Margaret and I planned to arrive in Cleveland on June 30 to see New Kids on the Block, who were performing that night. When Brad asked if he could tag along to see New Kids, how could I say no? Margaret offered to swap seats with him so he and I could sit together. It was then that I realized, *Wow! This guy is really special. Most guys make fun of me for liking New Kids, but he actually wants to join me. This one's a keeper!*

Margaret ended up heading back to South Bend the morning after the U2 show as planned, but there were still three full days of the long weekend left, and Brad and I wanted to spend more time getting to know each other. So he offered to drive two hours out of his way to take me back to Margaret's place, where my car was parked, on July 4. To say that made me feel special is an understatement. No other guy had ever gone so far out of his way—figuratively and literally—to spend additional time with me. I hated being away from Benny longer, but he was with Lori and I knew he'd understand. After all, if he wanted a daddy, sacrifices would have to be made.

Brad and I stood in the hotel lobby and watched Margaret make a less-than-graceful exit, rear-ending a concrete barrier as she attempted a three-point turn while leaving the valet drop-off in the ginormous SUV she'd rented. Then we made the most of our bonus time together. We cooled off in the breeze while riding bikes along the shore of Lake Erie, enjoyed a romantic yet steamy dinner in the Flats district, and strolled hand in hand under the stars on the banks of the Cuyahoga. On July 3, we left Cleveland and headed west, stopping at Cedar Point for a day of roller coasters, water rides, junk food, and fun in the sun. Mostly fun.

As they say, "It's all fun and games until someone pukes," and that just about summarizes our day. I always like to end any day at Cedar Point with a spin on the Raptor, which is an "inverted coaster," meaning that the cars are attached under the tracks rather than on top of them. The park likens the ride to how it would feel if "a bird of prey . . . snatches you up and then proceeds to take you on a terrifying journey to wherever it pleases." But to me, it's a smooth ride that makes me feel like I'm gently gliding through the air with the wind whipping through my hair—with a handful of twists, turns, rolls, and "loop-de-loops" thrown in for good measure. I could ride the Raptor all day and leave the park completely content.

But as Brad and I were making our way toward the exit, I noticed there was no line for the Blue Streak, a wooden coaster and the oldest at the park, so we decided to hop on board the rickety ride. Two minutes later, I seriously regretted that decision.

Unlike most coasters today, the Blue Streak only has a seat belt and a lap bar—there's no neck restraint or even upper back support. I guess because the ride doesn't go upside down, it doesn't need those creature comforts, but *I* need them. My head and neck thrashed back and forth and side to side as the vomit comet bounced up and down the multiple hills. Then, as we approached the station, the train slammed on the brakes with such force that I thought my neck might've snapped. As soon as we set foot on solid ground, I knew my equilibrium was off, but I hoped walking to the car would steady my swirling brain. Spoiler alert: It didn't.

Once we made it to Brad's car and began creeping out of the parking lot, I started feeling queasy. I rarely throw up (sorry if that's TMI) and have never done so due to an amusement park ride, so I just figured the nausea would wear off. But as we wound our way through the streets of Sandusky on the way to the toll road, I had to ask Brad to pull over. "I think I'm gonna be sick," I said pathetically through gritted teeth.

"Really? ... Are you sure?" Brad replied. I could tell he didn't want to pull over on a busy road, but he *really* didn't want this girl he was just getting to know to hurl all over his car like Linda Blair in *The Exorcist*.

I nodded vigorously, afraid to open my mouth lest I upchuck the corn dog I'd had for dinner.

After Brad pulled the car safely off the road, I opened the passenger door to exorcise the demon making its way from my belly up through my esophagus. When I tasted the salty saliva building up in my mouth, I knew it was only a matter of time. And then ... nothing. I don't know what it is, but like I said, I'm just not a puker.

Brad poured cool water on some napkins then patted my face and cooled my aching neck with them. By the time we got back on the road, it was well after eleven o'clock, which meant we weren't going to arrive at Margaret's to get my car until about three thirty in the morning. I knew it was too late to call her to see if we could stay over, but I didn't want Brad driving home that late. I also didn't want my dad to blow a gasket if he woke up in the morning and saw a strange man sleeping in his house. And I didn't want either of us spending money on a hotel in the area where so many of my family members lived, so I called the one person who I knew would still be awake: my night-owl sister Denise. She was gracious enough to let us sleep in her spare bedroom, no questions asked, even though she had no idea I was even dating anyone. In my defense, I didn't know either, but I hoped I was!

Brad and I left Denise and Bernie's house around ten the next morning and headed to Margaret's to retrieve my car. It was difficult saying goodbye to Brad after such an amazing weekend, especially since I didn't know when I'd see him again. But I was exploding with anticipation over the idea of this budding romance, so I called Dr. Bob, met him for brunch, and spilled the beans.

When I finally got home around four thirty, Lori and the kids weren't home, so Benny was by himself. As I opened the door and disengaged the security alarm, Benny zoomed toward me, skidded across the tile floor, then crashed into my shins.

"Hi, buddy! Mommy's home! Did you miss me? I sure missed you!"

Clearly ecstatic to see me, he treated me to his version of a happy dance, which I dubbed the Benny Boogie. With his entire body wiggling with glee, he bared his teeth in a toothy grin, squealed, snorted, smiled, stretched, sneezed, shook his little wigglebutt, and whipped his tail back and forth as he pranced around the kitchen.

It was good to be reunited with my baby boy, but I also missed Brad. From the way my heart skipped a beat, a tingle went up my spine, and my stomach did a flip whenever we kissed, I knew I was already falling head over heels for him. Yet I couldn't stop thinking, *How is this happening? I'm supposed to be happily retired from dating!*

With no plans to see each other until the U2 concert in Indy on September 10, Brad decided to drive up to my place on Friday, July 21, which was just a couple days after Lori and her kids moved into their own house. The time between Cleveland and that first visit was agonizing, but we texted every day and let each other know how excited we were to see each other again.

Brad was planning to arrive by eight o'clock my time, but due to Chicago traffic, it was nine thirty before he got there. Benny and I greeted him at the door, and while Brad and I gave each other a big hug and kiss, Benny skeptically sniffed him out. He was a little bashful at first (Benny, not Brad), but then he did what he usually did when we had company: with his little George Jefferson strut, he trotted over to his toy box and grabbed several of his favorites, one by one, then brought them to Brad, squeaking them exuberantly all the way.

By the time Brad arrived, we were both starving, so instead of going out to dinner, we made a frozen pizza, then the three of us snuggled on the couch and watched *Dirty Dancing*, one of my all-time favorite movies, which Brad had never seen and happened to be on TV. (Clearly, he'd lived a sheltered life until I entered the picture.) By then, Benny had warmed up to Brad a bit, but he wasn't quite ready to be his cuddle bug, so I lay sandwiched between them.

The next day, Brad and I went to a Cubs game. The Men in Blue won 3–2, but the highlight for me was being with Brad at Wrigley Field, which, since childhood, I'd described as my "happy place." Well, that and getting to see the World Series trophy live and in person.

After Brad made it home on Sunday night, he sent me a sweet and thoughtful text:

> **Brad 7/23/17 10:43 p.m.**
>
> Dear Jennifer, Thank you for the amazing weekend and having me over to your house. It was fun meeting and hanging with Benny Goodman. He's a gentleman, and he told me that his favorite hobby is, in fact, sleeping. The weekend went too quickly, and I didn't like leaving this afternoon. I can't wait 'til we do it again. —Bradley

I definitely experienced some Brad withdrawal when he left. I was bursting with anticipation and felt like I was floating on a cloud, thinking about what the future might hold for us. But at the same time, it felt like Brad took a piece of my heart with him. I'm pretty sure Benny missed him too because for the rest of the day, he moped around the house and didn't even finish his dinner.

Two weekends later, Brad visited my place again to celebrate my birthday. But he'd had enough of driving in Chicago, so this time he took a brief, thirty-minute flight, and I picked him up at the airport.

We had another marvelous weekend together. On Sunday morning, while we were strolling around my neighborhood with Benny, we ran into Francine, who was walking Jimmy and Sal. Without even thinking (which is rare for an overthinker like myself), I blurted out, "This is my boyfriend, Brad," when I introduced them. Then I started to panic.

After a quick conversation with Francine, we continued on our walk around the block. To me, the air suddenly seemed filled with a thick, awkward silence, until I finally addressed the figurative elephant in the room. With my palms sweating and my heart pounding so rapidly I could hear my pulse in my ears, I said, "Was that okay?"

"Was what okay?" Brad asked, completely unaware of my trepidation.

"Calling you my boyfriend.... I mean, we haven't actually had 'the talk' or anything." In my mind, Louisville was our first date, so this weekend was our fourth, but I had no idea what he was thinking.

"Absolutely!" he assured me. "If the situation were reversed, I would've introduced you as my girlfriend, without a doubt."

I breathed such a huge sigh of relief that I nearly passed out. It seemed like forever since I'd felt comfortable enough to relax in a relationship. For the rest of the walk, we discussed how we were going to handle the brick wall staring us in the face: the fact that we lived three and a half hours apart, in different states, and in different time zones. We quickly agreed to get together every other weekend and continue keeping in touch daily. And just like Michael Jordan and Ryne Sandberg, two of my sports heroes, I officially came out of retirement.

Chapter 13

"When Love Comes to Town"

Brad and I stuck to our promise to see each other every couple weeks, and suddenly the bendy bus that we rode the night we met in June seemed like a metaphor for our relationship as we would come together for a dreamlike weekend, then reality pulled us apart. Come together, move apart. Come together, move apart.

Somehow, when I'd least expected it, I'd finally met my match. Not only did we share a deep love for U2, we also had other common interests, and on countless occasions when one of us would be sharing something about our families or an anecdote from our lives, the other would respond with an open-mouthed look of surprise and exclaim, "Me too!"

Brad and I rendezvoused in Detroit over Labor Day and I visited his place the following weekend, both for U2 concerts. Unfortunately, Benny couldn't accompany me on either of those trips.

Often when I'd get out my suitcase and start packing to go somewhere, Benny would hop inside as if to say, "Hey, just a reminder to bring me along!" On those occasions, I'd channel my inner Bret Michaels and sing "I Won't Forget You, Baby" to him, replacing *Baby* with *Bunny*. I wanted to bring him to Indy, but Brad had a lot of events planned for us, plus several of his out-of-town buddies were staying at his place and we were hosting a U2-themed party the night before the concert. And because Benny often became so anxious and apprehensive around crowds that he demanded to be held then would cling to me desperately and quiver in my arms (think Scooby-Doo whenever he saw a g-g-g-g-ghost), it was better for him at my dad's.

"Sorry, Buns," I told him as I lifted him onto the bed and placed my clothes in the suitcase. "You're gonna stay with Grandpa. You can come with me to Brad's next time."

Benny's first visit to Brad's fell over Halloween weekend. Benny was a little timid at first, but when Brad presented him with a squeaky, plush soccer ball, he warmed up, surely thinking, *This Brad guy is all right.* After that, Benny hopped on the couch and quickly made himself right at home.

Although Brad had no trick-or-treaters and Benny had to stay behind when we toured a haunted house, the three of us wore costumes and had our own little party at the condo. I dressed as Little Red Riding Hood and Benny was the Big Bad Woof. I tried to get Brad to join in the theme, but he insisted on wearing a gorilla suit.

By this point in time, Benny was being crated whenever I left him for short periods of time, and that included when we were at Brad's or my dad's. Oftentimes, we'd come home to find him snuggled up in his blankie, sleeping peacefully. But other times, we could hear him as we approached the house, emitting a pitiful howl to voice his displeasure at being left in solitary confinement.

Even though Brad and I would go out and do things without Benny on our visits, we always made sure to leave plenty of time for cuddles. I'm sure Benny would've preferred to go with us, and if societal rules would've allowed it, we would have taken him. Nevertheless, Benny was clearly happy that Mommy had a boyfriend and he'd acquired a Braddy (Brad + Daddy).

Because our relationship was still in its infancy, Brad and I didn't spend Thanksgiving together in 2017. However, in early December when he came to visit, we were having a late dinner at a Mexican restaurant near my place when he asked a question that took me by surprise.

As I noshed on tortilla chips, he stammered, "Do you ... uh ... do you wanna ... uh ... come to my parents' house for Christmas?"

Flattered and shocked, I didn't know what to say, so I took a sip of my margarita to stall for time. "I would love to spend Christmas with you and meet your family, but I also want to spend the holidays with my family. Plus, would Benny be invited?"

"I'm not sure about bringing Benny," Brad admitted. "We had two Labs, Sam and Lilah, when I was a kid, but they were always outside dogs who were rarely allowed inside the house. So I'm guessing probably not."

As we discussed it, it was clear that we wanted to spend Christmas together, but we also had family traditions that we wanted to maintain, and, logistically, we couldn't figure out how to make it all work since South Bend and Cincinnati are about five hours apart by car. But we knew that in order to make our relationship work long term, we had to find a compromise, so we came up with a plan: We would celebrate Christmas Eve and Christmas Day with our respective families, then on December 27, I would fly to Cincinnati to meet Brad's family and spend a few days with them. Then Brad and I would drive back to Indianapolis to spend New Year's together before I traveled back to Chicago on the night of January 1.

We also decided it was time for Brad to meet my dad and Dr. Bob and get to know my sisters, niece, and nephew better. So we began planning an afternoon luncheon at Chez Bennifer for mid- to late January.

But first we had to get through the holidays. The thought of being away from Benny for so long was heart-wrenching; I hadn't been away from him for that amount of time since Denise and I went to California for our niece's graduation in June 2014, shortly after I adopted him. But I knew it was a sacrifice we'd have to make to see if my relationship with Brad was meant to be. Plus, I knew that when I came home, I'd get to witness the Benny Boogie and for the next several days, he'd literally attach himself to my side during the day while I worked, in the evenings when we watched TV, and as we slept at night. And those moments were priceless. Some sacrifices are worth making.

Chapter 14

Thumper

Back in March 2016, after living in the burbs for a year, Benny transferred to an animal clinic closer to home. By then, he'd seen more than a dozen veterinarians because we were assigned to a revolving door of doctors in the practice each time, so all they knew about Benny was what was in his chart. Nevertheless, every time we were introduced to a new doctor, I'd ask them how old they thought Benny was. Each doctor had a different opinion, ranging from a year and a half to seven, so I decided to make an educated guess and started putting his estimated birthdate as March 9, 2012, designating the day I brought him home as his second birthday. It might've been a bit Pollyannaish on my part to think he was only two when I got him, but I wanted him to be as young as possible.

For the first year I had him, Benny continued to struggle with ear infections, and we continuously came home from his doctor's appointments with ear drops, antibiotics, and a solution to flush any debris from his ears. When one of the vets—thinking that Benny's chronic ear infections might be due to a food allergy—suggested switching to a limited-ingredient diet and eliminating chicken, we did.

Aside from ear issues, Benny was thriving. But during the summer of 2016, he'd developed some hot spots on his paws, which were diagnosed as dermatitis. The vet said it was likely due to seasonal allergies and sent us home with more antibiotics, an ointment, and an allergy medication called Apoquel.

We continued with the Apoquel through November, when seasonal allergies should've ended. But when we returned from Michigan after Christmas break and Benny began scratching incessantly, I noticed we had some uninvited visitors.

"Aack! Oh my God!" I exclaimed with a shudder. I'd seen a tiny black dot skitter across Benny's chest while I was giving him a belly rub.

After catching the little booger between my index finger and thumb, I discovered a few more. "Oh no, Bunny! You've got fleas!"

How Benny had become the unlucky host of a colony of bloodsuckers when he was on a flea and tick preventative year-round was anyone's guess. But he did. I washed everything he'd come in contact with, took him to the groomer for a flea bath, and made an appointment with the vet, who didn't see any live ones on him but diagnosed him with flea allergic dermatitis and prescribed another round of antibiotics.

Three weeks later, Benny and I were out for his morning constitutional on a cold but sunny January day. As I bent down with a poop bag in hand, poised to pick up his deposit, I saw something move.

"Ewww! What *is* that?" I recoiled as what appeared to be a wiggling grain of rice emerged from Benny's poo. Although I'd never seen anything like it before, I instinctively knew it was a tapeworm.

Fortunately, I was able to get Benny in to see the vet right away because I was pretty grossed out after seeing the worm. I know a lot of dogs get them from eating poop, but Benny never did that. The vet assured me that tapeworms are often secondary to fleas and sent us home with deworming tablets and—you guessed it— more antibiotics.

After those setbacks, Benny's health was fantastic! In fact, he bulked up to an all-time high of eighteen pounds, so the vet wanted him to lose some weight. And, despite discontinuing the Apoquel, he was no longer itchy.

However, that changed in late 2017 when his itchiness really ramped up. As Benny scratched himself silly, trying to get some relief, his foot would pound the floor, making a *thump-thump-thump* sound, garnering him another nickname: Thumper. Because it started up again while we were at my dad's place for Christmas,

I thought maybe he was allergic to felines because my dad had taken in a stray cat after Sweetie passed away. But after the first of the year, when he was still itching like crazy and gnawing his paws like they were chew toys, I made an appointment at the veterinary clinic.

By this point, I'd started researching allergies in dogs and how to treat them. As a previous vet had mentioned, food is often the culprit for dogs, but environmental allergies are also possible. What I didn't like about the clinic we frequented is that every doctor just wanted to prescribe medications to treat Benny's symptoms rather than getting to the root of what was causing them so we could potentially eliminate that source and treat his itchiness more naturally. So when we saw the vet in early January 2018 and she recommended putting Benny back on Apoquel or trying a relatively new drug called Cytopoint and keeping him on them year-round, I wasn't really comfortable with the idea. I'd never heard of Cytopoint, but I had looked into the side effects of Apoquel and they included, among other things, skin and ear infections, which seemed to defeat the purpose since it could cause what it was supposed to cure.

The vet gave me her pitch for Cytopoint, which was likely the same spiel a pharmaceutical rep had given her. "It's completely safe," she said, "and unlike Apoquel, it's not an immuno-suppressant."

"Can you give me some time to think about it?" I asked.

"Of course," she said.

As soon as she left the room, my fingers were typing away on my phone, researching Cytopoint with Benny sitting on my lap. I had a bad feeling about putting Benny on a medication for the rest of his life, although I'm not sure where my anxiety stemmed from. I mean, I'd been taking allergy pills since I was ten years old, and I'd never second-guessed that or any other medication a doctor recommended for me. But with Benny, it was different. As his mom, his well-being was my responsibility and my top priority.

Over the holidays, I'd expressed my concern to my cousin Deb, who'd taken her dog, Cassie, to a homeopathic vet in Indiana, so she'd suggested that I ask about more holistic alternatives for Benny. When the vet returned to the room, I did just that.

"No!" she said emphatically. My cheeks flushed, and I was so taken aback by the harshness of her tone that my eyes fluttered and

I flinched, as if she'd just clapped her hands in front of my face. "I understand your concerns, but Benny needs to be on allergy medication year-round. That's the only way to stop his chronic itching and licking. Cytopoint is completely safe, and one injection will keep him itch-free for two to three months.

"Some dogs have elevated levels of a compound known as Interleukin 31 (IL 31), which causes them to be chronically itchy. Cytopoint works by inactivating IL 31. So, in other words," she said, "stop what's causing the itch and Benny will stop itching."

It made sense and seemed to satisfy my need for a solution that treated the root cause of his itchiness, not just the symptoms, but I was still on the fence. In hindsight, I wonder: *How did she know for sure that Benny's IL 31 was elevated?* But at the time, I felt shamed and intimidated into making a decision, so I agreed to let her give Benny the Cytopoint injection. However, I would soon regret it.

"What's the matter, Buns? Are you not feeling well?" I asked as I smoothed the soft fur on the top of his head. After receiving the Cytopoint injection, Benny was a bit tired and just not his usual perky self for the rest of the day ... or the next ... or the next. His appetite also decreased, which was always a sign that he was sick. I hadn't gotten very far in researching Cytopoint before the vet had returned to the room and pressured me to give Benny the injection, so when he was still out of sorts a couple days later, I did a deep dive, investigating this "miracle drug." What I read sent my anxiety through the roof.

One article backed up what the vet had told me, but it also went into greater detail about what she *didn't* tell me—most importantly that by inactivating IL 31, Cytopoint can cause long-term effects to the immune system, which can, therefore, lead to autoimmune diseases (such as lupus, rheumatoid arthritis, and Addison's disease) and even tumor growth. The author of the article, a holistic vet, went on to say that by inactivating or suppressing one part of the immune system, Cytopoint dysregulates the *entire* immune system. And when I scrolled toward the bottom of the article and saw a subhead that read "Cytopoint Killed My Dog!," I really freaked out.

My heart fell with a thud and a wave of nausea enveloped my body when I read that several owners had reported severe side effects shortly after their dogs received the Cytopoint injection. These ranged from gastrointestinal upset to epilepsy to immune-mediated hemolytic anemia (an autoimmune disease where the body attacks its own red blood cells) and even death. The author concluded the article by stating: "My advice is—avoid Cytopoint like you would the plague."

Well, of course, I *had* to look into these claims, which led me to story after horrific story of pets dying within days to a few weeks of receiving a Cytopoint injection. Needless to say, for the next few weeks, I watched Benny like a hawk. I could barely catch my breath as excessive worry and intrusive, fearful thoughts of impending doom invaded my brain. *What have I done? Why did I let the vet give Benny that stupid Cytopoint injection? What if he dies or suffers long-term side effects from it? I'll never be able to forgive myself if something bad happens to him.* Please, God, I prayed over and over, *please let Benny be okay and make sure the Cytopoint injection doesn't harm him in any way.*

Fortunately, after a few days with little appetite and depleted energy, Benny bounced back and returned to his normal, spunky self. *Thank you, God!* However, within two to three weeks—not two to three months as the vet had said—he was once again scratching himself in circles and nibbling his paws like a beaver chomping a log.

Who knows if the Cytopoint injection caused long-term damage, but I learned my lesson and vowed never to allow a vet (or any doctor) to pressure me into making a decision about Benny's health care—or my own—without first doing my research. This scare also lit a fire under my butt to find a new vet.

Chapter 15

Going Au Natural

By early 2018, Benny and I had been together almost four years. During that time, Benny frequently dealt with ear infections, skin infections, and allergic dermatitis. And despite the fact that he'd seen numerous veterinarians at three different animal clinics, the treatment options were always the same. We seemed to be stuck in a vicious cycle where the vet would prescribe Benny antibiotics to treat his symptoms, he'd be fine for a few months while the antibiotics were still in his system, and then the cycle would begin again. Dissatisfied that none of the doctors were getting to the root cause of Benny's issues and were only treating the symptoms, I decided to take a different approach.

Several of my cousins swear by a more homeopathic or holistic approach, but my parents always followed the route of Western medicine, which basically says, "If you have these symptoms, take this pill." Because that's how I was raised, that's the path I followed. But as I grew older and started making my own decisions and doing my own due diligence, I began to see the logic in treating the root cause of an illness rather than just the symptoms. So after thanking my lucky stars that Benny had survived the Cytopoint injection seemingly unscathed, I started seeking a holistic veterinarian in our area, one that embraced both natural remedies and modern medicine. And much to my surprise, I found one just a couple miles from our house.

When Benny started itching again following the failed Cytopoint experiment in early 2018, I made an appointment with Dr. Pam, the holistic vet on staff at this clinic. On March 1, during Benny's first visit with Dr. Pam, she performed a skin scraping and diagnosed the itchy crud on his paws and lower lip as allergic dermatitis, but she also sent a culture out to a lab to see if any bacteria was present. In addition, she recommended a saliva test for food allergies because she didn't think Benny's symptoms were environmental in nature. She also gave me a free copy of her book and discussed the importance of gut health in dogs as well as nutrition and detoxification methods to restore and calm the immune system to decrease inflammation. *Huh?* Yeah, that word salad made my head spin too.

She threw a lot of information at me that day, so I declined many of the tests and supplements she recommended. I was still new to this holistic or integrative type of medicine, so I needed time to process everything and do my research. But I did agree to test Benny for food allergies, and Dr. Pam sent us home with a bottle of oregano oil diluted with coconut oil (a carrier oil).

"This essential oil blend is a natural antibiotic," she explained. "Apply it to Benny's lips and paws once or twice a day. You'll also need to keep a cone on him at all times to prevent him from licking his paws or rubbing his face."

To someone who was unfamiliar with herbal remedies, this seemed a bit unusual and—I'll admit—kooky, but I'd asked for a more natural approach and that's what she'd offered. Plus, I was pleased that she was taking measures to pinpoint the root cause of Benny's itchiness. "Okay," I said. "Is it dangerous if he ingests the oregano oil? Is that why he needs to wear the cone all the time?"

"No, it's safe as a topical treatment for dogs. But you don't want it getting on your clothes or rugs or furniture, and if he licks it off, then it won't be effective."

"Oh, that makes sense."

After paying the nearly six-hundred-dollar bill, Benny and I left with nothing more than a small vial of oregano oil.

The next day, Brad came to visit for the weekend. As soon as he walked in the door, he eagerly asked, "Did you make spaghetti and meatballs for dinner?" (Like Benny, Brad is very food motivated.)

"No," I laughed. "That's Benny's new treatment. He has oregano oil on his face and paws."

Disappointed that I hadn't made spaghetti for dinner, Brad gave me a sideways glance and puckered his face into a "What'choo talkin' 'bout, Willis?" look. Then, practically salivating, he asked if I wanted to go to Olive Garden. Suddenly, he was famished.

From the get-go, Brad wasn't a fan of Dr. Pam, especially after he came with us to an appointment and the staff sent us outside with a ladle to collect a urine sample from Benny. Similar to the ER visit in 2014 after he ate paint, every time Benny would lift his leg, Brad would stick the ladle under Benny's belly to make a catch, but Benny would freeze up or knock the ladle out of his hand. We must've looked like the Three Stooges out there, and it seemed ridiculous to expect us to make the collection when the techs surely had more experience doing so. Charging me seven dollars for a ladle that they most likely spent a buck on at the Dollar Tree next door wasn't cool either.

Nevertheless, I stuck with Dr. Pam. Some of her treatments seemed a bit peculiar and unorthodox, especially when she kept trying to persuade me that Benny needed a fecal transplant. I'll leave you to mull that one over on your own, but I never could bring myself to make Benny undergo such a procedure. However, I liked that she wasn't just pushing drugs on him; she only did that when a more natural remedy wasn't available or effective. I also appreciated that she did titer tests to see how much of his vaccines were still active, and if he still had enough in his system, she didn't give him another one.

At our follow-up visit on March 19—our third appointment in less than three weeks—Benny's paws were doing better. But he was also wearing the cone all the time, so it was hard to say whether the oregano oil had helped. That day, we got the results of Benny's saliva test, which revealed that he was allergic to corn, oatmeal, and whitefish, and he'd also had a reaction to chicken and pork. At our first visit with Dr. Pam, she'd recommended switching Benny to a premade, commercial raw diet and adding a probiotic as well as LumaPet, a soil-derived supplement that promotes healthy digestion and immune function. By this point, I'd done some research and spoken to the nutritionist on staff, so I agreed to give those a try.

However, the culture taken from Benny's paws showed that he had a bacterial infection, so Dr. Pam sent me home with a bottle of antimicrobial spray to apply to Benny's paws several times a day and a two-week supply of antibiotics. *Ugh*, I thought. *Here we go again. More antibiotics.* She also had me stop the oregano oil since it wasn't doing anything besides making Brad and me crave Italian food.

As I've said before, Benny was always very food motivated. Whether he was that way since birth or just after he'd lived on the streets is anyone's guess. What I do know is that he rarely encountered a food he didn't like. In fact, about the only thing I ever offered him that he didn't eat was banana. He seemed interested while I was eating one, so I gave him a taste, but once he had it in his mouth, he quickly spit it out. Perhaps it was the texture that he found unappetizing. Still, that didn't stop him from "asking" me for some banana every time I had one, but I had to remind him, "You don't like banana. You *think* you do, but then you spit it out, so we're not playing that game."

Even though Benny loved food, I didn't really know how he'd react to the raw diet. He ate his breakfast and dinner every day—a mix of Merrick grain-free, limited-ingredient dry kibble and canned food with vegetables and gravy—but sometimes he didn't seem all that thrilled with it. So switching could be a good thing . . . or maybe not.

Because switching foods too quickly can cause dogs an upset stomach and diarrhea, the nutritionist advised me to slowly transition to the new food. Over the course of a week to ten days, I was to gradually increase the amount of raw food and decrease the other until he was fully acclimated to the new diet. I really had nothing to worry about because, from the start, Benny loved the raw beef patties and was soon licking his bowl clean at every meal, even pushing it around the room with his nose, trying to absorb every last morsel.

I want to make clear that the raw patties I gave him were not the same as going to the grocery store and buying raw hamburger. Premade, commercial raw diets—the good ones anyway—are processed under strict guidelines to prevent bacterial contamination and are packed with organic fruits and vegetables, vitamin and mineral supplements, and probiotics. At this point in my life, I hadn't eaten red meat in more than a decade, so if I was expected to give Benny a bloody, raw hamburger patty, I probably would've barfed. But I would've done it for my baby boy if that's what was best for him.

At our recheck appointment at the end of the month, Dr. Pam talked me into having Benny's blood drawn to test his thyroid and IgA, which is a protein in the blood and is part of the immune system. "IgA deficiencies often lead to chronic or recurring infections of the skin and other parts of the body," she explained.

Hearing that, it made sense that it could be the root cause of Benny's chronic skin and ear infections. *Finally, we might be getting some concrete answers,* I thought optimistically.

When the results came back in early April, Dr. Pam said both Benny's thyroid and IgA levels were low. She drew a complicated flowchart on a piece of paper and gave me a long, convoluted explanation for how this related to Benny's overall immune health and allergies, but to be honest, it went right over my head. She may have been a highly regarded holistic vet and a bestselling author, but she had difficulty explaining complex health issues in a language that someone without a medical degree could understand.

In a nutshell, Dr. Pam said she believed an autoimmune disease was causing Benny's itching. She threw around terms like *Addison's* and *Cushing's* disease, but she'd never come out and say that Benny suffered from one of them. Nevertheless, she prescribed a subcutaneous shot of adrenal cortex, an herbal supplement that's supposed to support hormonal balance and assist the body in adapting to stress and anxiety. And she was still pushing the fecal transplant, but once again, I declined.

Less than two weeks later, Benny and I were back at the vet. He'd been scratching his left ear, which had brown goop in it that smelled like Fritos, so I suspected he had another ear infection. Dr. Pam wasn't in that day, so we saw a doctor who wasn't as gung-ho on holistic medicine, and when she suggested that I go back to giving Benny Apoquel or Cytopoint injections, I lost all faith in her.

We made it almost four weeks before our next trip to the vet, but in late May, Benny went to the groomer, and when I picked him up, she said, "I think he has a yeast infection." She pointed out that his paws were red and irritated and he had some scaly crustiness on his chin and paws, all of which, until his haircut, his fur had been covering. The next day, he woke up with a greenish discharge from his eyes and nose, so I made an appointment to see Dr. Pam.

A skin scraping showed no signs of mites or yeast, but bacteria was present. However, instead of prescribing another round of antibiotics, she sent us home with an anti-itch shampoo and anti-microbial spray and told me to give Benny half a Benadryl at night. In addition, she wanted to rule out some other causes for Benny's issues, so she did a urinalysis and a complete blood work panel.

Benny's urinalysis was completely normal, but Dr. Pam said his T4 was slightly low, so she diagnosed him with hypothyroidism and prescribed medication. From that point on, much to my chagrin, Benny began a daily drug habit that would last the rest of his life.

"At this point, I'd also like to take Benny off the adrenal cortex and switch him to an oral form of hydrocortisone," Dr. Pam added.

I balked at this because I'd heard about the side effects of long-term steroid use, including greater susceptibility to bacterial and fungal infections, a predisposition to diabetes, and compromising the immune system. To me, knowing these potential side effects, it seemed counterintuitive to prescribe hydrocortisone for a dog who frequently got bacterial and fungal infections and might have an underlying autoimmune disease.

But when I brought up my concerns, Dr. Pam stressed, "He may only need to be on the hydrocortisone temporarily, and it's just a physiological dose."

"What does that mean?" I inquired.

"I means that we're only giving him enough to fill the gap of what his body should be producing but isn't."

I still didn't like the sound of it, but I told myself that she's the expert on animal health, so I had to trust what she was saying. And I have to admit that once Benny was eating the raw patties with his probiotic sprinkled on top and a 0.5 ml squirt of beef-flavored hydrocortisone mixed in at breakfast, he really began to flourish. He wolfed down his food at every meal, and even though he seemed constantly hungry (thank you, steroids), he actually lost some weight and got down to about fifteen pounds, possibly because the probiotic worked so well that he sometimes pooped three or four times a day, which prompted a new moniker: my super-duper pooper. He also had more energy and loved to chase after his toys when I'd throw them—although he still wouldn't bring them back to me. For the most part, he stopped chewing his paws, so he didn't have to wear the cone anymore, and his fur grew back thicker and fuller than I'd ever seen it. He was a happy, energetic boy.

We'd undergone some radical changes at Chez Bennifer during the summer of 2018: through multiple and frequent vet visits, Benny's allergies were finally under control; Brad and I were still going strong; and in June, I left my job at the children's book publishing company where I'd worked for five years. I'd been wanting to expand my horizons beyond the children's educational market, and a company-wide downsizing gave me the kick in the pants to branch out on my own. When it came time to name my new freelance editorial business, I didn't just want to use my name like a lot of people do. Besides, I was hoping that my surname would be changing sooner rather than later. (Wink-wink, Brad.) But truth be told, there was really only one name that I seriously considered and that's what I went with: White Dog Editorial Services. In life, Benny was my muse and my inspiration, so in business, I made him my spokesdog and fashioned a logo in his likeness.

Business quickly took off, and I couldn't have been happier being my own boss, choosing my own projects, making my own schedule, and working with Benny nuzzled right next to me every day. I even began toying with the idea of writing a series of children's books based on Benny's escapades.

With U2 gallivanting around Europe, Brad and I weren't traveling anywhere except to see each other, but in November, I was invited to his sister's house in Louisville for Thanksgiving. Unfortunately, Benny had to stay with Grandpa because Brad's sister wasn't sure how her cat would react to him.

Brad and I drove to Louisville on Thanksgiving morning and had a wonderful time with his family. I'd met everyone the previous Christmas, but I was really starting to feel more like part of the clan. I spent the rest of the weekend at Brad's place before heading back to my dad's on Sunday.

When I arrived around 6:00 p.m., Benny love-bombed me as if I'd just returned from a prolonged military stint overseas. He wagged his entire body, reared up on his hind legs like a spooked stallion to let me know that he wanted to be held, and smothered my face with kisses when I picked him up. After he settled down, I fed him his dinner, which he gobbled up, then Dad and I went to get something to eat.

When we came home an hour later, Benny's demeanor had made a complete 180. He was cowering, whimpering, and didn't want to leave his crate. That night, he wouldn't even sleep in bed with me, which he'd never done before. He only wanted to be in his crate, so I moved it into the living room and slept on the couch next to him.

Although Benny loved his raw food and the vet and nutritionist always assured me that it was completely safe, I'd been skeptical. So my first thought was that perhaps we'd gotten a bad batch and he had food poisoning. When we got up on Monday, I didn't want to give him the raw food in case it was the culprit, so I made him a scrambled egg instead. But he threw that up an hour later.

After I went to the store and got a new batch of raw beef patties, Benny ate a tiny bit and took his medication in a pill pop. But he still wouldn't come out of the crate. I practically had to drag him out just to take him potty. On Tuesday, I was able to get him into the veterinary clinic where Arnold and Sweetie used to go. During the exam, Benny yelped when they put moderate pressure on his belly, so they diagnosed him with gastritis, possibly from food poisoning or stress. They gave him fluids, an injection of vitamin B12, and Cerenia, a medication to prevent nausea and vomiting.

We ended up staying at my dad's house a few extra days until Benny's behavior and appetite returned to normal. Thinking that it was just a mild case of food poisoning, I didn't give it much more thought. But looking back, it might've been a harbinger of things to come.

Chapter 16

Benny's New Job

In 2018, as I'd done the year before, I flew to Cincinnati to be with Brad and his family after spending Christmas with mine. Again, I hated leaving Benny, but I had to respect Brad's parents' rules on no dogs in the house. However, when I arrived, I was greeted by a German shorthaired pointer. Apparently, Brad's brother, Dan, and his girlfriend had brought their dog, Mia, with them.

Confused and disappointed, I followed Brad upstairs when he took my suitcase to the bedroom where we were sleeping. On the brink of tears, I said, "Why is Mia allowed, but Benny isn't?"

"Um ... I never asked my parents if Benny could come," Brad confessed. "I just assumed since Sam and Lilah were almost never allowed inside that they didn't want dogs in the house. But obviously, Dan asked. I'm really sorry, Babe. I know how much you miss Benny when you're apart, and I should've asked."

Brad quickly learned his lesson and talked to his parents, and aside from a visit for a wedding in 2019, that was the last time Benny was excluded from a trip to Cincinnati.

After starting my own business in the summer of 2018, I spent a couple months working on branding and creating my own website. I didn't have the funds to hire someone to do it, and to be honest, writing my own copy, choosing my fonts and colors, finding photos, and learning how to put it all together gave me a sense of gratification. I'd taken a little coding in college—during the Stone Age of online newspapers and journals—and although I'd enjoyed it back then, I didn't have the time, patience, or wherewithal to code my website line by line. Fortunately, with website-building platforms such as Wix, I didn't have to. But in my naivete, I thought that once my website went live, people would magically find it. Spoiler alert: That's not how it works.

I still had a steady stream of work because I'd created a profile on Reedsy, a site that connects authors with publishing professionals, such as editors and designers—for a fee, of course. But I wanted to get more business organically, directly through my website. Obviously, the key to getting your website noticed is to show up on the first few pages of results when someone does a search. But in order to do that, you need to know something about keywords and search engine optimization (SEO). I purchased a copy of *Search Engine Optimization for Dummies* and soon learned that the more often you post new content to your site, the more likely you are to appear higher in the rankings. And an easy way to post new content is to blog.

Never in my life had I considered blogging. In fact, I'd only ever followed one blog and it belonged to an author I'd previously worked with who was very witty and funny. She mostly spun stories about interesting things that happened in her daily life, and I didn't think it was appropriate for me to do that since I was trying to promote my business. Besides, whenever someone would ask me, "What's new with you?" I could never think of anything exciting to say, and I didn't want to dish on my relationship with Brad all the time. So I needed to find a way to promote my business, be true to myself, and do so in a clever way that would attract potential customers. Then one day, it hit me.

I summoned Benny to our home office for a meeting. "As spokesdog and the face of White Dog Editorial," I began, "you're going to have to take on a more active role in the company. In addition to just snuggling next to me while I do all the work, you're going to be the voice of a new feature called Benny's Word of the Day."

The plan was for Benny to define a relatively uncommon word each weekday, so I found an app that would make my voice sound like that of a pet (or really a child). Basically, Benny just needed to pose for a picture where his mouth was visible because the app would also make it look like he was actually talking. It sounds relatively easy, and it was fun for a while, but it was also a LOT of work.

First, I had to come up with the word, then write a funny, punny, witty script for it. Next, Benny had to pose for a photo, which, again, is not as easy as it sounds. For an adorable guy who was super photogenic, he developed an aversion to having his picture taken, so whenever he'd catch sight of me picking up my phone and pointing it in his direction, he'd move or stop doing whatever he'd been doing that was so cute. After a photo shoot that could last up to half an hour or more, I would then upload the photo to the app and record the script. I'm a bit of a perfection-ist—which helps when you're an editor—but the recording stage was never accomplished in a single take. After that, I had to upload the entire thing to my website's blog, post it on my various social media pages, then write a brief description and ask people to share it. For each Word of the Day post, the entire process would take, at minimum, two hours to complete.

I kept up the daily pace for about a month, then it dropped to a few times a week. For the most part, these were short videos—about one or two minutes long—but hardly anyone shared them. Heck, only a handful of people even watched them!

My sister Lori is what we gently refer to as technologically challenged, so I had to give her a brief tutorial on how social media works. "When you see something in your feed that you want to share, hit the little share button," I began.

"What's the share button?"

I pressed my eyes tightly closed and let out a heavy sigh. "On Facebook, it looks like an arrow. Sharing allows *your* friends to view it and share it, and the more people share, the more views it'll get. And if the content is linked back to a website, the more action the website gets and the higher it goes in the rankings."

Lori still looked befuddled, so I decided to use a medical analogy since she's a nurse. "It's kinda like a virus. The more people pass the posts around and share them with their friends, the more those posts spread."

"Okay. Now I get it," Lori responded.

"Good. Now that you know, you can help out your friends on social media. It's really as simple as clicking a button."

I get that most people don't understand this unless they have their own business, but it was extremely deflating and disappointing that very few folks shared—or even watched—the videos I'd spent so much time creating. They were cute and educational, and I wasn't asking for anything more than a view, a share, and maybe a like or a comment. But that wasn't happening. So by mid-April, the return on the time I'd invested just wasn't panning out. We tried a short-lived feature called Fun Fact Fridays, but for the most part, Benny was relieved of his blogging duties after a few months.

Aside from Brad failing to ask his parents if Benny was welcome at their house, our relationship was rolling along like a boulder down a hill. We'd never had a single argument and hardly ever disagreed with each other. We thought so much alike and completed each other's sentences so frequently that we joked we had one mind and, like the U2 song, two hearts that beat as one. But it was getting harder and harder to say goodbye at the end of our weekends together, which always seemed to go by way too quickly.

From the get-go, I disclosed to Brad that I couldn't have children, but he didn't seem to mind. He fell in love with me for me. Like me, Brad always pictured himself as a parent, kicking a soccer ball with a son or daughter, so we occasionally discussed adopting. But I no longer felt I had the stamina to keep up with a newborn or toddler, and after my mom died, I'd started questioning my ability to raise a child without her there to guide me. As much as I'd always wanted children, I didn't have much experience with them, aside from a few babysitting jobs and a brief stint as a nanny in Boston. Brad had no experience either, so although I think both of us would've made wonderful parents, we ultimately decided it simply wasn't our fate, and we were content showering Benny with all our love as our four-legged child.

Benny had also grown quite attached to his Braddy. Whenever the two of them would be reunited on the couch after nearly two weeks apart, Benny would ambush Brad like a white lion, stand on his chest, pin him down with his paws, and smother his face, neck, and ears with kisses. Brad was a little unsure of this at first, and in some early photos, he looks like Lucy when Snoopy kisses her, with a grimace that says, "Ack! He's licking my face!" But since

Benny was never one to lick his nether regions, Brad soon came to accept this as an expression of Benny's love and affection for him.

Benny was also very selective about who he bestowed the gift of his kisses, and besides me, Brad was the only other recipient. In fact, when my sisters would try to get Benny to give them a kiss on the cheek, he'd put his paw on their shoulder and demurely turn his face to the side as if saying, "Not today."

But the kisses Benny reserved for Brad had a higher level of vigor. Benny would cover every square inch of Brad's face, neck, and forehead, often pulling out precious eyebrow hairs in the process. He'd spend so much time "cleaning Brad's face" and going so deep into his ears that I often asked Brad if he'd smeared peanut butter all over his head beforehand.

I'll admit that I sometimes got a little jealous when Brad would get more kisses than me, but I knew deep down that I was the one Benny couldn't live without. When Brad left after our weekends together, Benny would be mopey for a day, but when I went away and left him with Brad, my dad, or one of my sisters—even if just for a few hours—he would bark and cry and howl like his world had shattered. He would calm down after a while, but there was never a doubt that Benny was Mommy's Boy. And when I'd return, no matter how long I'd been away—whether it was a few hours or a few days—Benny would always be waiting with bated doggie breath to see me. He'd instantly perk up and break into the Benny Boogie. With his tail whipping around like a helicopter blade, he'd jump up and down, shake his little tushy, and give me that toothy grin. And if he was *really* ecstatic, he'd nab one of my slippers and zealously thrash his head from side to side as if it were his prey. If I tried to retrieve my footwear, he'd strut around the house with it in his mouth, always a step ahead of me, his little wigglebutt sashaying back and forth, before retreating to his bed like a lion taking his conquest to his lair. He'd never chew on the slipper, it was more about keeping it away from me, so it was a fun little game.

When Benny went for his annual checkup with Dr. Pam in April 2019, it had been nine months since she'd last seen him. In terms of his allergies, Benny seemed to be doing great, but I was concerned that he was still on the liquid hydrocortisone daily. However, whenever I'd ask Dr. Pam whether he needed it, she'd reiterate that the steroid was only a physiological dose. It was like listening to a broken record: physiological dose ... physiological dose ... physiological dose.

I couldn't really argue with her, though, because Benny's blood work showed that his kidney, liver, thyroid, and other levels were all within the normal range, and his IgA level had increased to 71. "His numbers all look good," she said. "This means we're on the right track and should stick to the protocol."

I dreaded keeping him on steroids that long, but my arguments fell on deaf ears. I knew stopping the steroids cold turkey was dangerous, so my options were to keep doing what we were doing or find a new vet and start all over from scratch. Reasoning that if things continued to go well with Brad, Benny and I would likely be moving to Indianapolis sooner rather than later, I decided to stick with Dr. Pam. The jury is still out on whether or not that was a wise choice.

Chapter 17

"Love Is All Around"

Love was definitely in the air in 2019 as Brad and I attended two weddings that year. In August, Brad's nephew and his college sweetheart were married in Cincinnati. It was a lovely, traditional Catholic ceremony with a modern rustic reception held at a former Gothic church, where I actually got Brad and his mom on the dance floor for a couple songs, including "The Twist" and "Shut Up and Dance." It was loads of fun, despite the fact that I got a bit banged up on some rides at Kings Island the day before, and I'm pretty sure I may have been mildly concussed. And that's not code for *hammered* or *intoxicated*. I mean I literally had a mild concussion from the whipping my head and neck took on a roller coaster called the Vortex, which was shut down for good later that year. Perhaps I should retire from concussion coasters.

In mid-November, Grant, one of Brad's closest friends in Indy, and his longtime girlfriend, Amanda, tied the knot. During the reception, I was chugging a glass of water after Brad and I returned from the dance floor when he leaned over and whispered in my ear, "We should go look at rings tomorrow."

I nearly did a spit take because I couldn't believe what I was hearing! Just a few years earlier, I'd given up hope that I'd ever find my soulmate and get married, but here Brad was, proposing a proposal. Wide-eyed and grinning from ear to ear, I looked at him to make sure he was serious—and sober. When I saw that he was smiling too, I knew he was sincere. I nodded excitedly in agreement.

When we got home from the reception, Brad took Benny for a walk while I changed into my pajamas. While Brad was changing, I gathered Benny in my arms and whispered, "Brad asked me to go ring shopping. That means he wants us to get married!"

When we were all settled on the couch for some TV and cuddle time, Benny bounced back and forth between Brad and me, bombarding us with kisses. Clearly, he was over the moon that he was finally going to have a daddy.

Christmas has always been my favorite holiday. After all, Santa brought me Arnold—the best Christmas gift I'd ever received—on that special day in 1979. Christmas Day forty years later was equally exciting, but for completely different reasons.

At this point, Brad and I had been dating long-distance for two and a half years, so for a while—especially after an engagement (and, therefore, a wedding) was on the horizon—we'd been discussing moving in together. As much as I loved the Chicago area and having Lori just a couple miles away, it simply made more sense that I would move to Indianapolis rather than Brad moving to Chicago. He'd been with the same company for over fifteen years, while I was self-employed and could work anywhere. Plus, Indy was midway between our families.

Therefore, a few days before Christmas of 2019, in preparation for putting my town house on the market, Brad came up to help me with some projects. Unfortunately, he arrived with a cold, so we laid low for the next two days while I nursed him back to health. On December 23, he woke up bright-eyed and bushy-tailed, clapped his hands together, and announced, "I'm cured! The malaise is gone! Let's paint the house!"

I really didn't think we had enough time to prep and put two coats of paint on my foyer, office, and living room, with its twenty-foot ceilings. The entire area amounted to about five- or six-hundred square feet, which seemed a bit ambitious, especially since Brad had been down for the count the previous two days. But we worked our butts off and got it done just before midnight.

The next day, we drove to my dad's house and dropped off Benny before going out for Christmas Eve dinner with Denise and Bernie, Lori, and my dad. Afterward, we went back to Dad's so Benny could open his presents from his aunts and grandpa, then we all went our separate ways. As Lori headed west back to the Chicago area, I drove Benny, Brad, and I south to Indy, clinging white-knuckled to the steering wheel in a fog so thick I could barely see Ruby's bright red hood. To alleviate some of my stress, I quipped, "Santa is definitely gonna need Rudolph's assistance tonight!"

On Christmas morning, the three of us opened gifts at Brad's condo. In his polka-dotted PJs with a hoodie adorned with reindeer antlers, Benny—the expert present opener—ricocheted across the couch, not unlike a metal orb in a pinball machine, ripping the paper off his own gifts and helping Brad and me with ours.

Just when I thought all the gifts were unwrapped, Brad presented me with a large box with a gift tag from Santa. "You should probably open this one by yourself," he suggested.

Santa thought he was being clever by nesting several increasingly smaller wrapped boxes into a larger one, until only a tiny little package remained. I had a feeling I knew what the smallest one was, so I set my camera to record as I unwrapped the gorgeous diamond ring I'd picked out a few weeks earlier.

Sensing the significance of the moment, Benny sat calmly by my side as Brad proposed. When he uttered the words I'd waited my entire life to hear, I really thought I'd cry tears of joy, but I didn't. Although I was overwhelmed with emotion, my response was a squeaky "YES!" as I giggled with elation and planted a juicy kiss on his lips. Then I picked up Benny and the three of us danced around the room together, proclaiming, "We're getting married! We're getting married!"

For Benny, there were more surprises in store as we packed up our suitcases and made the two-hour drive to Brad's parents' house. Not only was he getting a daddy, he was also getting another grandpa, a grandma, two bonus aunts and uncles, and more cousins. He quickly made himself at home at Brad's parents' house, but he was also on his best behavior and followed the rules, particularly the one that he was only allowed on the living room couch if he was sitting on someone's lap.

Speaking of laps, Benny was a bit timid around his new family members, but he immediately took a liking to his Uncle Dan. Brad's brother is six feet eight, and Benny found his lengthy lap especially comfortable. Benny would lay on his back in Dan's lap and instantly doze off while Dan rubbed his belly or massaged his neck and shoulders. He would stay like that for as long as Dan would, but if I left the room to use the restroom or get something to drink, Benny would promptly spring to his feet to keep an eye on me. Even in a deep sleep, he was always Mommy's Boy.

In early January, Benny came out of retirement to make a Word of the Day post—*affianced*—to announce that his mommy and Braddy had gotten engaged. We didn't intend for it to be his last post, but that's what it turned out to be. With all the changes, drama, and excitement that 2020 elicited, we were way too busy to blog.

Chapter 18

Road Warriors

By late January, my house was officially on the market. The next time we went to visit Brad, Ruby was so full of stuff that Benny had to ride in his crate. We looked like the Beverly Hillbillies, but we had to start packing up because the first person who saw my place put in a nearly full-price offer, and I accepted, meaning we had just over a month to move.

I called my dad on the drive down to Brad's on Friday, but when he didn't answer, I left a message and didn't think much of it. It was after 8:00 p.m. and sometimes he fell asleep early, so I figured he'd call me back the next day. But he didn't, so I tried calling him a little earlier that evening. Still no answer.

When he hadn't called back by Sunday night, I started to worry. I tried phoning him around noon on Monday, January 27, but at that point, calls were going straight to his voice mail. I left a message and sent him an email, asking him to call me. After speaking to my sisters, we realized nobody had talked to him since Friday. When four o'clock rolled around and he still hadn't responded, I started to panic. I tried to call him again around five, and when he didn't respond, Denise decided to go over to the house.

When she arrived and Dad didn't answer the doorbell, she enlisted the neighbors to accompany her into the house because she didn't know what she might find. Luckily, Dad was in bed, fast asleep. He said he'd started not feeling well on Friday, after returning from lunch with his friends, so he went to bed early. And since then, he'd only gotten up to use the bathroom and possibly eat once or twice—he really couldn't remember.

Sensing that something wasn't right, Denise called an ambulance. When the paramedics arrived, they took his blood sugar and it registered over 500, so it's possible he was slipping into a diabetic coma. The EMTs transported him to the hospital, where he was eventually diagnosed with double pneumonia. A day later, they also said he was septic.

I haven't mentioned it but, for a while, my dad, who was eighty-one at this point, had been undergoing chemo and radiation for lung cancer that had also spread to his brain. By then, he was finished with those treatments and was getting immunotherapy injections every few weeks, but when he was diagnosed with double pneumonia, his oncologist suspended those as well.

On Wednesday, January 29, Benny and I headed to the South Bend area to visit my dad and take care of Lulu, his cat. It was difficult to see my dad, who'd always been a strong and hardy workhorse, looking so frail and struggling to breathe. Despite the fact that he could barely sit up and was on full-strength oxygen and two very strong antibiotics, after he'd been in the hospital less than two days, they started pushing to release him to a rehab facility. I was appalled. He could barely breathe, even with the oxygen turned up full blast, yet they thought it was safe for him to leave!

But it really wasn't up to us, so on Thursday, at the recommendation of the hospital staff, Denise and I visited three different rehab centers. The hospital arranged for his transfer to our second choice, which wasn't ideal, but there was nothing we could do about it. And fortunately—whether it was due to lack of availability at the rehab center or because Dad needed additional time in the hospital—he wasn't released until a week later, on February 7.

The following weekend, Brad joined Benny and me in South Bend to celebrate Valentine's Day and visit my dad. Brad returned to Indy on Sunday, but I stayed at my dad's house for a few more days because I had some very important business to attend to: wedding dress shopping. My sisters and I went after work one day so Margaret could join us. We were also able to bring Dad in a wheelchair after taking him out of rehab for a doctor's appointment. I only tried on four dresses that day, and it's true what they say, "When you find the right dress, you just know." Same goes for the right guy, I suppose.

The next day, I woke up in my childhood bedroom, lying on my back and unable to move. As I gently opened one eye and peeked out from behind my sleep mask to see what was pinning me down, I caught a glimpse of the culprit—or culprits in this case. "Ack! I'm trapped under the weight of a black panther and a baby polar bear!" I giggled.

Lulu was in the habit of pouncing on my dad's chest and purring in his face to wake him up, so, apparently, I was a close substitute in his absence. Benny would always get a little jealous and territorial if another dog—or cat, in this case—was too close to his mommy, so he got in on the action too, standing on my chest and smothering my face with kisses.

"I can't move, you guys! If you want me to feed you, you have to let me up!" It felt good to be loved and needed.

A few days later, Benny and I resumed our roles as road warriors, cutting a triangular path across the Midwest as we made frequent trips between Indy, South Bend, the Chicago area, and back again. It was extremely stressful trying to work, pack up my town house to move in with Brad, visit my dad in rehab, and plan a wedding while coordinating dates with the venue we'd chosen, vendors, and our family and friends.

Brad and I really wanted to get married on September 25, the day U2—the group that we both loved so much and had essentially brought us together—first formed as a band in Dublin back in 1976, and, coincidentally, the fifteenth anniversary of the day I'd met Mike, who introduced me to Brad. However, we'd decided to have the wedding at a hotel in South Bend, and although we'd made sure the Fighting Irish didn't have a home game that weekend, with former mayor Pete Buttigieg running for president, a debate was scheduled to take place in town then. As a result, all lodging in the area was booked up, so we eventually settled on October 17.

In late February, after a few days in Indy, my copilot Benny and I hightailed it back to Chez Bennifer to continue packing. Brad arrived the next day and helped move some of my stuff into two climate-controlled storage units. On Sunday, we loaded up a U-Haul truck with my furniture and other items that I wanted close by, then Brad drove it to Indy as Benny and I followed. For those keeping score, I also had two storage units in Indy, so four total, but I also had a fifteen-hundred-square-foot town house (plus a basement) full of practically brand-new furniture that I didn't want to part with.

In early March, Benny and I made our final trip to our town house. We cleaned up the place, packed Ruby to the gills, and said goodbye to Chez Bennifer ten minutes before the buyer was scheduled for his final walkthrough. It was an emotional time, roaming around our empty home where we'd made so many memories. I could hardly believe that five years had passed since we'd moved in, thinking it would be our forever home. I adored that place and hated making Benny leave his friends, but what better reason could there possibly be to move than love? I guess it's true that life has a way of surprising us, and something nobody was expecting was lurking just around the corner.

Chapter 19

Tummy Troubles

As Benny and I embarked on a new chapter in our lives and watched our town house disappear in Ruby's rearview mirror, we hopped on the Indiana Toll Road and headed east to South Bend to visit my Dad, who was still in rehab. Admittedly, I don't watch the news very often, so I was only marginally aware of some pesky little bug going around, known as COVID-19. But my dad watched the news about five times a day with the volume turned up full blast, so there was no escaping it as Benny and I visited him at the rehab center. And when word broke that the first case of the virus had been confirmed in Indiana—Indianapolis specifically—I started listening a little more intently. After all, since the previous fall, Brad had been riding Indy's spiffy new electric bus line to and from work, so I didn't want him getting infected with this highly contagious disease.

On March 12, Benny and I returned to Indy, which was officially home base at that point. Four days later, Benny and I were sitting in the living room, working on an editing project, when Brad returned from work, fresh off the bus.

"Honey and Bunny, I'm home!" he called as he walked through the door.

"Hey, Babe! Welcome home!" I shouted back.

Moments later, Brad stepped into the living room, clutching his laptop, monitor, and his own personal Keurig.

"Oh my God!" I exclaimed. "Did you ride home on the bus like that? You look like you just ransacked a Best Buy!"

"I did, and that's exactly how I felt. I was worried someone might jump me," he laughed.

Little did we know that would be his last day in the office for more than a year and a half.

In a twist of fate, around this same time, my dad was released from rehab. Given the weakened state of his lungs, a hospital or rehab facility was the worst possible place for him during what was, by then, a worldwide pandemic. So even though he still had a long recovery ahead of him, home was the safest place he could be. My sisters and I took shifts staying with him for the first few weeks while he recovered at home.

With everything going on, Brad and I had to delay Benny's birthday party for almost two weeks, but he didn't mind. He waited patiently to tear into his presents with vigor when they were placed in front of him. And as usual, he had to sample each type of treat he received, ripping open each bag with his teeth. *I'll take one of those and one of those and one of those . . .*

By early summer, we'd settled into a routine—well, as much of a routine as you can get when you're working full-time, looking for houses, visiting a recuperating parent who lives more than two hours away, and planning a wedding during a global pandemic while doing your own invitations and floral arrangements. But in late June, it was becoming increasingly apparent that the likelihood of having a traditional wedding with more than a hundred guests was risky at best or, at worst, not going to happen. So we pivoted to Plan B, which was to have a small, intimate ceremony at an outdoor venue in Indianapolis in 2020 and reschedule the band and the venue in South Bend for 2021. It wasn't ideal to limit our 2020 guest list to twenty people, but at least we could get married on September 25, which only seemed appropriate since it was U2's anniversary.

Just like we had when we first moved to the Chicago suburbs in 2015, Benny and I took long walks and explored our new neighborhood. Unfortunately, there were hardly any small dogs nearby—and during the pandemic, people didn't want to mingle with strangers—so Benny didn't make any new friends (nor did I). But Brad's place was close to a park and the Indianapolis Art Center, which runs along the White River, so there was an abundance of wildlife, particularly squirrels and chipmunks, which Benny loved . . . or hated, depending on your perspective.

One time, Benny took off like a horse shooting out of the gates at the Kentucky Derby, dragging me behind him in hot pursuit of some invisible prey. With the leash extended as far as it would go and my arm stretched to the max, I struggled to keep up with him in my summer dress and flip-flops. Finally, after about a quarter mile, he stop in front of the ground-level window of an apartment building. With his tail wildly whipping back and forth like a windshield wiper on high, he began to yip and yap, emitting his squirrel-hunting yelp. But for the life of me, I could not see what he was barking at.

"Benny, are you barking at your own reflection in the window?" I asked quizzically.

Just as I began to question my boy's sanity, a chipmunk popped its little head out of a hole in the ground and hightailed it out of there. The chase was back on! As the chipmunk sped away looking for a safe place to hide, Benny yanked on the reins like a runaway horse towing a wagon—me being the wagon. Giddyup!

I'd come home from these walks exhausted and dripping with sweat, but seeing Benny's face light up when he took off after a pesky little critter made it all worthwhile.

It was a hot and humid summer, so in late June when Benny started having diarrhea almost every time he went outside, I thought maybe he wasn't drinking enough water. It's not easy finding a new vet (or doctors for humans either) during a pandemic, but when the Big D persisted for over a week—even after feeding him a bland diet of home-cooked turkey, rice, and sweet potatoes—I took Benny to a vet in the neighborhood. Due to COVID restrictions, I had to wait in my vehicle while the doctor examined him, did some blood work, and took a stool sample. When all was said and done, the vet prescribed metronidazole, which is used to treat infections and inflammatory conditions that cause diarrhea. In the meantime, he recommended that I continue with the bland diet, give Benny some Imodium, and drop his hydrocortisone down to every other day. *Finally, a doctor who agrees that he shouldn't be on the steroid daily.*

Despite the diarrhea, Benny's appetite, energy level, and joie de vivre remained robust. He was still a happy-go-lucky guy who loved to chase squirrels and chipmunks (even though I was clearly slowing him down and hindering his ability to hunt), bask in the sun, and roll in the grass. In fact, one day after work, Brad and I were taking him for a stroll along a quiet street in the neighborhood when he stopped to take a break and do his "roly-polies." With the scent of freshly mowed grass permeating the air, Benny had a huge grin on his face as he vigorously wriggled back and forth, scratching his back on the lawn. But with each twist and turn, he edged closer and closer to the curb.

There was no traffic on the street, so he wasn't in immediate danger, but as the mama bear, I was keeping a close eye on my little cub. "You better be careful or your gonna roll right off the curb," I warned him.

He kept squirming and wiggling, rubbing his back in the grass until, "Whooooaaa . . . ," he tumbled down the curb. I scooped him up just before he hit the ground. "You silly boy. I knew that was gonna happen. And now you've got a grass stain on your back."

By early July, Benny's diarrhea had gotten worse. He always let us know when he had to go potty, but one night, in the wee hours of the morning while Brad and I were fast asleep, he hopped off the bed, scurried into the closet, and pooped on the wood floor.

"Oh, Buns. . . . Are you okay?" I cooed as I met him in the closet and caressed his back.

With his tail hanging limply between his legs, Benny bowed his head, tucked his ears back, and looked up at me with sad eyes, ashamed and embarrassed by his accident. While Brad was getting dressed to take him outside, I continued, "You're not in trouble, Bunny. We know you wouldn't potty in the house if you could help it. And I'm really impressed that you went into the closet to go on the hardwood floor. The carpet in the bedroom would be much more difficult to clean. You're brilliant, Baby Boy!"

A few hours later when we got up, I called the vet and he was able to see Benny that day. He did a battery of tests, sent in another fecal sample, and gave Benny a vitamin B12 injection. It took a week to get the results of the fecal culture, and when they came back negative, the vet gave the okay for Benny to resume his raw diet. By this time, we'd switched to turkey as the main protein source, and when I fed him dinner that evening, he tore into his food like a fox in a henhouse.

Toward the end of July, Benny and I were back in the South Bend area to take my dad to a doctor's appointment. The day after we arrived, Benny had explosive diarrhea. And when I say explosive, I mean it literally shot out of him like a bowl of chili blowing up in the microwave. Fortunately, we were outside when it happened.

But as I said, aside from the tummy troubles, he seemed fine. He was still his perky little self and his appetite was strong—so strong that when we were at my dad's house, he'd try to sneak Lulu's cat food. I had to constantly be on guard to prevent my little bandit from gorging himself on Friskies and Sheba.

Given the persistent diarrhea, Benny's vet referred him to the VCA, a specialty and emergency animal hospital, for further testing. However, the first available appointment wasn't until the third week of August. In the meantime, I researched other specialty clinics where I might take Benny, but I soon learned that the VCA was the best in the area. Pet parents would literally drive hours to take their sick or injured dogs and cats there to get the best treatment possible.

By the time we went to the appointment at the VCA, Benny's tummy troubles had calmed down a bit; instead of having the Big D every time he went outside, it was only occurring about once a day. Still, I kept the appointment because, in my gut, I knew something wasn't right. Since Benny's last appointment with the holistic doctor in Illinois, he'd lost two pounds, which might not seem like a lot to a human, but for him, that was 12 percent of his body weight. Some of it might've been the switch from beef to the leaner turkey, but to have runny orangish-tan stool every day just wasn't normal.

Benny was scheduled for a drop-off appointment, which meant he would see the doctor, but I wouldn't. Dr. Hui, one of the internal medicine doctors at the VCA, called me after his initial examination of Benny. Dr. Hui offered up two options for determining the cause of Benny's persistent diarrhea: The more conservative route would be to start with a panel of blood tests. A more aggressive or assertive approach would be an abdominal ultrasound. I chose the more conservative approach because the ultrasound would require Benny to undergo sedation, which, to me, was the same as anesthesia. I was worried about putting Benny under anesthesia unless absolutely necessary because of the warning his first vet had given about him having a heart arrhythmia. I also recalled a conversation I'd had with Jerry, Chewee's dad, from our old neighborhood in Hanover Park.

As we rounded a bend near my town house while taking the boys for a walk, Jerry pointed to one of the single-family homes and asked in his Polish accent, "Do you remember Coco, the little dog that lived there?"

"Sure . . . she's a Yorkie," I said. "We'd sometimes see her wandering around in her front yard all alone."

"Well, apparently, she went to the vet last week to get her teeth cleaned (which requires anesthesia), and she died on the table," Jerry said. "She was only four."

"Oh my God! That's terrible!" I cried. "Poor Coco."

I knew I'd never forgive myself if something like that happened to Benny, so I told Dr. Hui to start with the blood work. I figured if the ultrasound was necessary after we got the results of the blood tests, we'd weigh our options then. In other words, we'd cross that bridge when we came to it.

Benny's blood work came back a few days later. The panel tested his B12, folate, and pancreatic levels, and everything came back within the normal range, except his B12 was slightly elevated, which could've been from the B12 shot he'd had a month earlier.

In the meantime, Benny was getting itchy again, so I took him to an animal dermatologist in the area. The dermatologist diagnosed Benny with bacterial and yeast infections on his paws and lip folds, so he prescribed two different medications to treat them. And based on Benny's recent bouts of diarrhea and history of allergies, the dermatologist also recommended weaning Benny completely off the steroids and starting a food trial with a novel protein, so we opted to switch to rabbit, which was something I'd never fed him before. Given that I love bunnies and one of Benny's nicknames was Bunny, it was a difficult decision, but there's nothing I wouldn't have done for his health and well-being.

We were supposed to follow up with the dermatologist in four weeks, which was the week of the wedding, but the universe had other plans.

Chapter 20

Are We in an Episode of Grey's Anatomy?

On the afternoon of Saturday, September 12, Brad, his friend Grant, and I were in the living room watching an IndyCar race. Benny was snuggled up next to me as I worked on my laptop, designing programs for the wedding, which was less than two weeks away. Since his visit with Dr. Hui and the dermatologist a few weeks earlier, Benny had been doing much better. Per the dermatologist's instructions, we'd been slowly weaning Benny off the hydrocortisone, which relieved a lot of my anxiety. He'd originally been taking 0.5 ml per day and we'd just gotten him down to 0.1 ml. We'd also been gradually switching him from turkey to rabbit, and for the past week, he'd been eating rabbit exclusively. He wasn't thrilled with the extremely limited diet required for the food trial—he missed his cookies and minty fresh dental chews—but we found some crunchy, freeze-dried rabbit snacks and the dermatologist said he could also have bite-sized pieces of apple for a treat. He devoured anything we offered him, and that Saturday morning in September was no exception. He wolfed down his breakfast like a ravenous beast, had pep in his step, and didn't even have diarrhea.

However, later in the day, while we were all gathered in the living room watching the race, Benny flew off the couch and vomited, which is something he rarely did.

I ran to Benny's side and comforted him, "Poor Baby Boy. Are you okay? Did you eat your breakfast too quickly?"

Brad took him outside while I cleaned up, and we hoped it was just an anomaly.

Benny laid low for the rest of the day, but he did drink a lot of water. However, whenever we'd take him outside to potty, he'd just sit on the ground, looking a bit out of sorts. As a result, throughout the day, he had a couple accidents on the floor, which also wasn't like him. When dinnertime rolled around, Benny refused to eat anything, which—if you haven't already realized—was highly unusual for him. By nine o'clock, he was lethargic and completely sapped of the energy he'd had in the morning, and by the time we were preparing to go to bed, he'd thrown up three times.

Brad always tries to look on the bright side and come up with a practical reason for things, so he tried convincing himself—and me—that there was a logical explanation for Benny's illness. "Maybe he just Hoovered up a stray crushed red pepper flake from the pizza last night," Brad speculated.

I try to maintain a positive attitude too, but I knew this wasn't normal behavior for Benny. "I admire you thinking outside the box," I said to Brad just before midnight, "but the red pepper theory just doesn't seem plausible to me. I'm gonna take Benny to the ER at the VCA."

Brad wanted to wait until morning, but I pushed back. "I know Benny, and something is definitely wrong, so I'm taking him to the VCA with or without you."

Brad reluctantly agreed to go.

When we arrived, they immediately took Benny to the back to examine him while we waited in our vehicle due to COVID restrictions. I'd brought my tablet and tried to read a book, but it was difficult to concentrate because I was worried about my little boy.

Around 2:45 a.m., we received a call from Dr. Stephanie, the emergency vet working that night. "We gave Benny subcutaneous fluids and Cerenia, an antinausea med," she began. "But our VetScan—which is a machine to run blood tests in-house—isn't working properly, so we'll have to send those to an outside lab, which means we won't get the results until Monday."

"So, can we take him home?" I asked.

"Yes," Dr. Stephanie replied, "but call us or bring him back if he doesn't improve or gets worse."

Our butts were dragging all day on Sunday. Benny continued to drink water, but he still wouldn't eat. At that point, the food trial was the least of our concerns, so I offered him his favorite foods, but he refused them all, even peanut butter, which, under normal circumstances, he loved to gently lick off my fingers.

On Monday morning, the results of Benny's blood work from the outside lab came back, and it didn't sound good. Several of the counts were elevated, indicating possible pancreatitis, so they recommended that I bring Benny back after 6:00 p.m., when Dr. Stephanie's shift began.

When we arrived, Dr. Stephanie ran another comprehensive blood panel. I was sitting in Ruby, waiting in the parking lot, when she called with the results. "Some of Benny's liver and pancreatic values are slightly higher than they were in the blood drawn on early Sunday morning," she began, "so I still can't rule out pancreatitis or an underlying GI issue. At this point, I recommend admitting Benny to the hospital so he can get an abdominal ultrasound in the morning."

Knowing how much we'd miss each other and that he'd be uncomfortable in a kennel, I didn't want to leave him overnight, so I asked, "Could I just bring him back first thing in the morning for the ultrasound?"

"You could, but if he stays overnight, he'll already be in the queue for the ultrasound," Dr. Stephanie explained. So basically, the inpatients got first dibs.

Ultimately, I agreed to keep him there overnight, knowing that he'd be able to get the ultrasound sooner rather than later and he'd be on fluids and monitored all night. Leaving him there was heart-wrenching, but I knew it was for the best.

The tech was kind enough to bring Benny out to the SUV so I could say goodnight. My eyes welled with tears as I hugged him, gave him a kiss on the head, cupped his cheeks in my hands, and said, "You need to have a test in the morning, so you're gonna spend the night here, Bunny. You be a good boy for the doctors and nurses, get some rest, and try to eat and drink something, okay? Mommy and Braddy will miss you SO much, but we'll see you tomorrow."

By the look in his eyes, I could tell he was a combination of scared, anxious, and just downright weary. Once he and the tech were inside and out of view, I started Ruby and drove away as the waterworks began to overflow.

At six o'clock on Tuesday morning, Dr. Stephanie called to let us know that Benny's ultrasound was scheduled for around eleven. She also said he'd been stable overnight, was better hydrated, and had even eaten a few bites of canned chicken. At that point, I didn't care that he might be allergic to chicken. I was just glad he was eating.

A little after noon, Dr. Stephanie called back with the findings from the ultrasound. "Benny has severe, acute necrotizing pancreatitis," she announced.

My heart sank as I asked, "Oh my God. That sounds scary. What does that mean?"

"It means that the linings of his stomach and pancreas are inflamed. Plus, the central area of his pancreas shows decreased blood flow, which means the tissue is dead," Dr. Stephanie explained.

I let out a breathy gasp, but words escaped me. Eventually, the vet filled the silence. "He needs pretty advanced care, so he'll have to be hospitalized for at least seventy-two hours. And if he doesn't start eating on his own, we many need to insert a feeding tube."

"Could weaning him off the steroids have caused the pancreatitis?" I wondered.

"No. I don't think so," she answered.

After hearing Dr. Stephanie's diagnosis, I became a guilt-ridden nervous wreck. From the moment I'd become Benny's mommy, I tried my hardest to give him the best life and keep him healthy, safe, and strong. My stomach and neck muscles tensed as I slumped on the couch, wrought with worry that something I'd done had caused this. I bawled as I wondered, *Should I not have taken him to the holistic vet? Should I have insisted a long time ago that I wanted him weaned off the steroids? Should I not have fed him a raw diet, despite Dr. Pam and the nutritionist insisting that it was best for him?*

God, please let Benny recover from this, I begged as I stared into space, my glasses speckled with tears, *and help me make the right decisions for his health and well-being going forward.*

Fortunately, Benny started eating extremely well when they offered him chicken, so he didn't need to have a feeding tube inserted. He was also drinking on his own and his vitals were stable, so on Wednesday, they transferred him from the ICU to internal medicine, where he was placed under the care of Dr. Hui.

When we were finally given permission to visit Benny, I couldn't wait to see him! He and I were so attached to each other that being apart, even for a couple days, was unbearable. When we arrived, I immediately relaxed because he looked much better than he had on Saturday. He had a little IV attached to his arm and he seemed a bit drowsy, but his eyes were bright and alert and he was clearly happy to see us. Brad and I took turns holding him, and after about thirty minutes, a tech came in to take him back to his "room," aka kennel. It was difficult leaving him, but I felt confident that he was going to pull through and would be home soon.

The next day, I was out running errands in preparation for the wedding. I was leaving Dick's Sporting Goods, where I'd just purchased a wagon for Benny in case he couldn't walk down the aisle with me and my dad as planned. As I drove to my next stop, my cell phone rang through Ruby's speakers. It was Margaret.

Margaret and I had been friends for twenty years at that point, and I wanted her to be my maid of honor, but she didn't want such a visible role in the wedding, nor did she want to wear a brides-maid's dress, so she offered to be our photographer instead. But as we talked, she became choked up. "I'm really sorry, but I'm not going to be able to attend your wedding."

"What???" I exclaimed. "Why not? What's going on?"

We wept together over the phone as she explained that she was dealing with some serious medical issues. "I'll be having surgery, but the hospital can't get me in until early October. And right now, I just feel too weak to travel, even with Scott doing the driving."

I wanted so badly for her to be there that I said, "Let me talk to Brad tonight about postponing the wedding until you're feeling better." But Margaret wouldn't dream of it.

I couldn't believe what was happening. First it didn't look like my dad would survive to walk me down the aisle and then Benny ended up critically ill and in the hospital. But the two of them were finally on the mend, and now I was worried that something had to be seriously wrong with Margaret if she couldn't attend the wedding. All this medical drama seemed surreal, like I was watching an episode of *Grey's Anatomy*.

A couple hours later, Brad and I were on our way to the VCA to bring our little boy home from the hospital. We were told that his prognosis was very good and that his pancreas could still function well, despite the fact that part of it was necrotized. They sent us home with a small pharmacy of meds, including Cerenia for nausea, an appetite stimulant, pain pills, and an antacid. We were told that he should continue with his previous diet of raw rabbit, but it was recommended that we completely wean him off the hydrocortisone, which I was all for.

Benny was a little weak when we left, but he was on the road to recovery. I think we all breathed a sigh of relief as we turned a corner on our way to the finish line, i.e., our wedding day, when the three of us would officially become a family.

Chapter 21

A Beautiful Day

On the morning of September 25, 2020, despite the fact that I'd only slept a few hours, I woke up bright-eyed and bushy-tailed. Okay, maybe I was more bleary-eyed and Benny was bushy-tailed. Either way, I was filled to the brim with excitement because the day I'd always dreamed of had finally arrived: I was about to marry my soulmate and become Mrs. Jennifer Schaeffer.

As a traditionalist, I felt strongly that Brad and I shouldn't see each other until we met at the altar, or in this case, under our wedding arch at Fort Harrison State Park, so Benny and I had spent the previous night at a hotel. Benny wasn't quite at 100 percent yet, but he'd made a tremendous recovery in the week since we'd brought him home from the hospital, and he was clearly excited for the day that Braddy officially became Daddy.

Around noon, I was bouncing around the room like a Ping-Pong ball, trying to get ready for the momentous occasion. I'd already showered, had my hair styled, and dressed Benny in the suit I'd had customized for him. In its original form, it was a toddler-sized gray suit vest and pants with a lavender button-down dress shirt and a matching plaid clip-on tie. A few weeks earlier, I'd taken him to a tailor in the neighborhood. After getting Benny's measurements, the tailor removed the sleeves from the dress shirt and combined the vest and shirt into one, so I could easily slip it on my handsome little boy. I promised Benny I wouldn't make him wear the pants, even though that would've made him over-the-top adorable. As it was, Benny looked downright dapper in his suit.

Lori and Denise were running late because they'd been scrambling to finish decorating the arch at the park, so I needed someone to help me get into my dress. My dad had recently arrived at the hotel, but he was struggling just to get himself dressed. *I wish Mom or Margaret were here,* I thought to myself, and not just because I needed help zipping my dress.

Just then there was a knock on the door. I looked through the peephole and saw Laura—the wife of Brad's best man, John. From the moment we met, Laura and I became instant friends. She'd also graciously stepped in at the last minute to fill Margaret's role as our photographer.

"I was just stopping by to see if you need any help getting ready," Laura greeted as I opened the door.

"You read my mind," I said as I ushered her in. I was still in my bathrobe and my makeup was only halfway complete. I probably looked like Two-Face, the villain from the Batman comics.

"What can I do?" Laura asked.

"After I finish my makeup, I could really use some help getting into my dress."

"Sure. No problem."

"Could you help me button my shirt and fasten my tie?" my dad asked Laura. "These damn sausage fingers don't work like they used to."

Laura laughed and, without hesitation, she patiently buttoned my dad's shirt and helped him put on his suit coat, even though she'd never met him before.

With my makeup complete, Laura helped me don my dress and all the accoutrements, which was more difficult than I'd expected.

Despite being a bit late to my own wedding, the day went off without a hitch. We couldn't have asked for more perfect weather; I just wish Margaret could've been there. Benny and my dad successfully walked me down the aisle, Grant served as officiant, Dr. Bob recited my favorite Bible passage (1 Corinthians 13), and Scott read a heartfelt tribute that Margaret had penned. Throughout the ceremony, Benny sat patiently by my side.

After the wedding, we held a luncheon and reception under a pavilion in the park. While Brad and I had our first dance to U2's

"Slow Dancing," Benny sat next to my dad nearby. He beamed at us with pride as if thinking, "That's my mommy and daddy!"

Next up, we had the traditional father-bride dance, followed by the mother-groom dance, and then it was time for something special: a bride and son dance. I often sang the song "You Are My Sunshine" to Benny, so when it was time for our special dance, it was the perfect choice. I chose the winsome yet haunting version that Christina Perri had released the year before as a sort of lullaby.

As the song began, I crouched down and cradled Benny's face in my hands, caressing his cheeks as I serenaded him. Then he stood on his hind legs and I held his hands as we swayed back and forth. Toward the end of the song, I scooped him up in my arms, then he rested his paws on my shoulders and nuzzled his face close to mine. And as we danced cheek to cheek, I whispered the lyrics in his ear. It was one of the most tender moments we ever shared and one that I'll always cherish.

Brad and I didn't take a honeymoon. With all the travel restrictions during the pandemic, it was difficult to plan anything. Plus, we wanted to go someplace where we could take Benny with us. So we put it on hold and concentrated on finding a house.

We'd been looking at houses all summer and had actually put in a couple strong offers, but both were rejected. I don't take rejection well, so it was hard to get back on the figurative horse after our offers were turned down, but we hopped right back in the saddle. A few days after the wedding, I was performing my morning ritual of scrolling through listings on Redfin during morning cuddles with Benny, when two in particular—both in the suburbs—caught my eye.

Brad was initially resistant to the idea of moving to the suburbs. He really liked the walkability of the Broad Ripple neighborhood, but the houses and lot sizes there didn't correlate with what we— mostly me—were looking for. I wanted a newish home (built in the 1990s or later), preferably Craftsman or modern farmhouse style, with a pool or the room to build one. Brad wanted a basement, a reasonably sized yard, didn't want to increase his commute by much, and wanted to be close to the bike trail where he and Grant rode nearly every day.

These two houses met all those criteria. Well, one did. It had a gorgeous deck with an inground pool, a spacious kitchen, and a finished basement with lots of storage. It was built in 1996 and was a short bike ride away from the trail. The other house was newer (built in 2014), was Craftsman style, and was a little closer to the trail, but it had an unfinished basement. The yard had space for a pool, but we had no idea if the HOA would allow us to build one, although two homes in the subdivision had them. After discussing it with Brad, we contacted our realtor to set up some showings. Since this wasn't our first rodeo playing the home-buying game during the 2020 real-estate boom, our realtor got us in to see both homes that same day.

On the way home, Brad and I discussed the two, very similar, homes we'd just toured.

"Obviously, I like the one with the existing pool and a price tag that's $20K less," I admitted.

"But the Craftsman house is newer and closer to the trail," Brad countered.

"We're literally talking about a difference of a half mile," I scoffed.

"I know," Brad replied. "But something about the house with the pool just rubs me the wrong way."

"What do you mean?" I questioned.

"I don't know. I can't really put it into words," he said. "I just get a bad vibe from it."

"I'll happily get a sage stick and cleanse it of any evil spirits, if it makes you feel better," I chuckled.

But he had his heart set on the Craftsman house. And when I saw that it literally went on the market while we were getting married, I took it as a sign that it was meant to be. I deferred my dream of having a pool and we made an offer on the Craftsman house just a few hours after seeing it.

The next day, Brad and I were sitting in the stands at the Indianapolis Motor Speedway, watching an IndyCar race, when our realtor called. If you've never been to an auto race, let me preface this by saying that it's extremely loud, like 130 decibels, which is louder than a jet taking off or a jackhammer striking concrete. We always wear earplugs when we're at a race, so when Brad answered the phone vibrating in his pocket, it was difficult for him to hear what our realtor was saying.

When he hung up, I asked impatiently, "So, what did he say?"

"Well, I had a hard time hearing him," Brad replied.

"Obviously."

"But I'm pretty sure he said that our offer has been accepted. We just bought a house!"

We called the realtor on the way home to make sure Brad had heard him correctly. He had. When we got home, I picked up Benny and the three of us danced around the living room as we excitedly told him that we'd bought a house—and that two of our favorite drivers (Josef Newgarden and Alexander Rossi) had come in first and second in the race. It was a good day in the Schaeffer household.

Brad, Benny, and I moved into our new house just before Thanksgiving in 2020. Due to the pandemic, we weren't able to celebrate with our families, so it was a quiet day, just the three of us. We had a lot to be grateful for that year: our health, our new home, each other, and that we'd pulled off a pandemic wedding without anyone getting the dreaded virus. Plus, Benny and my dad were recovering from their health scares, and even though we'd learned shortly after the wedding that Margaret had cancer, she was in treatment and doing well. And so, after packing and unpacking my four storage units and Brad's condo, we were thankful for a nice, relaxing day in our new abode.

After settling in to our new place, Brad and I made the tough decision to cancel the vow renewal ceremony and wedding reception that we'd planned to have in South Bend, which would've included all the guests we couldn't invite to our 2020 wedding due to COVID restrictions. We didn't want to cancel it—in fact, we were very much looking forward to it—but a series of events led us to that decision.

First, the members of the U2 tribute band that we'd hired—whom I'd been friends with for years—had a falling out and broke up due to irreconcilable differences. But more importantly, COVID-19 was still rearing its ugly head and we didn't want our celebration to potentially cause an outbreak among our family and friends. Plus, my dad was growing increasingly weaker even though his cancer seemed to be at bay, Margaret was still undergoing chemo, and my elderly friend Dr. Bob was declining healthwise.

There were just too many variables out of our control. And even though it wasn't quite what we'd dreamed of with all our friends and family there and a U2 cover band playing during the reception, our 2020 wedding had been beautiful and nobody had gotten sick from attending. We'd been lucky in 2020, so we didn't want to roll the dice and take a chance with COVID still hanging around.

Chapter 22

Thunderbolt, Needles, and Simone Biles, Oh My!

In late 2020, Benny seemed to be thriving after being weaned off the hydrocortisone and recovering from his bout of pancreatitis. But at the beginning of 2021, his allergies came back with a vengeance. It started off with another ear infection and a skin infection on his belly. We left the vet with more ear drops and antibiotics.

After a few weeks, the infections cleared up and the itching subsided, but by April, Thumper was back and nibbling his paws like they were carrots. It got so bad that I had to put booties on him. If Brad and I went somewhere, we had to wrap Benny's paws with breathable medical tape (hot pink or purple was all I could find) to keep him from biting them and scratching himself bloody. With his paws wrapped, Benny reminded Brad of a racehorse, so we gave him a competitive nickname: Thunderbolt. And to hinder him from removing the tape with his teeth—which he did until we learned our lesson—he had to wear the cone of shame when left alone. So back to the vet we went. When we came home with more antibiotics, it was clear that the vicious cycle we'd been trapped in back in Chicagoland, prior to seeing the holistic vet and starting the hydrocortisone, was starting anew.

That summer, I found a holistic and naturopathic vet in the Indianapolis area and took Benny there specifically for his allergies. That vet even tried acupuncture, but nothing worked. When a new veterinary practice offering both traditional and holistic treatment options opened about a mile from our new house, we decided to give it a try.

From the moment we met Dr. Steve, I knew he was Benny's new vet. With his salt-and-pepper hair and kind eyes, even behind the N95 mask, I could tell that he cared about the health and well-being of each and every one of his patients. Not that Benny's former doctors didn't, but it was a relief to find someone who was genuinely interested in finding the source of Benny's allergies rather than just treating the symptoms with whatever medication the pharmaceutical companies were pushing. Plus, Dr. Steve sat down on the floor and got to know Benny on his level.

"Who's a good boy?" Dr. Steve said as he scratched Benny's velvety ears.

Benny, who, moments earlier, had been trembling in my arms while we waited in the pristine, cinnamon-scented room, quickly warmed up to Dr. Steve. Benny rolled on his back and tapped Dr. Steve's hand, which was his way of saying, "That feels good, Mister, but I'd prefer a belly rub instead."

During our appointment, Dr. Steve explained, "In dogs, allergies are often the biproduct of an unhealthy gut biome, so I'd like to switch Benny to a higher quality probiotic and add colostrum, which helps combat allergies by boosting the immune system."

I greatly appreciated the fact that Dr. Steve respected my concerns about not overmedicating Benny and said he would only prescribe pharmaceutical meds when absolutely necessary.

But after about six months of Dr. Steve's individualized treatments, Benny was still struggling with allergies and his itchiness was out of control. Nothing seemed to help, despite the fact that every weekend I was cleaning the house from top to bottom, vacuuming, washing our sheets, blankets, and Benny's beds with a naturally derived, fragrance-free detergent, and bathing Benny with a gentle, anti-itch shampoo. I was also washing his paws every time we came inside after a walk. The only thing that gave Benny a little relief was applying a skin-soothing balm to his paws. So, in the spring of 2022, Dr. Steve referred Benny to Dr. Lori, an animal allergist and dermatologist in the area.

I immediately liked Dr. Lori with her cheerful smile, bubbly personality, genuine concern, gentle demeanor, and love for her patients. I secretly wished she could be my dermatologist/allergist.

Benny needed a little more convincing. As he stood on the metal table while she examined him from nose to tail, his entire body quivered with fear, causing the table to shake and rattle like a pair of maracas.

"You're okay, Bunny," I reassured him. "Mommy won't let you fall."

"Oh, Benny, you're so handsome!" Dr. Lori cooed. "Just relax. . . . I'm not gonna hurt you."

After her examination, Dr. Lori said, "I'd like to start off by testing Benny for environmental allergies, but first I'll need to do a skin scraping to see if these crusties between his toes contain yeast."

I was all in, so she took the scraping and then went to review it under a microscope. When she returned a few minutes later, she said, "Well, he definitely has a yeast infection, so we'll have to hold off on testing for environmental allergies until the infection clears."

"Okay," I replied. "His vet back in Illinois tested him for food allergies and said he was allergic to corn, oatmeal, whitefish, and possibly chicken and pork. Do you need a copy of those results?"

"No, unfortunately, the only *true* test for food allergies in dogs is an elimination diet."

In other words, the test that Dr. Pam had done was pretty much bunk.

After Benny's yeast infection cleared up, Dr. Lori tested him for environmental allergies in much the same way that I had been years earlier, although he needed minor sedation. While Benny was deeply relaxed, a large patch of fur was shaved from his side and a grid of eighty-one black dots was drawn on his skin. On each of those dots, a small amount of a potential allergen was inserted under the skin to see which ones caused a reaction.

A little while later, Dr. Lori came back to the room with my groggy doggie. Benny sat on my lap, looking a bit stoned, as Dr. Lori went over the results, which were quite revealing.

She handed me a copy and went over them with me. "So, as you can see, Benny is allergic to a handful of molds, grasses, trees, and weeds."

"Just like me," I said. *Like mother, like son.*

"Do you know if you have any of them around your house?" Dr. Lori inquired.

"Not that I'm aware of."

Benny was also allergic to cats, horses, and sheep, which may not sound like an issue since we don't have any of those animals, but he was occasionally around my dad's cat, Lulu, and our house was built on a former horse farm. But the most astonishing revelation was that Benny was allergic to humans! When I saw that on the list, I exclaimed, "Benny is allergic to humans?! I guess it makes sense, since people can be allergic to dogs, but I had no idea that dogs can be allergic to people. Huh ..."

Armed with this newfound knowledge, Dr. Lori went to work formulating three vials of serum containing small amounts of antigens of the things that caused Benny the greatest allergic reaction. Brad and I would need to inject a gradually increasing amount of this "allergen-specific immunotherapy" into Benny's scruff every day and keep track of his itch level. Sounds easy, right?

It should've been.

When I'd first mentioned to Brad that we might have to give Benny allergy shots, he bragged, "I can do it. No problem. I had to give my snake vitamin and antibiotic injections when I was a kid." (I'm not using the word *snake* as a euphemism for anything. When he was younger, Brad actually had a ball python, which ate dead mice. God bless his mother! I thank my lucky stars he grew out of that phase!)

But when it was time for us to actually give Benny the first injection, Brad grew pale and clammed up. "I don't think I can do it. How 'bout I hold Buns and you give him the shot?"

I rolled my eyes, pursed my lips, and shook my head but reluctantly agreed. I'd given Arnold subcutaneous fluids toward the end of his life, and even though that was more than twenty years earlier, I figured I could do it. After all, when the tech demonstrated how to do it at Dr. Lori's office, she'd made it look so easy. But I failed to remember two things: 1) Benny was a *very* sensitive little guy; and 2) He was still coming out of sedation during the demonstration.

Nevertheless, the three of us got comfortable on the love seat with Brad holding Benny in a loose headlock while I positioned myself behind him. I parted Benny's white fur, took a deep breath, and prepared for the poke. I'd barely touched Benny with the needle, much less pierced his skin, when he let out a yelp and lunged toward Brad and away from me as if he'd been stung by a bee.

I wasn't about to give up, though. I was determined to make this work and treat Benny's allergies naturally. So I walked to the fridge, got an ice cube, then used it to numb the scruff of Benny's neck. When I inserted the needle and gave him the shot, he didn't feel a thing.

But as time went on and we had to increase the amount of antigen in each injection, we learned to distract Benny with treats. Brad would hold a handful of freeze-dried rabbit treats in his palm and Benny would snarf them down while I injected the serum into him.

Over time, we got much better at the process, but Brad was always the most stressed of the three of us. Although I wasn't thrilled about poking my little guy with a needle, I knew it was for his own well-being. Plus, by numbing him and feeding him treats, he didn't really notice. *You wanna give me a handful of treats? Sure. Sign me up.* But whenever it was time to give Benny his injection, it was Brad who I practically had to wrangle and wrestle to the ground. He'd get anxious, his heart rate would increase, and he'd practically start hyperventilating. This from a guy who, as a child, wanted to be a veterinarian when he grew up. Good thing he changed career paths.

Around this same time, Brad and I also started noticing that Benny's rear legs seemed to be getting weak. He'd be standing at his food station, eating dinner or getting a drink, and his legs would just start slipping outward until he'd practically be doing the splits and then his butt would plop on the floor. During Benny's next visit to the vet, I mentioned it to Dr. Steve.

As Dr. Steve examined Benny and squeezed his little legs to gauge his muscle strength, he said, "He seems fine. It's normal for senior dogs to lose some muscle tone."

Despite his jovial smile and friendly demeanor, I took slight offense at Dr. Steve referring to Benny as a senior—even though I knew, on paper, that he was. Although Benny's exact age was a mystery to me, it had been eight years since I'd adopted him, and unlike a lot of dogs whose fur turns white with age, Benny had been all white since birth, so there was no telling that way. I'd often ask him, "How old are you, Buns? Just tell me. We have no secrets between us." But he was as tight-lipped as Zsa Zsa Gabor when it came to admitting his true age.

Even so, it was hard for me to think of him as old. Sure he'd pretty much stopped playing with his toys, had lost a couple teeth, and he loved his naps, but he wasn't struggling to get up and move around. To me, he was still my baby boy.

By then, his hearing loss had gotten to the point where we thought he was completely deaf. His ears were such a defining part of his character that it was hard to believe they didn't function properly. Sometimes, he'd perk up both ears, like they were standing at full attention. Other times, he'd pin them both behind his head, like a bunny, or to the sides of his head, like Yoda. He also had this uncanny ability to rotate his ears independently in different directions. So one might be pointing upward while the other was periscoping toward my voice, the TV, or some other sound.

And then one night, Benny surprised us. While the three of us were snuggled on the couch, watching a horror movie—which is something I rarely do—Brad and I were so startled by the sudden appearance of something scary on the screen that we both screamed and jumped into each other's arms. Benny turned around to face us from his perch near our feet and glared at us as if saying, "What is *wrong* with you two? You woke me up from a sound sleep!"

By then, his vision was also starting to wane, not so terribly that he was running into things, but it was impaired enough that he was unable to spot the occasional bunny romping across our path on our walks. Nevertheless, despite the inevitable onset of age, he was still the same delightful little guy.

But in the late summer of 2022, an incident occurred that caused Brad and me to implement some ground rules to keep Benny safe. One evening, we were eating dinner in the dining room, which, in our open-concept lower level, looks into the living room. Benny was perched on a pillow on the couch so he could keep an eye on us while we watched *Wheel of Fortune* and *Jeopardy*. But all of a sudden, Benny stood up, walked across the pillows lining the back of the couch, and took a flying leap off the arm of the sofa. As if it were happening in slow motion, I watched him channel his inner Simone Biles by rotating a couple times in an aerial twist. I sprang from my chair and vaulted toward him with my arms outstretched, like a center fielder diving for a baseball. But before I could reach him, he went *KERSPLAT!*, fell about three feet off the couch, and landed on his belly on the hardwood floor, with his arms and legs splayed outward.

"Oh my God! Are you all right, Bunny?" I shrieked, feeling him all over to see if he was hurt.

He just sat there on the floor for a moment, stunned—like a boxer who'd taken one too many blows to the head. Then he got up, shook himself off, and wandered over to his bed.

I think he just got the wind knocked out of him, but he seemed a bit sore for the next couple days and was limping a bit, so I took him to the vet. Dr. Steve did a thorough exam, manipulating his arms and legs and touching him for signs of pain, but Benny didn't make a peep. Even so, Brad and I decided that Benny's days of jumping off the couch were coming to an end.

That weekend, Brad found some boards and a carpet remnant in our basement and fashioned a ramp out of the scraps. Then he proudly placed it next to the couch. With those trusty freeze-dried rabbit treats in hand, Brad coaxed Benny to walk up the ramp and then back down as I filmed the momentous occasion for posterity. After a couple trips up and down while we praised him and bribed him with treats, Benny got the hang of it and never attempted to jump off the sofa again. Our boy was a genius. Maybe I should've named him Albert after all?

Chapter 23

A New Diagnosis and
Two Crushing Losses

As usual, Brad, Benny, and I dressed up for Halloween. The year before, we'd gone as cowboys and a cowgirl, but since I was a kid, I'd always loved the movie *Grease,* so in 2022, to honor Olivia Newton-John, who'd recently passed away, Brad and I dressed as Danny and Sandy. Benny also got his own little T-Birds "leather" jacket and went as Kenickie, Danny's best friend and sidekick in the movie.

However, just four days after the fun and revelry of Halloween, Benny started exhibiting symptoms similar to those he had in September 2020. Late on that Friday afternoon, he vomited, then peed on the floor and refused dinner. By the following day, he'd thrown up three more times and still wouldn't eat, plus his poops were soft with a yellowish tinge. When he tried to walk, he tottered back and forth like an inebriated fan stumbling out of the infield at the Indy 500. This time, Brad and I wasted no time getting him to the VCA.

Given Benny's history of pancreatitis, Dr. Stephanie, the ER doctor, immediately ran a panel of blood tests and started him on fluids and antibiotics. We were hopeful that he would be fine after getting some fluids and wouldn't have to stay overnight. Unfortunately, that wasn't the case.

Dr. Stephanie delivered the news. "Benny's lab results reveal that his white blood cell count is elevated, indicating an infection, and his ALP, ALT, and bilirubin (liver values) are off the charts."

"What do you mean by 'off the charts'?" I asked as I pet Benny, who was resting on my lap.

"Our machine only registers so high and Benny's ALP, ALT, and bilirubin are all above that, so we can't get an accurate reading," she explained. "That being said, I'd like to schedule him for an abdominal ultrasound in the morning."

We knew from previous experience that having Benny stay at the hospital overnight would secure his place in line for the ultrasound, while also getting him the fluids and meds he needed, so Brad and I made the difficult decision to leave him there. As I'd done in 2020, I kissed him goodnight and tried to explain what was going on and why he needed to stay overnight. He gave me a sad look that seemed to say, "Okay, Mommy. I just want to go to sleep anyway."

When Benny's ultrasound was compared to the one from 2020, there were changes to his liver and gallbladder, which led the doctor to a diagnosis of something called cholangiohepatitis, which is inflammation of those organs due to a bacterial infection. Based on the ultrasound, it was also determined that Benny had severe chronic kidney disease with cortical cysts. The doctor let me know they were going to continue treating Benny for an acute bout of pancreatitis, as well as cholangiohepatitis and chronic GI disease, and give him something for his belly pain. He was on a laundry list of meds, but she told me that if he continued to remain stable, he would transfer out of the ICU and to the care of Dr. Hui and his team in internal medicine on Wednesday.

I tried to keep a positive attitude, knowing that Benny was getting the treatment he needed, but he was constantly on my mind. Sitting at home without him, my heart literally ached. I couldn't help but contemplate the unfairness of the situation: *If he were a human child, I could be sitting by his side in the hospital all day and staying overnight. But because he's a dog, we can only visit him for short periods of time each day. I certainly don't blame the hospital; it's just the world we live in. I just wish it were different.*

Sunday evening, Brad and I visited Benny in the ICU. When Benny entered the room sporting an IV attached to his arm with hot pink medical tape, Brad exclaimed, "Thunderbolt is back!"

Benny seemed a little loopy, but he was content just to cuddle and sit on my lap. Tears came to my eyes as I held him in my arms, but whether it was from seeing him so weak, relief that he seemed to be doing better, or joy from being reunited with him, I can't say. Probably all of the above.

While we were there, one of the ICU doctors updated us on Benny's condition. "We're still treating Benny for cholangiohepatitis and a flare-up of pancreatitis, but his blood pressure spiked this morning, so we also gave him a drug to treat hypertension."

"What was it? His BP, I mean," I said.

"It was 220 at one point and should've been between 90 and 150."

"Oh my God!" I'd feared that being away from us and being sequestered to a kennel would cause Benny additional stress, and it sounded like that's what was happening. I probably shouldn't have asked my next question, but I needed to know. "What could happen if his BP doesn't stabilize?"

When I heard the doctor utter the words *stroke, congestive heart failure, seizures, enlarged kidneys,* and *blindness,* I became lightheaded. My heart clenched as I closed my eyes tightly to hold back tears.

"Benny, you have to relax while you're here," I said emphatically as he snoozed on my lap and likely couldn't hear me anyway. "Mommy and Daddy don't want to be away from you either, but until you get better, you have to stay here, so please try to be calm, get some rest, and let the medicine do its job."

After that, in addition to praying for Benny's health and safety every night, like I had since I'd adopted him, I stepped up my game, obsessively praying—begging really: *God* please *keep Benny calm and his blood pressure stable. And please, please, PLEASE let him make a full and complete recovery from this disease that I can barely say, much less spell, as well as his kidney disease and any other health issues he has going on.*

While driving home from visiting Benny, Brad and I were both in a state of disbelief and confusion. "I just can't believe this is happening again!" I whined. "Just two days ago, our little boy ate his breakfast and seemed like his spunky little self. But now he's back in the hospital, where the doctors are throwing out medical terms that I don't really understand and names of illnesses that I've never heard of."

"I know," Brad agreed. "Trying to parse through all this information is making my head spin."

"Mine too."

From the moment I adopted Benny, I'd tried to remain in control of his health, well-being, and health care decisions, but all of this was way above my pay grade, so I had no choice but to put my faith in the doctors, trust what they were saying, and pray that they were correct with their diagnoses and treatment plans.

On Monday, November 7, Dr. Stephanie called to say that Benny's values, although still skyrocketing, were trending downward. "When you brought him in on Saturday, his bilirubin was 5.4 but it's down to 1.2."

"What should it be?" I asked for some context.

"Ideally, it should be 0.1 to 0.6," she clarified.

"Oh . . . , so it's still really high," I said solemnly.

"It is, but it's much, much better. Also, his ALT is now 1,360. It should be between 10 and 118, but before it was over 2,000, which is as high as our machines go. And his ALP, which was 1,603, has dropped to 1,487. Normal is between 20 and 150," she explained as I scribbled it all down on a piece of scrap paper. "On a positive note, his kidney values are within the normal range, and his blood pressure is holding steady at around 150."

"Well, that's good news," I said, breathing a little sigh of relief.

"Benny ate well for us last night, but then he started barking and howling excessively in his kennel unless one of the techs was petting him, so we had to give him an antianxiety med to calm him down."

Ugh . . . it's just one thing after another, I lamented internally. *I knew being away from us would hinder his recovery. You gotta chill out, Buns!*

As I'd mentioned to those rescue organizations years earlier when they wouldn't let me adopt a dog with separation anxiety, the less a dog with SA is left alone, the worse his issues get. And, ironically, that's what happened with Benny after I started working from home 100 percent of the time in 2018. Since then, Benny's anxiety had intensified whenever he was away from me. Even if he was with Brad, my dad, or one of my sisters, he'd start with a whimper that would gradually grow to a piercing, high-pitched tone that rivaled Mariah Carey in "Emotions" and eventually morph into a whine that sounded like, "REOW!" But that medley of sounds was just the warm-up act. When he really got going, he'd raise his snout in the air and vacillate between a mournful howl that sounded like he was saying "OW ROO!" to a warbly, deep bass shout of, "OH ROOOAR!" I imagine that in his language, he was crying out: "I want my mommy!" just like I did when I was a youngster.

So when Benny had to be given antianxiety meds to keep him calm, I started worrying that us visiting him, then leaving, was exacerbating his separation anxiety. *Is he wondering why we left him at the hospital and haven't taken him home with us? Is he worried that we've abandoned him?*

I tried not to let my anxiety and feelings of guilt overshadow the reality that Benny's blood work indicated he was improving or the fact that Dr. Stephanie said if he started eating reliably and would take oral meds, there was a chance he could go home the next day and just follow up with Dr. Hui as an outpatient.

Brad had gone into the office that day, so we met at the VCA to visit Benny around four o'clock. When the tech brought Benny into a room to visit us, he was wrapped in a plush, blue blanket. He could barely keep his eyes open, so I just rocked him in my arms while he slept and reminded him to relax, rest, and recuperate.

The next day, I went to see Benny around noon, then Brad and I went back after dinner. Although Benny's liver values were still high, they had dropped some more. He also seemed less sleepy than he had been the day before, and he even ate some food out of my hand. These little baby steps were all signs of improvement, but the doctors weren't ready to discharge him quite yet.

We knew Benny would be transferred to the internal medicine team the next day, so we were hopeful that Dr. Hui would send our little guy home. We were told that it might happen around noon, and since Brad was working remotely, we went to visit over lunch.

When the tech carried Benny into the room, wrapped in a tie-dyed blanket, he was more alert than the last time we'd seen him. Even so, he was content to lie peacefully on my lap with his chin resting on my arm. While we visited with Benny, anxiously awaiting word that we could take him home, Dr. Hui popped in the room to give us an update.

It was the first time Brad and I had actually met Dr. Hui in person. Until that point, all our communication with him had been over the phone. He was a slender man with a boyish face, kind, warm, brown eyes hidden behind a pair of spectacles, dark hair, a reserved manner, and, as we would come to find out, an endless supply of bow ties.

"Benny's appetite is coming around. We gave him some turkey and he ate that well," Dr. Hui began.

"That's good news!" Brad and I said in unison, petting Benny and praising him.

"It is," Dr. Hui continued. "His blood pressure is stable at 125, his kidney values are still normal, and his liver values are moving in the right direction. This morning, his bilirubin was down to 0.6, which is in the normal range. His ALT was 598 and his ALP was 1,154. Both of those are still high, but they're getting better.

"Even so, I'm concerned that Benny might have an underlying intestinal disease, but I'm not sure what's causing it," Dr. Hui added. "So, in order to rule out cancer or a tumor, I'd like to do an endoscopy of Benny's upper and lower intestinal tract and take some biopsies. We could do that tomorrow, but it does require anesthesia.

"The good news is that despite Benny's chronic kidney disease, his values are normal, so I think it can be managed with a diet change, which we'll discuss after the endoscopy, when we have more information about his GI issues."

Despite my concerns about Benny undergoing anesthesia, Brad and I consented to the endoscopy for the next day, so we went home empty-handed. Again, this was a lot to process, but there was nothing I could do except pray, so that's what I did.

In the morning, Dr. Hui called to let me know that Benny was stable, so they were planning to do the endoscopy and biopsies in the afternoon. I wanted to go visit Benny before the procedure, but I was worried that it might get him worked up. Dr. Hui said it was okay, so I arrived around noon. Although Benny seemed a little more attentive, I just cradled him in my arms, petted him, and gave him a pep talk, willing him to be Schaeffer Strong and hang tough.

He kissed my hand and slept in my arms for almost an hour, which I cherished.

Dr. Hui called a little before four to let me know that Benny's endoscopy and biopsies went well and he was in recovery. Although the results of the biopsies would take a few days to come back, Dr. Hui started Benny on prednisone based on the inflammation he saw during the procedure. Yes, it was another steroid, but this time it seemed absolutely necessary.

The next morning, Dr. Hui called to say that he was releasing Benny. After being separated from him for almost a week, we were ecstatic to have him home. His ALT and ALP were still high (361 and 918, respectively) but much improved from what they had been, and since Benny was eating well, Dr. Hui felt he would be more comfortable recuperating at home. Dr. Hui was right: Benny was much happier being in his own house, in his own bed, and snuggled right between Mommy and Daddy. But our poor little guy was down to twelve and a half pounds! He'd lost an entire pound during his six days in the hospital and was a few pounds shy of his ideal weight.

Benny came home on about half a dozen new meds, including the aforementioned prednisone, two antibiotics, Cerenia to combat nausea, ursodiol, which is used to treat liver and gallbladder diseases, and an appetite stimulant that he ultimately didn't need. Dr. Hui recommended switching him to a hydrolyzed protein diet, so after some trial and error, Benny chose Royal Canin hydrolyzed protein canned food, Hill's z/d dry food, and Hill's Hypo treats. Despite another change to his diet, he ate with gusto like he was making up for lost time.

A few days after Benny returned home, Dr. Hui called with the biopsy results. "Fortunately, there are no signs of cancer or tumors," he began, "but his stomach and small intestine are moderately inflamed, which is on par with a diagnosis of irritable bowel disease (IBD). I'm honestly not surprised by this. In fact, it's likely what caused Benny's bacterial cholangiohepatitis."

"Okay, so how is it treated?" I asked.

"Ideally, the IBD can be managed with diet alone," Dr. Hui replied, "but I won't be sure until we see how Benny does after weaning him off the prednisone. However, some of the other meds, like the ursodiol, he'll need to stay on long term."

The following evening, Brad, Benny, and I were all nestled on the couch, watching TV, when our friend Scott called. Based on the hour of his call and the agony in his voice, I knew immediately what was coming.

"I really hate to be the one to tell you, but Margaret is gone. Her sister just called and told me she passed away early this morning," he said, his voice cracking.

Brad pulled me close as I immediately began to wail and a guttural "NOOO!!!" escaped from somewhere deep inside me. Through my choking sobs, I cried out, "I just spoke to her a couple weeks ago, and she sounded like her usual chipper and upbeat self! I asked how she was feeling and she said she was fine. And when I asked how her treatment was going, she said she was doing immunotherapy to help boost her immune system to fight the cancer."

But we soon learned none of that was true.

Margaret was a very private person—so private that she didn't even share her terminal diagnosis with Scott and me, two of her closest friends. Some of her other long-time friends didn't even know she was ill. I tried to visit her whenever I was in South Bend, but she always had an excuse why I shouldn't, so I just figured she was worried about catching COVID. But we found out later from her sister that the cancer had spread to her liver and brain.

I was devastated. Margaret was like a sister to me. She was only fifty-six and had so much life left to live. She was the best human friend I'd ever had, and I felt like I'd lost a limb.

In the days and weeks that followed, I simply couldn't believe she was gone. But then reality would smack me in the face, and a wall of anguish would overtake me. I tried to focus on all the fun times we'd had over the years, but I was filled with regret and mired in guilt that I hadn't been more insistent about visiting her or even calling, but neither of us really liked talking on the phone.

To top it all off, a year earlier, Dr. Bob had passed away at age ninety-four. Like Margaret and me, he and I had been friends for more than twenty years. To have two of my dearest and closest friends die in a year's time was a staggering blow that sent me into a depressive spiral, the kind of which I hadn't experienced since losing my mom. I felt like the walls were closing in on me as my circle of friends—my family—was shrinking.

A week after losing Margaret, we celebrated Thanksgiving. Once again, we had a lot to be thankful for, including the fact that our little boy was out of the woods, but my heart was breaking over the loss of my dear friends. Despite these crushing losses, I kept up my nightly prayers for our health and safety and that of our family and friends and continued asking God to let Benny recover and live a happy, healthy life for many years to come.

Chapter 24

A Christmas Miracle

"C'mon, Buns. Get out of the suitcase. You get to come this time! You'll get to see Grandpa, your aunts, and a bunch of cousins." It was Saturday, December 17, 2022, and we were packing to head to a family holiday party at the home of my cousins Jim and Rich, where we would also spend the night.

Benny removed himself from the suitcase and plopped down in his bed. "What do you want to wear to the party? Your red Snoopy Christmas T-shirt, your green Ho Ho Ho fleece, or your snowman sweater?" I asked, not really expecting an answer. Benny didn't seem to have an opinion, so I chose the Snoopy T-shirt and dressed him.

Since his return from the hospital, Benny had been eating well and doing much better. Although he'd thrown up once, it seemed like a fluke because he immediately bounced right back. At this point, he'd finished taking the antibiotics and antinausea meds, but he was still taking a small dose of prednisone while we slowly weaned him off it.

Benny was fine throughout the two-hour drive to Jim and Rich's place. He loved going for rides in the car—as long as he wasn't going to a doctor's appointment. We got to the house just before the party was scheduled to begin, so we scrambled to unload Benny's crate, a large cooler with his food, and our suitcase before the other guests arrived. Shortly after Ruby was unpacked, Benny tinkled on the floor, which wasn't like him. However, Brad and

I blamed ourselves because in the rush to get our stuff unloaded before the party started, we'd failed to take him potty.

During the party, Benny was a bit clingy and wanted to be held, but that was nothing unusual. He loved being part of the action, i.e., at human eye level, and didn't like being relegated to the floor like a common animal. Plus, there were probably about forty people at the party, and he could be apprehensive in crowds.

Benny was sitting on my lap later in the evening while we were all gathered in the living room for a "white elephant" gift exchange. All of a sudden, Benny started jerking his head forward and making gagging sounds, the telltale sign that he was about to vomit. I got him off the expensive rug and onto the hardwood floor just before he tossed his cookies—and his dinner. Brad took him outside while I cleaned up the mess.

A little while later, it happened again. Brad and I repeated our roles, but at that point, Benny just wanted to lie in his bed. By then, the wheels were already turning in my head, and while everyone else was laughing at their various gifts and having a jolly time, I started to panic. *This doesn't feel right. Something is wrong. Should we drive back tonight to be closer to the VCA?*

"I'm worried Buns is having another flare-up of pancreatitis or cholangiohepatitis," I whispered to Brad, who was sitting next to me. "How would you feel about driving back tonight? I think I'd sleep a lot better if we were at home in case we need to take Benny to the hospital."

Brad doesn't like driving late at night, and by this time, it was after eleven. "You'll have to drive," he replied, motioning to the beer in his hand.

"I don't mind," I said. I hadn't had anything stronger than iced tea to drink.

When the gift exchange wrapped up a few minutes later and people started to leave, we let Jim know our decision. And when Benny threw up a third time—this time all over his bed and his Snoopy T-shirt—we accelerated our departure. After removing Benny's T-shirt, wiping off his bed, and placing both in a trash bag, we gathered up our belongings and headed out. It was after three by the time we got home, but I slept better knowing we were closer to Benny's doctors.

In the morning, Benny was pretty lethargic. I made his break-fast while Brad took him outside for his morning potties. "How did he do?" I asked when they returned.

"He pooped, but it was yellowish and surrounded by white mucous," Brad reported.

"Ugh. . . . That doesn't sound good," I replied. "Benny, will you eat some breakfast for Mommy?"

By this time, he'd walked up his ramp and gotten comfortable on the sofa. I took his food bowl to the couch and placed it in front of him, but he turned his nose away from it. He did the same with his water.

"I think we need to go to the VCA," I said to Brad. He agreed.

When we arrived, a tech carried Benny to the back and took some blood for a panel of tests. Brad and I waited in the lobby until they put us in a room and the ER doctor came in with the results.

"Benny's ALP, ALT, and bilirubin are off the charts again," Dr. Stephanie informed us. "Plus, he's running a fever, his heart rate is elevated, and his white blood cell count is high, indicating some sort of infection. I'd like to admit him, get him started on fluids and the same meds as last time, and add something for pain because his belly is tender. He yelped when I examined him. And then tomorrow, I'd like him to have an abdominal ultrasound to compare it to the one he had back in November."

A feeling of déjà vu swept over me. *Why does this keep happening to our little boy?* I screamed internally.

Benny's ultrasound revealed no significant changes, so they continued to treat him for a flare-up of cholangiohepatitis.

Brad and I visited Benny every day, but it was difficult to get into the Christmas spirit with our Benny Boo Bear in the hospital. The house felt cold and quiet without Benny there. I mean, he was never a noisy guy, but just having him next to me and hearing him breathe or snore soothed my soul. And we often referred to him as our Little Burrito because when he'd nestle his small furry body next to us, it would keep us warm, like a pack animal—or a furnace. So even when Brad was home with me, it just wasn't the same without Benny.

Our prayers were answered on December 22, when Dr. Hui called to say that Benny was being released. "His liver enzymes are still elevated, but they're going down each day, so I think he'll be much more relaxed recuperating at home over the holidays."

That's an understatement, I thought.

I picked him up a little before eleven, and we left with a Santa sack full of meds. When we got home, I made sure Benny was comfortable in his little nest on the sofa, then I drew a chart to keep track of the little canine pharmacy that was building on our countertop.

It felt like a Christmas miracle to have Benny back home with us. But around four o'clock, while I worked next to him on the couch, Benny started moving around in circles like a whirling dervish, kicking and pawing and fluffing his blanket as he tried to get comfortable. He soon settled down, but then he began whining and howling. He was clearly in pain, so I called the VCA and asked if they could prescribe some of the pain meds he'd had in the hospital. We were under a winter storm warning with several inches of snow expected, so I was hoping it was something they could call into a nearby pharmacy. It wasn't, so I hopped in Ruby and slowly made my way to the hospital.

With snow falling in steady, heavy crystals, the roads were pretty desolate and eerily quiet. The only sounds I heard were the squeak of my windshield wipers and the crunch of Ruby's tires over the freshly fallen powder. It took over two hours to go what would normally be less than an hour round trip, but I knew the weather was going to get worse before it got better, and I couldn't bear to have my baby boy in pain.

Chapter 25

"Running to Stand Still"

Brad, Benny, and I spent a quiet Christmas of 2022 at home, just the three of us. Benny wasn't 100 percent, so I wanted to stick close to home and the VCA; plus the weather was bad and we'd just seen my family the week before at Jim and Rich's party.

We showered Benny with gifts as usual, but since he was no longer playing with toys and was on such a strict diet, he was limited to his prescription food and treats and apparel. Even so, he opened his presents with vigor to the sounds of Bing Crosby crooning in the background. We got him a sweatshirt with "Love Rescued Me" printed on it, which was true, but it was also a play on "Love Rescue Me," one of my favorite U2 songs. Truth be told, he probably took more delight in tearing apart the blue tissue paper it was wrapped in, and when all was said and done, he had so much of it stuck to his face that we christened him Benny Bluebeard.

Brad took a quick trip to see his folks after Christmas, but Benny and I stayed home to give him more time to recuperate. By New Year's Day 2023, he was doing well. The sparkle had returned to his big, brown eyes, and he was eating so much better that he'd bulked up to fourteen and a half pounds. Although he was tooting more frequently and would often have a little diarrhea in the evening, I was generally pleased with his progress.

At a follow-up appointment in late January, Benny's cholesterol and triglycerides were super high, so Dr. Hui prescribed fenofibrate to keep them in check. He also had me start giving Benny a Metamucil capsule daily to stiffen up his stool. We were supposed to see Dr. Hui again on February 21, but two days before the appointment, Benny became ill. Shortly after doing his morning potties and eating a cookie and a pill pop with his meds, he threw up. For the rest of the day, he refused to eat, plus he was lethargic, as wobbly as a newborn fawn taking his first steps, and arching his back as if his belly hurt. He vomited a second time later in the afternoon and was straining to poop; whatever small amount came out was covered with mucous. Just when we thought he was over the hump and had a regimen of meds that was working, the cycle started all over again.

Brad and I took Benny to the hospital that evening, and once more, they admitted him and started him on fluids and meds, suspecting a flare-up of IBD, cholangiohepatitis, or pancreatitis. They also scheduled him for another ultrasound the following morning.

By then, I was starting to wonder if it could be his gallbladder. My mom had endured frequent bouts of similar symptoms until she eventually had hers removed, so I thought maybe that's what was going on with Benny. I mentioned my suspicions to Dr. Stephanie the next day.

"The results of Benny's ultrasound are consistent with a recurrence of cholangiohepatitis and pancreatitis," she informed me, "but cholangiohepatitis can be caused by gallbladder issues, particularly if the normal flow of bile through the liver and from the gallbladder is disrupted, so it's not out of the realm of possibilities."

She recommended something called a cholecystocentesis, which is just a really complicated way of saying that they'd take a sample of the fluid in Benny's gallbladder to see if it contained bile. Although Benny would have to undergo mild sedation for the procedure, we agreed to have it done the following day.

"If it's his gallbladder," Dr. Stephanie warned us, "given the frequency of these flare-ups, Benny might need to have his removed."

I certainly didn't like the prospect of Benny having surgery to remove his gallbladder, so I just prayed that it wasn't necessary.

Benny came through the cholecystocentesis like a champ and ate well afterward, so they released him on the condition that I bring him back the following day to have his blood work checked again. I wholeheartedly agreed and brought Benny home after less than one day in the hospital, which seemed like a cause for celebration.

As planned, Benny and I returned to the VCA the next day to have his blood drawn, but we were told that the results from the gallbladder culture could take up to a week. Apparently, they have to wait to see if any bacteria grows in the culture and, if so, what kind, so they know which antibiotics will destroy it.

Meanwhile, back at home, Benny was slowly getting better. His energy level was sapped and he was sleeping more, but just a few days after being in the hospital, he was galloping down the sidewalk, ready to get inside the warm house after doing his business on a frigid and blustery winter morning.

Ultimately, bacteria was found in Benny's gallbladder, and on March 1, Dr. Hui called in a prescription to a local apothecary to have doxycycline compounded for someone of Benny's size. After a few days on the antibiotic, Benny started to return to his normal self.

On March 9, we celebrated Benny's eleventh birthday, which was the ninth anniversary of the day I brought him home. He was less enthusiastic than in years past, but in his defense, the first present he opened was a bag of cookies. After that, he was distracted and only wanted to sample the treats. If I were a dog, I would've done the same thing.

Again, due to the circumstances, we didn't have a lot of gift ideas, so in addition to the treats, he got a tube of doggie toothpaste, a bathrobe, and a doormat that said, "Home of the World's Cutest Dog." Lest anyone think we're terrible gift givers, Benny actually enjoyed brushing his teeth each night and he would always shiver after a getting a tubby, so he loved the bathrobe.

The next day, Benny and I returned to the VCA for a follow-up appointment with Dr. Hui. Since December, Benny had been eating the hydrolyzed protein diet well and hadn't vomited or had diarrhea since his last checkup.

"Is it possible that all the symptoms Benny's exhibited in the past few months—even dating back to 2020—are related to the gallbladder?" I asked. "Like maybe he had a gallbladder infection that didn't totally heal because he was on the wrong antibiotic for that type of bacteria?"

"It's a definite possibility because we didn't sample his gallbladder back then," Dr. Hui admitted. "So while we were treating him with antibiotics for cholangiohepatitis, the bacteria in the gallbladder could've just been sitting there, festering, until it caused this most recent episode."

As Dr. Hui continued to explain how the gallbladder works, I could see how all of these issues were related and how Benny could have the trifecta of a gallbladder infection, IBD, *and* cholangiohepatitis.

"The gallbladder secretes bile into the intestine every time you eat to help you digest fat. Normally, that bile only goes in one direction—from the gallbladder into the intestine via the bile duct—and the process runs nice and smooth," Dr. Hui elaborated as he illustrated a diagram on the whiteboard. "But when you have chronic inflammation in the GI tract, even if the inflammation goes down a bit with medication, you can still have some scar tissue built up. And all that can cause the bile duct to close up a bit, so maybe it's only 60 or 70 percent open compared to normal. When that happens, the bile can't exit properly, which means it sits there longer and is more prone to infection. So instead of the gallbladder acting like a nice gate where the bile just passes through to the intestine, when inflammation is involved, bacteria is more likely to travel in the *opposite* direction and end up in the gallbladder.

"Due to Benny's IBD and the chronic inflammation in his gut, he'll always be susceptible to this to some degree, so the best thing we can do is minimize any pancreatic problems or any intestinal inflammation to decrease the chances of that happening. That's what we're currently doing now with his meds."

The way I understood it, the goal was to clear the gallbladder of any infection by keeping Benny on the doxycycline for a while, and then they would just continue treating his IBD to prevent another gallbladder infection from happening in the future.

"In an ideal world, we'd sample the gallbladder again in a few weeks to make sure all the bacteria has cleared up," Dr. Hui continued, "but that requires anesthesia and there's a little bit of risk every time you sample the gallbladder. Especially when you have a diseased gallbladder, you don't want it leaking bacteria into the belly because that would turn into a surgical emergency."

I trusted Dr. Hui's expertise, and I definitely did not want Benny to end up in a surgical emergency, so we agreed to just continue treating him with the doxycycline and check his labs again in a month.

We also discussed whether the hydrolyzed protein diet was best for Benny or if we should consult with a nutritionist who would make up a special homemade diet catered to his needs. My question was, "Do you think the hydrolyzed protein food *won't* prevent this from happening again, or do you think it happened because he just wasn't on the right antibiotic?"

In hindsight, it was an unfair question because Dr. Hui didn't have a crystal ball, so I shouldn't have been surprised that his answer was a bit vague.

"It's hard to say," Dr. Hui admitted. "Was it the wrong antibiotic for that specific bacteria, or did he have it cleared up and then have a flare-up of his bowel stuff and that pushed bacteria in there again, which caused a relapse? I don't think we'll ever know for sure.

"Instead of contacting the nutritionist to discuss changing his diet, we could take a more conservative approach and assume that he had a relapse because he was on the wrong antibiotic. With that option, we'd keep him on the hydrolyzed protein diet and give him more time on the antibiotic and see how he does. I'm not opposed to that because he seems to be doing very well. I'm surprised his liver enzymes are as good as they are, and he just looks better to me all-around than he normally does."

We opted for the conservative approach and planned to regroup in a month.

By the time we went to see Dr. Hui in April, Benny was maintaining the status quo. He'd gained a tiny bit of weight and was almost back to his "fighting weight" of fifteen pounds. Although his poops were still a little soft, he was no longer having diarrhea. But he had thrown up once, about half an hour after eating his breakfast, plus, he'd become more of a grazer with his meals. Before, he'd wolf down his food in a minute or so. Now, he would eat a little bit, then come back to it later. Some days, he wouldn't finish breakfast until three in the afternoon or dinner until bedtime.

Dr. Hui kept Benny on the prednisone but felt that it was time to take him off the doxycycline and switch him over to Tylan, which, although it's also an antibiotic, is frequently used to treat IBD and is considered safer for long-term use. Overall, Dr. Hui was pleased with Benny's progress and decided we didn't need to follow up for three months.

In the meantime, we continued living life as usual. Brad and I tried to spend as much time as possible with Benny. He was our little cuddle bug and my constant companion and work buddy. I even bought an upholstered bench for working at my desk because the two of us crammed into an office chair was getting a bit uncomfortable.

By this time, we'd accepted that Benny had full-blown separation anxiety, and I didn't want to be apart from him either. If I went to places that allowed dogs, like TJ Maxx or Hobby Lobby, Benny went with me. He'd sit so patiently that people would do a double-take and say they thought he was a statue and didn't realize I had a dog in the cart. When Brad and I went out to dinner, we'd always try to go somewhere with outdoor seating so Benny could join us. (Weather permitting, of course.) We were even planning a family vacation together.

When we saw Dr. Hui again in July, he was pleased with how well Benny was doing. He was eating well and his poops had improved, but he was a bit gassy. Sometimes Benny's toots were "silent but violent," but it no longer seemed to mortify him. Brad and I would giggle when he'd let 'em rip—especially when he'd sneeze and fart (or snart) at the same time—but we tried not to let him see us laugh so we wouldn't embarrass him.

Benny's weight was also holding steady, and although his liver enzymes were elevated, Dr. Hui believed that was due to the medications, so we discussed decreasing his dosage of prednisone.

I also asked Dr. Hui if I should move forward with the home-cooked diet for Benny. He said that because Benny seemed to be doing so well, he didn't want to change his diet, and I wholeheartedly agreed. When Dr. Hui said he didn't need to see Benny again for four months, I took that as a great sign.

That night, while Brad and I were making dinner, we had '80s music videos playing on the TV. When The Bangles's video for "Eternal Flame" came on, I serenaded Brad and Benny, and the three of us slow danced together, with Benny in my arms. At one point, I sang directly to Benny, altering the lyric to: "Close your eyes, give me your paw, Benny. Do you feel my heart beating?" I kid you not, Benny put his paw on my heart, leaned his head on my chest, and closed his eyes. It was one of the most precious moments we ever shared as a family, and it's something that, hopefully, I'll never forget.

Chapter 26

Road Trip!

With COVID safely in the rearview mirror (mostly), Brad and I decided to venture out of the Midwest and take a vacation. We wanted to take Benny along, so we knew it needed to be somewhere close enough to drive. When one of Brad's college buddies announced that he and his bride were having a reception in DC in September (the wedding had taken place in Scotland in May), we decided that was the perfect opportunity for us to get out of Dodge. I'd never been to DC, but Brad's brother, Dan, and Rodney, one of my good friends from the U2 universe, both lived in the area, so we figured it would be nice to explore and catch up with friends and family.

Before the trip, I ordered Benny a new set of wheels. He loved his Snoopy stroller, but he needed a little more room to maneuver. The Snoopy stroller required him to remain in a seated position at all times, but at this stage of his life, he needed something that enabled him to relax a bit more. I found a nice model online that would allow him to sit up or lie down. It also had a seat belt to clip to his harness, ample storage for his food and water bowls, a retractable canopy with mesh windows, and two cupholders. What more could you ask for in a doggie stroller?

As soon as it arrived, Brad unboxed it and put it together, then we added Benny's cushy bed and away we went on a stroll around the neighborhood. Brad was a little embarrassed at first, but Benny absolutely loved it. He still enjoyed being outside, but he tuckered out faster than he used to. In fact, he'd often just sit down in random people's yards while we were out on walks and refuse to go any further. Brad and I would humor him for a minute or so and let him lie in the sun or do his roly-polies, but if he still wouldn't budge, one of us (usually Brad) ended up carrying him home.

In late September, we rented an SUV and headed east. Always an excellent traveler, Benny rested patiently and comfortably in his bed on the back seat. He hardly made a peep, but we made sure to stop every couple hours to let him potty and get something to eat and drink.

We spent three nights at an Airbnb just outside the nation's capital. The house we rented was built in the 1920s, but it seemed much older; I honestly would've guessed it was from the eighteenth century. The floors were extremely slanty and the upstairs hallway was the narrowest one I'd ever seen—we practically had to walk down it sideways. But the place had charm and, despite the fact that it was in an urban area, the wooded backyard gave it a fairy-tale-like atmosphere, with several deer stopping by every day to greet us. We also saw a lot of squirrels, but they seemed to make themselves scarce whenever Benny was around. Clearly, his reputation as a ferocious squirrel chaser had preceded him.

Our first full day there, Brad and I spent a few hours at the Smithsonian Museum of American History, but we made sure not to leave Benny alone for extended periods of time. In fact, we'd brought along a tiny nanny camera so we could keep an eye on him while we were out. We knew if he started barking and howling in his crate, it was time to head back to home base. We weren't worried about him bothering the neighbors; that's why we chose detached homes rather than apartments or condos. We were more concerned with him working himself into a tizzy. Each night, we either got carryout or went to a pet-friendly restaurant, then we'd go home, cuddle on the couch, and binge-watch *Suits*, which had recently dropped on Netflix.

On our final day in the DC area, we took Benny into the city. After meeting my friend Rodney for brunch, he played tour guide and showed us the sights, including the Washington Monument, the Lincoln Memorial, the White House, and the Vietnam Wall. I don't know how many miles we walked that day, but Benny rode in style. By the end of the day, I wanted to ride with him in the stroller and have Brad push us both.

The next day, we headed north to Phoenixville, Pennsylvania, about thirty miles northwest of Philadelphia. Our home for the next few days was a quaint carriage house on a serene farm, and when we arrived, the owners' very friendly beagle, Sarge, greeted us in the driveway. The place was actually 220 years old, but it felt much newer than the last place we'd stayed because it had been recently updated.

Until we arrived, Brad and I had no idea that Phoenixville is just minutes from historic Valley Forge, where George Washington and the Continental Army spent the brutal winter of 1777–1778. After unloading our luggage at the carriage house, we headed down the road and purchased a self-guided audio tour, then drove around the national park with Benny in tow.

When our tummies began to grumble, we headed to downtown Phoenixville and found a burger joint that allowed dogs on the spacious patio, where the booths were actually wooden gliders. I fed Benny while we waited for our food, then he zonked out in my arms, weary from a day of sightseeing.

Before we departed Phoenixville for Gettysburg, our final destination, Brad walked Benny around the farm to do his potties. That's when Benny encountered something he'd never seen before: chickens. I didn't get to witness it, but Benny took off chasing them like they were squirrels. Apparently, he forgot that his ancestors were terriers, not herding dogs, but Brad said the joy on Benny's face was unforgettable.

The next day, we hired a licensed guide to give us a tour of the battlefield from the convenience of our car. Brad drove while Benny and I sat in the back seat and the guide told us all about the Battle of Gettysburg. Later in the day, the three of us embarked on a ghost tour.

On our final day in Gettysburg, Benny stayed at the Airbnb while Brad and I toured some local museums. I'm pretty sure Benny was okay with that, though. Like a sullen teenager, after tootling around Valley Forge twice and the Gettysburg battlefield, he had a glazed look in his eyes that said, "I've learned enough about American history! Go. . . . Do your thing. Just leave me alone so I can sleep!"

After returning home, the three of us made our annual visit to Fort Harrison State Park to celebrate our third wedding anniversary. Life was good. We were a happy little family bursting with love for each other while enjoying life's milestones and cherished moments. But in the back of my mind, I couldn't help but wonder how long it would last. Perhaps it was a premonition, or maybe I have this deep-seated notion that I'm not deserving of such happiness, but I had a sinking feeling in the pit of my stomach that the other shoe was about to drop.

Chapter 27

A Mother's Intuition

As was likely the case for many, in the fall of 2023, Brad and I traveled more than we had in the past five years. A few weeks after returning from our family vacation out east, Brad and I hopped on a plane and headed to Vegas to see a couple U2 shows during the band's residency at the new, state-of-the-art Sphere.

It's no secret that U2 is my all-time favorite band (sorry New Kids). Heck, it's because of our mutual love of the Irish lads that Brad and I even found each other. And since my first U2 show in 2001, I've never missed a tour. But I just wasn't feeling this one. I'm not a gambler or much of a drinker, so Vegas isn't exactly my kind of town. And because Larry Mullen, Jr.—U2's drummer and the founder of the band—had to sit this one out due to an injury, I felt that it wasn't authentically U2 without him. Plus, it wouldn't be the same without Margaret, and I didn't want to leave Benny, even though it was only for three nights and I knew he'd be in good hands with his Aunt Denise.

I could tell Brad really wanted to go, so I acquiesced. Our friend Scott and his girlfriend, Rachel, were also going, and our match-maker Big Mike planned to drive up from LA to see us, so I knew I'd have a good time. Yet given all of Benny's hospitalizations in the past year, I was really reluctant to spend any time away from him. The way I saw it, every day with him was a blessing, and days we spent apart, we couldn't get back.

Brad and I did have a good time, and I called Denise twice a day to check on Benny, even calling before bedtime to tell him goodnight. When we were reunited with Benny, he was so ready to go home that he might as well have had his bags packed and waiting by the door. He very much enjoyed being an only child, so after spending three days with his cousins, Angel and Binky, and Denise's foster dog, "Hurricane" Harvey, Benny was ready for family time, just the three of us.

When we got home, I noticed that Benny was limping, so I asked Denise if anything had happened that might cause him to limp. The only thing she could think of was that he'd jumped off her bed one night. That was most definitely the cause. Since Benny had started using the ramp Brad built for him a year earlier, he no longer leaped off any furniture, so he probably tweaked something dismounting Denise's bed.

Even though Benny didn't seem to be in any pain, when he was still limping a week later, I took him to see Dr. Steve, who performed a thorough exam but found nothing wrong.

For the past month, Benny had started vomiting occasionally, about once every week or so. It was almost always in the morning, in the window between the time when I'd give him his meds in a pill pop and feed him his breakfast. Brad thought the pill pops were either getting stuck in his throat, causing him to regurgitate, or they were forming a glob in his gut, giving him a tummyache and making him sick. When I started rubbing his throat to ensure that the pill pops went down all right, that seemed to help, but I was still concerned that something more serious was going on.

We'd also noticed a change in Benny's eating habits. Not only had he become a grazer, there were times when he would only finish his breakfast or dinner if we hand-fed him, which seemed odd. Obviously, he still had an appetite or he wouldn't eat when we hand-fed him, but why wouldn't he eat *unless* he was hand-fed? That was the conundrum.

When I mentioned these things to Dr. Steve at our appointment on Halloween, he ran a panel of tests, but they all came back relatively normal—at least they were normal for Benny's conditions and the meds he was taking. His liver values had improved since Dr. Hui had tested him in July, and his kidney and thyroid levels were within the normal range.

Later that day, Benny, Brad, and I dressed up as Snoopy, Linus, and Sally and handed out candy to trick-or-treaters in our neighborhood. I've loved Snoopy for as long as I can remember, and it was an easy costume for Benny; he already had the white fur, so I just had to attach some black felt ears to a piece of ribbon and tie it around his chin and one around his belly. Naturally, he looked adorable and was a big hit with the kiddos.

In early November, I headed back to Vegas with my sisters, this time to celebrate Denise's birthday by seeing Rod Stewart, one of her all-time faves. Again, I didn't want to leave Benny, but at least this time he'd be in his own home and sleeping in his own bed with his daddy.

Despite returning to my not-so-happy place twice in less than a month, I had a great time with my sisters. When I came home, Brad was out with John and Laura, who were visiting from Ohio, so after I parked in the garage, I readied my phone's video camera, hoping to capture the Benny Boogie accompanied by the toothy grin and snorting combination.

I didn't hear Howler Monkey making any sounds, so I assumed he was fast asleep. But when I walked in and approached his crate, he was sitting upright as if he'd been waiting for me. "Hi, Honey Bunny! Mommy's home! Mommy's home!" I said in a high-pitched voice.

As I let him out of his crate and removed his cone of shame, he shook his body, wagged his tail a little, and sneezed—a subdued version of the Benny Boogie.

"I missed you, Baby Boy! Did you miss me? Do I get to see your cute little teeth?"

But he just toddled to the door and grumbled like an old man saying, "I gotta pee. Take me outside."

"No toothy grin? Oh well . . . let's go potty."

As the days grew short, the temperatures dropped, and pumpkin spice wafted through the air, we celebrated Thanksgiving at home again, just the three of us. As usual, we were grateful for each other, for our health and safety, and for that of our family, friends, and loved ones. Benny seemed to be doing really well, and Dr. Hui and I discussed this at our follow-up a week later.

"Benny's lost a little weight since his visit in July, so he's just under fourteen pounds," Dr. Hui revealed. "But his ALT and ALP, although still high, are much better than they were in July. Plus, his blood sugar and kidney values all look good."

"That's great news about his blood work!" I said. "I thought Benny might've lost more weight, and I'm concerned because he seems to be losing muscle mass too. Is that just normal for a dog his age?"

"It certainly could be age-related," Dr. Hui replied. "How long has it been since Benny's last GI episode?"

"He hasn't had a major once since he was hospitalized back in February," I answered. "But he has been vomiting once every week or so, and it always seems to happen after I give him his morning meds. There's no rhyme or reason to it; it's almost like they went down wrong or they're giving him an upset stomach or something."

"Hmm . . . ," Dr. Hui continued. "I think the chronic steroid use could be making him weaker, so I want to get him off them or lower the dosage. To do that, we have a couple options. Option one is to keep him on his current diet and lower his prednisone from a half to a quarter tablet and see how he responds. If he does pretty well, maybe he'll regain some weight and muscle mass. Option two, we switch him to the home-cooked diet, and if he seems to be doing well with it, we'll drop his steroids down at that point. The hope is that if he does really well with the home-cooked diet, we could wean him completely off the prednisone."

"I'm definitely in favor of getting him off the steroids, but I want to discuss these options with my husband first."

"Sure. Of course."

This was a bit confusing to me, so I commented, "But last time we met, back in July, you didn't want to change his diet because he seemed to be doing well on the hydrolyzed protein food."

"Yeah . . . with home-cooked diets, the risks and the benefits are both a little bit higher," Dr. Hui explained. "Some dogs do really well on the home-cooked diet, but others end up doing worse than they were on the hydrolyzed diet. So there's a higher risk but also higher potential benefits. So if he was doing extremely well right now and he wasn't losing weight, then ideally, we'd keep him on the hydrolyzed diet and decrease his prednisone down to a quarter tablet and eventually take him off it. But I'm not sure we're going to be able to do that, so I think we have to potentially consider changing things.

"My guess is that we won't be able to get him completely off steroids, but we'll definitely try. I'm not opposed to keeping him on the hydrolyzed diet and dropping his steroid dosage down to a quarter tablet, but we'll need to keep an eye on him—you know, monitor his weight and see how he does clinically."

When Brad and I discussed it that evening, we decided to stick with the hydrolyzed protein diet. Even though Benny was vomiting occasionally, that didn't necessarily seem related to his food because it always happened *before* he ate, right after he took his meds. And although we sometimes had to hand-feed him, Benny liked his food, so it was kind of like the old adage: is it better to stick with the devil you know or the devil you don't? Besides, I don't think either of us really understood how the home-cooked diet would be better for him.

By then, I was keeping a log of exactly how often Benny was throwing up and what the circumstances were. On December 7, just over a week after we saw Dr. Hui, Benny barfed up his pill pops before he had breakfast. The same thing happened a week later, then again on Christmas morning. He typically bounced back fairly quickly, but that day, he wasn't really in the mood to open his presents until early evening. The day before, we'd driven to South Bend and back to spend Christmas Eve with my family, and we were all pretty exhausted, so I didn't read too much into it.

However, over the course of the next month, I logged seven different days when Benny vomited. It was usually after he'd taken his meds but before he ate breakfast or shortly after. It was definitely escalating, and when he threw up three times in four days in the latter part of January, I made an appointment to see Dr. Hui.

We agreed that Benny probably needed another abdominal ultrasound, and fortunately, they were able to get him in that week. Unfortunately, it was a drop-off appointment, so Dr. Hui would call me to discuss his findings.

After handing my baby over to Andrea, Dr. Hui's tech, I headed up the road to suppress my anxiety with some retail therapy at a nearby shopping center. Andrea had told me Benny should be done by noon, so when I left Costco, my final destination, around twelve thirty and hadn't heard from Dr. Hui, I decided to go back to the VCA and wait there.

Apparently, Dr. Hui had called while I was in Costco and either my phone didn't ring or I didn't hear it. Whatever the case, it worked to my advantage because they put me in a room to speak to Dr. Hui about his findings, which I was grateful for. He began with the good news: Benny's liver enzymes and blood work all looked good. Then came the bad news.

"The ultrasound shows that Benny has a mucocele of his gall-bladder," Dr. Hui said.

"A what?" I'd never even heard the word *mucocele* before.

"So if you recall, the gallbladder stores bile and moves it along. But when the bile doesn't flow out properly, it can start to solidify, and it eventually forms a ball or mucocele," Dr. Hui explained.

"Okay ...," I said, scrutinizing Dr. Hui as I tried unsuccessfully to digest what he was saying.

"Mucoceles typically occur because the gallbladder just isn't pumping out as much stuff as it should be, which isn't surprising in Benny's case, given his history. He's on the ursodiol and predni-sone to decrease the inflammation of the bile duct, which connects the gallbladder and intestine. And sometimes when there's a secondary infection, it can also produce a mucocele.

"His is a pretty mature mucocele, and if you look at the text-books for what to do for a mature gallbladder mucocele, almost inevitably, the recommendation is surgical removal."

"Oh ...," I muttered, a bit shocked. I bit my lower lip and my heart began to pound at the idea that Benny needed surgery.

"But that's a big surgery, given his age and everything else he has going on. We'd have to open him up and take out the gallblad-der, which is not without potential complications."

Looking defeated and dumbfounded, I just sat there mute. My tongue felt swollen, as if I'd had an allergic reaction, and left me unable to speak, so I just nodded my head at the appropriate times. I was grateful that Dr. Hui had given me permission to record the conversation because my head was swirling with everything he was throwing at me. I felt like I was in a black hole, unable to see any-thing around me except a small sliver of light, and Dr. Hui's voice seemed warbled and far away. Without recording the conversa-tion, there's no way I would've been able to remember anything to repeat it back to Brad when I got home.

"I've had some patients whose owners didn't want to do the surgery, either due to the risks or the cost or whatever, and in those cases, we just treat them with antibiotics and see how they do. But the risk is that if the antibiotics don't work, the gallbladder can rupture, and if that happens, it's a life-threatening emergency and the prognosis is a lot worse than if the gallbladder is still intact when it's removed."

I wanted to ask what his recommendation was, but I was still numb from the shock of hearing the word *surgery* and couldn't find the words. He must've read my mind, though.

"Part of me is reluctant to jump into surgery with him because it's such a big surgery and he's got a lot going on internally, so I worry a bit about his recovery. But at the same time, if we don't do the surgery right away, we take a risk that the gallbladder could rupture. And if that happens, you'd either have to let him go or still do the surgery. But if you took him to surgery *after* it ruptured, he'd be in an even worse state. You know what I mean?"

Unfortunately, I understood all too well what he meant. I nodded as a tear trickled down my cheek. I was trying not to cry, but this one escaped.

At that point, I found my voice and began to formulate some questions. "Are there any other options besides surgery, like lasering the mucocele to break it up?"

"No. You wouldn't be able to laser an area like that. Kidney stones and stuff like that can be lasered in people, and we laser bladder stones here, but the mucocele is not really like a stone; it's a hardening of mucinous secretions. So if you take it out, it's solid like a ball, but it's not actually mineral material."

"Is this related to what he had before?" I asked, unable to think of the strange word for one of Benny's diagnoses.

"He had cholangiohepatitis, which is an infection of the gallbladder (or liver or bile ducts). But he did not have a mucocele before."

"So how big is the mucocele?"

"It's as big as his gallbladder. So, basically, the mucocele is filling up his entire gallbladder."

When Dr. Hui said that, I knew surgery was the only option. Thinking back to the large fibroid I'd had in my uterus, I said, "I'm guessing you can't remove the mucocele without removing the gallbladder, right?"

"Correct. It's called a cholecystectomy."

"And what does that mean for him long term?"

"Like humans, dogs can live without a gallbladder. Actually, it'll probably make him a little less susceptible to cholangiohepatitis because he won't have a gallbladder."

"But how will it affect his diet and what he can and cannot eat?" I wondered. "I mean, he's already on such a limited diet."

"The main thing is the lower the fat, the better," Dr. Hui answered before laying out the options. "So, 1) I could put him on antibiotics, then you could come back soon—within the next couple days or even sooner—to get the surgery. I'd have to talk to the surgery department to see what their schedule is like. Or 2) we could put him on antibiotics, reimage him in two weeks or so, and see if there are any changes—improvements or worsening—and go from there."

"Is there any chance that the antibiotics will just clear it up?" I knew the likelihood was slim, but I had to ask.

"There's a chance," Dr. Hui replied hesitantly. "I've treated this with antibiotics before and some patients have gotten better. It's few and far between, but it does happen. The main thing, of course, is the risk of potential rupture between treating it now and coming back for a recheck."

"Okay. . . . So what causes this?"

"The mucocele is usually caused because a) he either got an infection of the gallbladder that persisted, or b) which is more likely . . . so the gallbladder usually pumps bile into the small intestine as you digest fat. So if the gallbladder is only squeezing at like 50 percent instead of 100 percent every time, the mucousy bile material just slowly builds up and starts to solidify.

"The reason why the gallbladder doesn't empty all the way is either because a) they have primary GI disease, so there's inflammation in there and the gallbladder can't push the bile through completely, or b) they have a little bit of inflammation on the pancreas, or c) they have primary liver disease. Benny has all those things to some degree, so he has all the predisposing factors. Also breed-wise, small dogs like Yorkies, West Highland terriers, and shih tzus are more likely to develop gallbladder mucoceles as they get older, regardless of the other contributing factors that Benny has."

Hearing this made me feel yucky inside. I instantly felt a stitch in my side and a burning sensation in my gut, the likes of which I hadn't experienced since college when my mom thought I had an ulcer. *How did this happen? When did this mucocele begin to grow and overtake Benny's gallbladder if there was no sign of it on his last ultrasound? Did it start a couple months ago when he began vomiting once a week or so?* I knew there was no way Dr. Hui could answer those questions, so I didn't bother asking.

"Okay," I said as I steeled myself to ask the difficult question. "Given his sort of unknown age, but he's at least ten . . . , I mean, as of March, I will have had him for ten years, and he wasn't a newborn puppy when I got him . . ."

Dr. Hui knew what I was beating around the bush trying to say. "Yeah. . . . The risks of surgery?"

"Yes," I eked out.

"Certainly, it's a little riskier because he's older."

"But, like, is his heart in good shape? His lungs, his kidneys, all that?"

"Those are good questions. We would do blood work, of course, and take chest X-rays before surgery to make sure he doesn't have any heart enlargement. I'd have to look back because I think he has a slight arrhythmia, but sometimes that's normal as they get older, so it's not a big deal. But if his heart is enlarged, then yes, that would make him more predisposed to having issues during the anesthesia and at a higher risk for complications.

"I think, for him, it's not necessarily his age. Age is a factor to some degree, but it's more that he has a lot of internal issues. During the surgery, the pancreas has to be manipulated in order to remove the gallbladder—you know, the pancreas sits right here (he shows me on a diagram)—so the likelihood of him developing post-op pancreatitis is always a risk. That's not uncommon with gallbladder mucoceles, and he has a history of it too."

"Okay," I said as I exhaled deeply, terrified of making the wrong decision. "Well, this is a lot to take in. I'll need to talk it over with my husband."

"Of course. So why don't we do this: I'll ask the surgery department to prepare an estimate, and we'll email it to you later today or tomorrow. In the meantime, I'll send him home on antibiotics and see how he does and then you can let us know what you want to do."

I agreed, but it didn't matter what the estimate was. In my mind, money was no object where Benny was concerned. I was just worried about making a life-or-death decision for my little boy and knowing I'd have to accept the outcome either way.

On the way home, as I looked at my precious Benny Boo Bear in the back seat, I could no longer hold back the tears. My heart felt like it was being squashed in a vice and I was angry—angry at God. Every night, I prayed for Benny's health and safety and specifically asked that he never needed to have surgery. I was terrified of Benny having surgery, but the thought that his gallbladder could rupture and cause a life-threatening emergency was just as bad. It was a no-win situation.

When we got home a little after two o'clock, Brad greeted us at the door.

"How did it go?" he asked right away.

"Not good," I replied. "Not good at all. I don't even know what to say, so let me get Benny something to eat and then we can listen to the recording."

Benny had been required to fast prior to his ultrasound and blood work that morning, so he hadn't eaten anything since dinner the night before. He immediately walked into the kitchen, stared at his empty bowl, then looked up at me with hungry eyes as if to say, "The service in this place has really gone downhill. What's a guy gotta do to get some food around here? I'm starving!"

Once Benny was fed, Brad and I sat at the dining room table and listened to the conversation I'd just had with Dr. Hui. My head was spinning and my mind was a blur.

After listening to the recording, Brad and I discussed the situation. Even though we were concerned about the risks surgery posed for Benny, it seemed better than doing nothing but keeping him on antibiotics, which could ultimately lead to surgery anyway, but then it would be a life-threatening, emergency situation. In other words, surgery sooner rather than later seemed like the lesser of two evils.

That afternoon, I did some research and reached out to Dr. Steve, who encouraged us to have the surgery. After Brad and I talked it over some more, we started feeling more optimistic about it. Surgery seemed like a tangible step that would remove the source of what was causing some of Benny's ailments. As Brad said, we had to be optimistic about it because there really was no other option.

We also knew time was of the essence since Benny's gallbladder could burst at any time. So I called the VCA and scheduled a consultation with Dr. James, the best surgeon on staff, for the next day.

Chapter 28

"A Coalescing Glob of Pretty Gelatinous Stuff"

Brad and I were sitting in a treatment room, anxiously waiting to meet Dr. James, the top surgeon at the VCA. Brad was bouncing his knee, which is something he rarely does, and the scent of antiseptic wafted through the air. It was ten o'clock on the morning of Thursday, January 25, 2024—less than twenty-four hours since Dr. Hui told me Benny needed surgery. Our little guy was in the back getting his vitals taken.

When Dr. James entered the room, he immediately got down to business. He seemed to be about my age, with closely cropped hair and an athletic build. For the first fifteen to twenty minutes, he talked almost nonstop, explaining to us in detail how a gallbladder should function and precisely how Benny's wasn't. "Based on the ultrasound, Benny's gallbladder is enlarged for someone of his size," Dr. James stated, "and it's formed a coalescing glob of pretty gelatinous stuff."

He informed us that, although Benny's gallbladder didn't appear to be in imminent danger of bursting, he recommended surgery in the near—not distant—future because medication was unlikely to help, and a rupture could lead to something called septic bile peritonitis, where bile leaks into the abdominal cavity and essentially burns everything around it. "If that happens, the mortality rate approaches 50 percent," Dr. James warned. "So I've got a fifty-fifty chance—a coin flip—on a successful outcome, and the moms and dads know it."

In other words, doing nothing—or, in this case, treating it with antibiotics—would be like ignoring a ticking time bomb, which is what Brad and I had already concluded.

Brad and I sat quietly, trying to absorb everything Dr. James was telling us. Through red-rimmed eyes, I gazed vacantly at Dr. James with a forlorn frown on my face, my countenance and body language betraying my emotions. Feeling like my arms weighed a thousand pounds, I sat in the hard plastic chair with my shoulders slumped and my hands primly folded on my lap, desperately trying to suppress the urge to cry, which was causing a burning sensation in the back of my throat.

Dr. James walked us through the day of surgery step-by-step, stating that someone would inform us when the procedure was about to begin, then he'd call us post-op to let us know how it went. We'd get a couple more calls that day with updates from his techs, but he stressed that we did *not* want to hear from him after that because he would likely be bearing bad news. "We don't want any excitement," he emphasized. "We want a boring case."

Brad and I silently nodded in agreement.

Dr. James looked at me and said, "I want you to keep your cell phone on all night. If my techs call me in the middle of the night, and I think you need to wake up, I *will* wake you up. No questions asked. You'll get a call directly from my cell phone."

I certainly didn't want us to get a call from him with bad news, but I respected that he'd be the one calling if the situation arose.

It was clear that Dr. James had done this many times before and had learned to anticipate all the questions pet parents were going to ask, so he just laid it all out up front. He was a straight shooter who didn't mince words just to placate us, and I appreciated that. I found him down-to-earth, confident but not cocky, and definitely not arrogant—the ideal combination for a surgeon of any kind.

"You should know that gallbladder disease is very painful, and I speak from firsthand experience because I had mine removed when I was eighteen," he revealed. "My dad found me on the floor at two o'clock in the morning, sweating profusely and as yellow as a school bus. I had septic bile peritonitis, and they gave me about a 30 percent chance of surviving."

"Oh, geez! Wow! So this really hits home for you," Brad said with surprise as I looked at Dr. James wide-eyed with my mouth agape.

"Yeah, I take gallbladder disease very personally and seriously. I know some surgeons who like to take a wait-and-see approach, but I know that time is of the essence."

Because he wanted us to go into this with a healthy dose of concern and worry, Dr. James also shared stories of successful outcomes and some worst-case scenarios from his background of performing cholecystectomies on dogs. When he finished, he said, "So, I just dumped a lot on you. How're you doing?"

Still looking dazed, I responded with a half-hearted laugh. But Brad replied, "Good. . . . I mean, I think moving forward with the surgery is the right decision—the only decision, really."

"Yeah, I haven't sugarcoated it," Dr. James continued. "But that's the kind of commitment you'll get from me. I'm always on guard and take the approach that nothing is ever easy. I do a lot of worrying. It keeps me out of trouble, and it usually means that I've amped you up a little bit, but it's for good reason because I know that not all cases go perfectly. I'd be foolish to tell you not to worry. It's okay to worry—you should be worried."

"Oh, we're definitely worried," I assured him, finally finding my voice.

Despite Dr. James's best efforts to anticipate all our questions, I still had more, but he answered them all effectively.

"You said that based on the ultrasound, it doesn't look like Benny's gallbladder is close to rupturing," I began, "but if it does burst before he gets in for surgery, how will we know?"

"He'll be vomiting, have diarrhea, no appetite, and be lethargic. You'll know something is wrong," Dr. James replied. "I don't worry about you. I know you're watching him. I can tell. And if that happens, there's always a surgeon on call."

"I was told when I first adopted Benny that he has a heart murmur or arrhythmia, so will you be checking his heart before surgery?"

"Absolutely. He does have a sinus arrhythmia, and that's okay. It means that his heart rate increases and decreases with his breathing, but it's pretty textbook."

"Oh!" Brad and I said in unison. It was always unclear whether or not Benny had an arrhythmia, so hearing it confirmed scared us a bit.

"It's fine. I have one, actually," Dr. James said reassuringly.

"It said on the estimate that you'll be using fentanyl. Is it an anesthesia you can immediately get him out of or reverse to wake him up?" I asked, the horror story of the Yorkie in our previous neighborhood still on my mind.

"Yes, fentanyl is quickly digested; that's why we like it so much," Dr. James explained. "And we can do such small micro-doses that in a drip, it goes in really slowly. So if we turn it off (snaps his fingers), he's awake."

"Okay," I breathed a sigh of relief. "I think we've just heard bad things on the news about fentanyl, so—"

"Haven't we, though? And it takes very little to be effective, so that's why we use micro pumps."

"You said earlier that the surgery could take twenty minutes or it could take two hours. So, I'm guessing you won't know for sure until you get in there and see what you're dealing with?" I asked.

"Twenty to thirty minutes is typical; it all depends on what his body does, how willing he is to give up this organ that he no longer needs, and then I have to make sure I leave the environment in a way that's conducive to keeping him alive.

"If Dr. Hui wants me to get biopsies, then things get trickier because every biopsy is a hole that I have to sew up and leak test. I need to get the samples and make sure that the hole left behind— whether it's this big or this big (he demonstrates with his hands)— is closed properly and tested for leaks. So I make Dr. Hui prioritize his list because if the dog can't tolerate the extra time in surgery, we're done. I'm closing up and getting out of there. So sometimes, I don't get Dr. Hui everything he wants. That's on me. But it's done for the right reasons because I need your little one to go home."

After all our questions were answered, Brad said, "Well, it sounds like this is the right thing to do." I nodded in agreement.

"It's risky, but it's worth it. And the alternative is that it might rupture," Dr. James reiterated. "And even if it doesn't go well, you're still doing the right thing by attempting it. I know that's not what people would think. They'd think, 'My dog was fine. Why did I do this?' But remember, this is a ticking time bomb, just waiting to go off."

By that time, Dr. James had spent forty-five minutes with us, which exceeded our expectations and seemed unprecedented in this day and age of rushed appointments, so we thanked him for his thoroughness.

After Dr. James left the room, Brad took my hand and said softly, "Benny's going to do great."

A minute later, Jessie, one of Dr. James's techs, entered with Benny in tow. She had a wide smile on her face as she lovingly nuzzled Benny close to her. Jessie's voice was bubbly and peppy, like a cheerleader, as she went over the estimate with us and echoed Dr. James's words about what we could expect before and after Benny's surgery. When she let us know that they could put him on the schedule for Monday, I was filled with conflicting emotions. On the one hand, I wanted to get this "ticking time bomb" out of my little boy. On the other hand, I was worried about the risks of surgery and Benny's recovery.

"Yeah, I think we do it Monday," Brad said.

I heard myself croak out a weak, "Okay."

After Jessie went over everything, she asked if we had any questions. Dr. James had answered most of them, but I thought of one more. "I'm sure you've heard Benny barking and howling back there—we could hear him from in here. Clearly, he has a lot of anxiety, so I think one of the keys to his recovery will be keeping him stress-free. I know Dr. James said Benny would be given fentanyl and possibly a sedative during and *after* surgery, but will he be given anything prior to it to keep him calm beforehand?"

"If he needs it, definitely, because it'll be easier for him if he's calm before going under full anesthesia, so we'll definitely keep that in mind."

Jessie told us to have Benny there Monday morning between seven and seven thirty. She also said he needed to fast after bedtime Sunday night, however, he could have a pill pop with his morning meds. Before walking us to the lobby, she handed me a packet with the estimate and a pamphlet titled "What to Expect When Your Pet Needs Surgery."

On the way home, Brad and I discussed the consultation. We agreed that surgery was the best option for Benny, and we both felt confident that he was in excellent hands with Dr. James, who seemed fact-based, experienced, and very passionate about his work. It was also evident that he makes every effort to get the best possible outcome for his patients. Plus, it was reassuring that he understood that for us, Benny was our child, and he'd gone through gallbladder surgery himself.

We were also hopeful that Benny would bounce back quickly and be able to come home on Wednesday, two days after the surgery, which we were told was the best-case scenario. But that was out of our hands. We would just have to wait and see.

Chapter 29

Dismantling a
Ticking Time Bomb

I've never been a very confident person, so it should come as no surprise that after we met with Dr. James and scheduled Benny's surgery, I started second-guessing that decision. Benny seemed fine the rest of the day as he snuggled up next to me while I did some work on my laptop and later that evening during family time with Brad. But the next morning, he vomited shortly after taking his pills. That was enough to convince me that we were doing the right thing moving ahead with the surgery. We didn't want Benny in pain every time he ate, nor did we want to put him in a position where he needed emergency, live-saving surgery.

Not surprisingly, my nerves were frayed all weekend. My hands were shaking, I had to keep taking deep, cleansing breaths to slow my wildly pulsating heart, and erratic, negative thoughts so consumed my mind that all I could do to overpower them was pray, pray, pray that Benny's surgery and recovery would go well and he'd be home with us as soon as possible.

I'd planned to clean the house that weekend, but with Benny's surgery looming over our heads, all I wanted to do was cuddle with him on the couch. So that's what we did. We even watched *The Secret Life of Pets 2*, which I'd told Benny a long time before that we'd watch together. I tried to entice him to eat something before bed on Sunday night, since he had to arrive at the hospital on an empty stomach, but he wasn't interested.

I hardly slept a wink that night. I just wanted to hold Benny close and watch him sleep. The VCA pushed back Benny's arrival time to between seven thirty and eight, so I wanted to get there as late as possible, using the extra half hour to spend more time with Benny. But Brad, the early bird, wanted to arrive at seven, so we decided to split the difference.

Of course, Benny wanted breakfast before we left. "I'm sorry, Buns," I told him, "but you can't have anything to eat besides your pill pops. You're having surgery today, and your tummy has to be empty. That's why I tried to get you to eat a bedtime snack last night."

Not understanding, he just stared at me with pleading puppy dog eyes.

Brad drove to the VCA while I sat in back with Benny, petting him to keep him calm. As much as he loved going for rides, he always instinctively knew when he was going to the vet. This day was no exception: his entire body was quaking and quivering with fear. When the three of us arrived at the hospital around seven thirty, Benny summoned his courage and walked in on his own, then a staff member promptly put us in a room.

After singing "You Are My Sunshine" to Benny, I told him to be Schaeffer Strong and to avoid any bright lights and angels—even if it was his Grandma Judy, his older brother, Arnold, Aunt Margaret, Uncle Bernie, Uncle Steve, or Dr. Bob—and reminded him that he had a lot more life to live, love to give, adventures to have, and stories to write.

When the tech took him from my arms, I held back my tears so Benny wouldn't see me cry, but as soon as Brad and I stepped outside, the dam broke. Leaving him at the hospital that day was the most difficult thing I'd ever had to do as his mommy.

When Brad and I returned to the house, he went to his home office to work, but that wasn't an option for me because 1) my focus was on Benny; and 2) I hadn't taken on any editing projects in the new year, which turned out to be a blessing in disguise because I couldn't concentrate.

When we'd dropped off Benny, they weren't sure what time his surgery would begin, so we went home and waited for the phone to ring. Around 9:20 a.m., a tech on Dr. James's team called to say the surgery was about to start. I spent the next hour and a half praying nonstop that the surgery would go well, there'd be no complications, and Benny would make a full and complete recovery.

A little before eleven, Dr. James called with an update. "The surgery was successful and Benny's gallbladder was ready to come out. It could've burst at any moment."

"Well, I guess we made the right decision," Brad said.

"Uh-huh," I agreed.

"We did have some trouble keeping Benny's blood pressure stable, so I got in and out pretty quickly," Dr. James added. "But I was able to get the liver biopsy Dr. Hui wanted."

"How did Benny's kidneys, liver, and pancreas look?" I asked.

"His kidneys and pancreas look good for his age and his issues, but his liver was a bit inflamed and sensitive," Dr. James replied. "Once Dr. Hui gets the results of the biopsy, he'll have a better idea of how to treat Benny going forward.

"Benny is resting peacefully right now, so we'll offer him some food later. A tech will call you tonight with another update, but you can call anytime to check on him."

"Thank you so much, Dr. James. We're so relieved that it went well," I said and Brad agreed.

A tech called a little before five to report that Benny was resting comfortably, and his vitals were stable. She also sent us a picture of him. He was chilling out in his kennel, swaddled in an array of soft, plush blankets, and although his ears were perked in the air like two isosceles triangles, his eyes were only open a tiny slit, a sure sign that the drugs were keeping him mellow.

We called and checked on him again before we went to bed and were told that he was still relaxing and his vitals were good, but he hadn't eaten anything when they'd offered him food. That didn't surprise me, though, because he looked pretty doped up in the photo the tech had sent earlier.

Brad was working from home again on Tuesday, so we went to visit our little guy over lunch. When the tech carried Benny into the room and placed him in my arms, my heart flooded with love, relief, and gratitude that he'd made it through the surgery. Brad and I were a bit taken aback by the five-inch-long wound on Benny's belly, which stretched from the bottom of his sternum to his wee-wee. More than a dozen sutures zigzagged down his abdomen. "Now you and Mommy have matching scars," I told him, blinking back tears.

While we were visiting Benny, Dr. James came in and spoke to us, which was an unexpected surprise. He said Benny's gallbladder was "very angry," and when I asked how big it was compared to how big it was supposed to be, he replied, "It's hard to say because small dogs have smaller gallbladders than big dogs. But to put it into perspective, Benny's gallbladder was so enlarged that it was the size of a German shepherd's."

"Oh my God!" I gasped. Brad and I stared at Dr. James incredulously with our eyes bulging and our mouths open.

Dr. James said Benny's vitals were good, and, overall, he was pleased with his progress. He told us Benny hadn't eaten yet, but he wasn't surprised, once again using his own personal account as an example. "When I had my gallbladder removed, I didn't eat for three days."

Although Benny was still pretty loopy during our visit, the techs brought in some food to see if he'd eat for us, but he just snoozed in my arms most of the time. They said he'd been sleeping so much that they weren't even making him wear a cone because he hadn't tried to lick at his stitches once, which was highly unusual for a guy who would gnaw on his paws any chance he got.

Brad was unable to join me for a second visit that day, so around four o'clock, I returned equipped with some apple chunks—one of Benny's favorite treats. But he turned his nose away at them and the canned dog food the tech left with me to try, so I just held him while he slept. Despite the hum from the fluorescent lights, the silence in the room was practically deafening, so I whispered encouraging words to Benny. "Keep hangin' tough, Bunny, and be Schaeffer Strong. Mommy and Daddy need you to fight to survive and make a full recovery, so you can come home as soon as possible."

Given that Benny wasn't eating, the initial assessment that he might come home on Wednesday seemed a bit unrealistic. When I spoke to the tech that morning, she pretty much confirmed it, stating that Dr. James and Dr. Hui were going to discuss transferring Benny out of the ICU to internal medicine under Dr. Hui's care.

I went to visit Benny around noon. He still refused food and seemed very weak, which wasn't surprising since he hadn't eaten anything since Sunday evening. While I was there, Dr. Hui stopped by with a progress report. He recommended another ultrasound of Benny's belly because his bilirubin and kidney values were elevated, so he wanted to see if he'd developed some post-op pancreatitis.

"If he does have acute pancreatitis, we'll probably give him a medication to reduce inflammation in the pancreas and prevent it from developing into something really, really bad. Because, as you already know, severe pancreatitis can be life-threatening," Dr. Hui explained. "The other thing I would do is place a nasal esophageal tube in him, a temporary one just to trickle feed him food to get his gut going, give him nutrition, and make him stronger. Hopefully, that'll stimulate him to eat as well.

"They took him off the fluids last night, but I'm going to put him back on them to try to drive down his kidney values. Then we'll give him another forty-eight hours and see how he's doing and go from there.

"After forty-eight hours, if he's showing signs of recovery—like his kidney and liver values are stable or improving—but he's still not eating, we can talk about placing a temporary feeding tube in his belly. With that, he'll get his meds and some nutrition and be able to recover at home. However, that kind of feeding tube does require sedation. It's a very quick procedure, but we need to be careful about his kidneys every time he goes under."

My head was spinning with all this information, and I was starting to feel pretty beaten down. With a heavy sigh, my shoulders slumped and my lips turned downward as I stared at the floor, disappointed about this negative turn of events. "Okay," I said defeatedly. "Go ahead and do the ultrasound and the nasal esophageal tube and put him back on the fluids."

"For sure. . . . The other thing, and I hate talking about this . . . ," Dr. Hui paused momentarily. It was only for a second or two, but in that time my heart constricted and my muscles tensed because I thought he was going to suggest I sign a DNR for Benny. I was relieved when he said, "But we'll have to let you know where you're at cost-wise and how much it'll be for those additional forty-eight hours."

"Oh, of course," I said, relieved that he just felt uncomfortable bringing up the subject of money.

"Any other questions?" Dr. Hui inquired.

"Yeah. Does anesthesia affect the kidneys?" I wondered.

"So, during surgery, the doctors and techs maintain the patient's blood pressure the best they can. But under anesthesia, any small dips or changes in blood pressure mean that blood flow to the kidneys is compromised, so they take a hit. Same with the pancreas. The kidneys and pancreas are the two organs that are most sensitive to blood pressure changes."

"Okay. Thanks for explaining that. Dr. James said they had some issues maintaining Benny's blood pressure during the surgery, but I wasn't sure how that affected his kidneys."

"He's still got a bit of a recovery ahead of him, but we'll do what we can to get him through this," Dr. Hui assured. "He's a trooper. . . . He always is."

"Yes, he is," I agreed as I gazed down at Benny and stroked his head, which was resting on my forearm as he slept serenely. "I hated putting him through the surgery, but it sounded like it was just a matter of time before his gallbladder would burst."

"Yeah, Dr. James said it needed to come out. You know, we do the gallbladder removal because mucoceles need to come out, even though sometimes it doesn't necessarily look horrible in there. But he said Benny's was really bad. In that case, I highly doubt the antibiotics would've worked by themselves. So, unfortunately, that was the only real choice he had."

Just then, Dr. Hui's phone rang. He looked down at it and abruptly stood up. "Sorry. I need to go. I have a patient in distress. Thank you."

After thanking Dr. Hui as he rushed out of the room, I hugged Benny and kissed the top of his head, grateful that he wasn't the patient in distress. Then I said a silent prayer that the pet who was would be okay.

Chapter 30

Spinning in Circles

"Hello?" I said into my phone with trepidation. It was two days after Benny's surgery and Brad and I were eating dinner when I saw the VCA's number pop up on my caller ID. Every time I saw the VCA calling, my heart stopped until they told me Benny was okay.

"Hi, it's Dr. Hui. I was just calling with an update on Benny. Is now an okay time?"

"Oh, hi, Dr. Hui. Of course," I replied. "I have you on speakerphone so my husband can listen in."

"That's fine," Dr. Hui confirmed. "So, we did a chest X-ray on Benny, which looked good, and the ultrasound only showed minor pancreatitis and some fluid around his liver. Both were to be expected because, as you know, the pancreas was manipulated and a liver biopsy was done during the surgery.

"I also wanted to let you know the insertion of the nasal esophageal tube went well, so Benny will start getting some nutrition that way, but we'll keep trying to get him to eat on his own."

This was all good news, and when Brad and I arrived at the hospital to visit Benny later that evening, he actually walked into the room—although he was a bit unsteady on his feet, which wasn't surprising given the amount of pain meds he was on and the fact that he'd just started getting some nutrition after not eating for three days. However, he had to wear a cone to prevent him from knocking out his nasal tube. As small as the tube was, it took up his entire left nostril, so he was having some difficulty breathing. He sounded like he had a cold and was only able to breathe through one side of his nose. They actually sewed a stitch into his nose to keep the tube in place, so Brad, ever the jokester, said, "Benny, you got your nose pierced!"

The tepid expression on Benny's face made it clear that he did not find Brad's joke the least bit amusing. I'm sure if he could have, he would've rolled his eyes and said, "Not funny, Dad. Not funny."

While I was holding him, Benny seemed unable to get comfortable, so I put him on the floor, and as soon as I did, he peed. Then he just kept pacing around the room in circles. It was difficult to see him that way, but Brad—always the optimist—kept commenting on how great it was that Benny was walking. He even found a silver lining with the feeding tube, saying it was giving Benny the calories and nutrition that his body needed to heal. I couldn't argue with that.

On Thursday, knowing that Benny would be in the hospital until at least Friday afternoon, Brad went back into the office. Around nine o'clock, Dr. Hui called with an update. "Benny's bilirubin has spiked up to 6.9. (It should've been between 0.1 and 0.6.) I'd like to do another ultrasound and take a sample of the fluid in Benny's belly to see if he's leaking bile."

Dr. Hui is pretty reserved and keeps his emotions close to the vest, which is likely a defense mechanism to avoid getting too close to patients who are seriously ill. It also makes him difficult to read, so I didn't really pick up on the concern in his voice. When I told him I was planning to visit at noon and asked if I should wait until after the ultrasound, without hesitation he said solemnly yet resolutely, "No. You should come now."

The tone of his voice scared the bejesus out of me and had me concerned that Benny didn't have much time left. I gulped to swallow the burning tension mounting in my throat, then croaked out, "Okay." As soon as we hung up, tears gushed from my eyes.

I called Brad, but when he didn't answer, I grabbed my purse to rush to the VCA. Just as I was getting into the car, Brad called. When I told him what was going on, he said, "What should I do?"

"I can't tell you what to do. That has to be your call," I said as I backed out of the driveway. "But the concern in Dr. Hui's voice has me worried, so I'm on my way there."

Brad said he'd be there as soon as he could.

On the half-hour drive to the hospital (which probably only took twenty minutes because I was pushing the speed limit), I bawled my eyes out and pleaded with God to save Benny. A part of me knew that Benny had to have his gallbladder removed, but another part of me felt guilty that he was going through this because we'd elected to do the surgery. "Why are you doing this, God?! Why are you doing this to my baby boy?!" I lashed out in anger, punching the steering wheel. "Please let Benny make it through this, God! He's such a good little boy, and he brings so much love and joy to so many people! Please heal him!" I screamed.

When I got to the hospital, one of the front desk clerks saw my tear-soaked face and immediately put me in a room. But when the tech brought Benny into the room, I was shocked to see him walk in, especially given the concern in Dr. Hui's voice only thirty minutes earlier. Once again, Benny seemed uncomfortable when I held him, so I sat on the floor while he wobbled around the room. When Brad arrived a few minutes later, we both agreed that Benny actually looked better than he had the night before. They let us visit for about an hour, then it was time for Benny to get ready for his ultrasound and fluid draw.

Brad decided to work from home the rest of the day, which helped me relax a bit. He's my rock, especially during difficult times, so without him there, I would've been even more anxious.

When my phone rang a little after four, Brad came running down the stairs when I hollered, "Dr. Hui is calling!" We sat on the love seat as Dr. Hui explained that the ultrasound and fluid draw had gone well, however, he still wasn't sure whether Benny had post-op pancreatitis, was leaking bile, or something else was going on. As a result, the plan was to treat him with three different antibiotics and keep him in the hospital a couple more days, with him possibly going home on Sunday. When he started to cautiously say, "I hate to bring this up . . . ," I thought he was going to bring up the additional costs again. In my mind, I was prepared to hear him say that, so when he actually said, "But you currently have listed that you want Benny resuscitated if his heart stops. Given everything that's going on, you may want to consider making him a DNR."

I couldn't speak. I just shook my head, held myself in a self-soothing hug, rocked back and forth, and silently sobbed. After a beat of silence, Brad stepped in and stoically said, "I don't

186 | *Jennifer Huston Schaeffer*

think we're ready to make that decision yet, but if and when we are, we'll let you know."

After the call with Dr. Hui, Brad held me as I wept on his shoulder, and we both willed Benny to be strong and keep fighting.

We didn't know what to do with ourselves the rest of the day. Brad tried to work and I tried to keep busy by doing some crafts, but neither of us could concentrate. Around five, we took a long walk around the neighborhood, then decided to get something to eat at Wolfie's, the restaurant next to the VCA. I was trying really hard not to cry, but every song that played over the restaurant's speakers—even love songs—seemed to remind me of Benny or the situation we were dealing with. Under normal circumstances, I would've loved the selection of '80s music, which included "Right Here Waiting" by Richard Marx, "I Remember You," by Skid Row, and "We Belong" by Pat Benatar. Billy Joel's "The Longest Time" also made me think of Benny, especially the lyric that mentions having music left to write because every time Benny had a medical setback, I would tell him to keep fighting because he has many stories left to write, thinking of the children's books I planned to pen about him someday. And when "You're the Inspiration" by Chicago started playing, I lost it and quietly sang the words to Benny, who was lying in the hospital across the street.

As tears streamed down my face, I could tell other diners were gaping at me, wondering what was wrong, but I didn't care. Besides, I figured it didn't take a rocket scientist to figure out why a woman would be weeping uncontrollably at a restaurant next to an emergency animal hospital.

After dinner, we walked over to the hospital. We'd brought Benny some leftover rotisserie chicken, a slice of apple, and a couple chunks of his cookies to see if we could coax him to eat. We couldn't, but he actually seemed a bit peppier and stronger than he had when we'd visited earlier in the day, so we were trying to be hopeful.

He was spinning in circles again, though. I agreed with Brad that it was good to see him walking, but the fact that he was taking a circuitous route around the room and couldn't seem to get comfortable concerned me. But Brad, Mr. Brightside, who always tries to put a positive spin on things (no pun intended), thought the nasal feeding tube was causing the circling because it was in his left nostril and Benny always seemed to go in a counterclockwise direction, i.e., leading with his left. I didn't really buy into that theory, though.

The next morning, Friday, February 2, Dr. Hui called around eight thirty. He said Benny seemed perkier than he did before he left the night before, so that was encouraging. But he also reported that, although some of Benny's values had improved, his bilirubin was even higher at 7.6 than it was the day before. As a result, Dr. Hui wanted to do another ultrasound and take another sample of the fluid in Benny's belly, which meant more sedation, albeit mild. It literally was Groundhog Day, and I felt like Bill Murray in the movie of the same name, whose character keeps repeating the same day over and over again.

Brad and I went to see Benny at two and stayed for over an hour, then we went back for another hourlong visit at eight. Benny did seem more alert, but he still refused the chicken, apple, and treats we'd brought him.

After a moment of silence, I pointed out something that seemed obvious but was difficult to address. "Have you noticed the color of Benny's skin and the whites of his eyes?"

"Yeah," Brad replied. "You mean the yellowish tinge?"

"Yeah . . . , I noticed it last night too," I confessed.

"Me too," Brad said.

Apparently, neither of us wanted to admit that Benny was jaundiced. Instead, we preferred to think we were just imagining it. But, this time, there was no denying it. It wasn't a super bright hue—it was more of a pastel yellow—but it was definitely noticeable.

Fortunately, the ultrasound revealed the fluid in Benny's belly was going down, which meant his color should return to normal soon. However, he continued to pace in circles until he finally plopped down on a blanket on the floor. I scooped him up, blanket and all, and gently rocked him in my arms for a while before handing him over to Brad, who hadn't held him since Monday morning when we'd dropped him off for his surgery.

When Benny started whining in Brad's arms, we thought maybe he was uncomfortable or in pain, so Brad put him back on the floor. Then I noticed something.

"What's on your pants?"

"Oh my God! Benny peed on my lap!" Brad exclaimed.

"Are you sure? It looks like *you* peed your pants!" I giggled so hard that I nearly peed *my* pants. But it felt good to laugh after shedding so many tears.

Before we left, Brad and I gave Benny his nightly pep talk, "Stay Schaeffer Strong, Buns!" Brad encouraged.

"Yes, and hang tough, Baby Boy. You have many more adventures to have, walks to take, apples and broccoli to eat, and squirrels, chickens, and bunnies to chase," I reminded him. "Just relax, rest, recuperate, let the meds do their job, and, as always, avoid any white lights and angels."

Brad was very chatty on the drive home. It was his way of dealing with the stress and worry we were both experiencing with our little guy in the hospital. But I tended to zone out and get very quiet on our drives to and from the VCA, pouring all my attention into thinking positive thoughts about Benny and praying incessantly for God to heal him and let him come home to us ASAP.

Dr. Hui called around nine thirty on Saturday morning. Lucky for us, he was working and on call that weekend. "I just wanted to let you know that Benny's labs have improved since yesterday. His bilirubin went from 7.6 to 6.3, and his kidney values are almost back to normal. And today's ultrasound showed less fluid in his belly, so he's trending in the right direction.

"I also got the results of Benny's gallbladder culture," Dr. Hui continued. "His gallbladder was infected with a type of bacteria that's very resistant to all but a couple antibiotics. One of those antibiotics can cause kidney failure, so it's not an option for Benny. The other one has to be compounded for Benny's size at the local apothecary, so I'll call in a prescription. In the meantime, Benny seems to be responding to the doxycycline, Baytril, and metronidazole, so we'll continue with those for now."

After a brief pause, Dr. Hui admitted that he was cautiously optimistic about Benny making a full recovery. I was elated because he doesn't say things just to make us feel better.

But my elation wore off that afternoon when we went to see Benny. A tech greeted us in the lobby and told us that Benny was feeling very "dumpy," so rather than moving him into a treatment room to visit, she took us back to where all the kennels are located. It seemed highly unusual, but Brad and I appreciated it.

Benny's kennel was somewhat larger than his crate at home, and it was on the lower level, which was good since he was afraid of heights. The tech opened the crate door and unhooked his IVs while we were there, but Benny didn't seem up to visiting. At first he was facing us, so I sat on the floor and stroked his fur. Even in the darker room, it was apparent that his skin was still a tad yellowish, like the Scarecrow from *The Wizard of Oz*. A few minutes later, he turned around and lay down on his side, facing toward the back of the crate. After visiting for only about fifteen minutes, the tech came and said it was time for Benny's treatment, so we knew that was our cue to leave.

We went back to see him again around eight. Following our afternoon visit, Dr. Hui had removed Benny's nasal esophageal feeding tube, hoping it would alleviate his stuffiness and stimulate him to eat on his own. However, after the feeding tube was removed, Benny really struggled to inhale through his nose, so he was mostly breathing through his mouth. He took a drink of water, but most of it went up his nose, and when we tried to get him to eat some of the chicken and apple we'd brought with us, he seemed confused, like "How am I supposed to eat and breathe through my mouth at the same time?"

"We're a little concerned that pneumonia or a respiratory infection could be causing his breathing trouble," the tech told us, "but we're hoping his nasal passages are just irritated from the tube."

"It kinda looks like he has some canned food wiped all over his nose, maybe even up his nostril," I said. "Could you clean up his face a bit to see if that helps?" She said she would.

After seeing Benny struggle to breathe like that, it was even harder for me to leave him than it had been on the day of the surgery. Brad and I gave him his nightly pep talk, and as I did every day, I told him how blessed I am to be his mommy. While I softly sang "You Are My Sunshine" to him, silent tears trickled down my cheeks. My heart felt like it was being shattered in a million pieces as I wondered if that would be the last time I'd ever see him and hold him in my arms. I desperately wanted to stay and lay next to him all night, even if it meant sleeping on the cold tile floor. Knowing that wasn't possible, Brad and I said that if we ever win the lottery, we'll open an animal hospital with rooms where parents can sleep next to their pets overnight.

Hearing the tech mention pneumonia or a possible respiratory infection was like a punch in the gut. *How much more can Benny's little body take? How much more stress can Brad and I take?*

Not surprisingly, I couldn't sleep that night. In fact, when Brad went to bed, I stayed up later and watched TV. My mind was racing with negative thoughts, so I prayed obsessively to battle them. I was also paranoid that if I fell asleep, we'd get a call in the middle of the night informing us that our worst fears had come true.

Chapter 31

How Benny Got His Groove Back

On Sunday, February 4, Brad drove us to the VCA under a blanket of clouds and a leaden sky. The temperature was in the mid-forties, but it might as well have been zero; anything below seventy and I'm freezing.

When we arrived, we were relieved to see that Benny was no longer struggling to breathe, which made me breathe easier as well. "Hi, Bunny!" I cooed. "You look so much better than you did yesterday!"

"After you guys left last night, I wiped off his nose and sprayed some saline up his nostrils to clear his nasal passages," the same tech from the night before told us. "Then I started giving him nebulizer treatments."

"Thank you *so* much!" I gushed. "I'm sure he wasn't thrilled with that, but it certainly worked! I'm so relieved. Mommy was really worried about you, Buns."

"Yeah, I thought about texting you overnight to let you know his breathing had returned to normal," the tech admitted. "But it was around 1:00 a.m., so I was afraid I'd wake you."

I'd been so worried about Benny that I hadn't even gone to bed until after three, but I didn't want to make her feel bad for not texting me. Instead, I casually said, "You could've. I was still wide awake, so it would've been a welcomed surprise if you had."

Benny's bilirubin was still high, but it had dropped again, down to 5.0 from 6.3 the day before. And he finally ate for us: some chicken, a little bit of apple, and even a few bites of his cookies!

Dr. Hui called later and gave us the great news that Benny's latest ultrasound showed the excess fluid in his belly was almost completely gone. "I took him off the pain meds, which should—fingers crossed—increase his appetite," Dr. Hui said optimistically. "If he continues to eat well and his numbers continue to improve, you could possibly take him home Monday or Tuesday." Then in a rare show of emotion, Dr. Hui added, "He's a tough little guy!" Even though we were talking on the phone, I could tell he had a smile on his face.

When Brad and I returned that evening, Benny looked fantastic! He was still a little weak and his skin was a light buff color, but he ate some more chicken for us and he'd eaten more in his crate earlier.

"Great job, Buns!" Brad praised.

"Mommy and Daddy are *so* proud of you for finally eating something!" I raved. "Keep up the good work so you can get stronger and come home soon."

We were overjoyed that our little Benny Boo Bear had taken a positive turn.

On Monday morning, Dr. Hui called with an update. "First, I got the results of the liver biopsy Dr. James took during the surgery. It only showed some inflammation, which we'd expected.

"Second, Benny's bilirubin is down to 2.7, which is still high (less than 0.6 is normal), but it's much improved," he began. "However, Benny's creatinine level, which was normal yesterday, is now 2.0. (Less than 1.5 is good.) But that might just be Benny's new normal. I'm not too concerned about it because he could live for several more years at that level. It could also be the chicken he's been eating because it's higher in protein than the hydrolyzed diet he was on before." Apparently, higher levels of protein negatively affect kidney values, at least in those with kidney disease.

"I'd like to get Benny's creatinine level back down before discharging him, so I'm going to keep him on fluids one more day."

"Okay," I murmured. "I really appreciate you calling and taking such good care of our little guy."

Although I was disappointed that Benny wouldn't be coming home that day, knowing that he'd turned a corner in his recovery journey and should be coming home the next day gave me the jolt of energy I'd been lacking since learning that he needed surgery. I finally got the house cleaned, but I still made time to visit Benny during the day, then Brad and I went back in the evening after dinner.

With Benny off the pain meds, he was starting to look and act more like himself. He was still weak and super skinny, but his color had improved and it seemed like he was tracking in the right direction. Brad and I were pumped for Benny's homecoming the next day. He'd been gone eight days, but it felt like a month.

At ten the next morning, Dr. Hui called to say we could pick up Benny at noon. His bilirubin was down to 1.6, which was still slightly elevated, and his creatinine went up to 2.7 from 2.0 the day before, but Dr. Hui was optimistic that those levels would come down at home.

It took us about an hour to check out and go through all of Benny's discharge instructions with Andrea, one of Dr. Hui's techs. They'd basically been throwing the whole pharmacy at him to see what worked, so he had to take ten pills in the morning and five in the evening, including three types of antibiotics, two appetite stimulants, and an antinausea medication. I thought back to when I'd tried so hard to take a more natural approach to treating Benny's medical issues, but that was no longer an option. Even so, I was a bit concerned about him taking all those meds in a pill pop because he hadn't shown any interest in the treats since his surgery. When I expressed my apprehension to Andrea, she tossed a pill shooter into our goody bag as well as a syringe that we could use to squirt ground-up pills mixed with water or broth into his mouth. She even demonstrated how to do it and made it look easy-peasy.

Brad held Benny while I put his harness and coat on him and went over the paperwork with Andrea. Benny started getting a little squirmy in Brad's lap, so when Andrea left the treatment room, he set him on the floor.

"What is *that*?" I asked, pointing to a blob of something bright yellow smeared on Benny's blue parka.

"I don't know," Brad replied.

But when we noticed it was on Brad's jeans too, it dawned on us. "Ack!" Brad said, taken aback. "Benny leaked squishy poop on me!"

Brad doesn't handle the three Ps (pee, poop, and puke) well, so I found this hilarious. Brad freaked out a bit, grabbing a wad of paper towels and vigorously scrubbing his jeans with soap and water. But he wasn't upset with Benny. We got them both cleaned up, and fortunately, I had anticipated that Benny might have some post-op leakage issues, so I'd already placed a pee pad over his bed in the car, just in case he had any accidents on the way home.

Brad drove home so I could sit in the back seat with Benny to make sure he was comfortable and didn't accidentally fall. When we got home, Benny wandered around the kitchen and dining room area, taking everything in and making sure his food and water bowls were right where he'd left them. Then he made his way to the living room, sniffed his toys in his basket, walked up his ramp, and plopped on the couch. I imagine he thought to himself, *Ahhh . . . It's good to be home.*

Dr. Hui wanted Benny to stop eating chicken, so it was decided that we'd try turkey and rice. After we got Benny settled, I went to the grocery store and bought a frozen bone-in turkey breast and a couple packages of pee pads. The only turkey I'd ever cooked was a small, boneless breast, so this was unchartered territory for me. After removing it from the packaging, Brad attempted to drop it in the Instant Pot.

"It's too big!" he announced.

"Well, crap. What are we gonna do?" I replied.

We tried every which way to get it in the pot, but because it was frozen, we couldn't shove it in. Then Brad had an idea: we held it under the faucet and ran hot water over the slippery sucker until it was pliable enough to stuff in the pot.

I also didn't have instructions on cooking a frozen turkey in the Instant Pot, so I had to wing it. I found a recipe that said to cook for five to six minutes per pound until it reached 165 degrees. This was a six-pounder, so after thirty minutes, I released the steam and Brad took the temp. The bird was still frozen solid. I ended up putting it back in for another thirty minutes, and it came out mouthwateringly juicy.

Dr. Hui hadn't specified what type of rice to use, so I cooked up some organic brown rice, which I'd heard was healthier than white. Benny loved the turkey, but he left most of the rice in his bowl. Because he was turning up his nose at pill pops, as I'd feared, we tried wrapping his meds in turkey to mixed results.

Over the next few days, Benny ate like a champ, although he mostly cherry-picked the turkey out of the rice. Even so, there were a couple times when he ate too much and got a bellyache. When that happened, he would moan and then let out a shriek that sounded like a fussy baby. It broke my heart to see him in pain, but there was really nothing we could do to comfort him; we just had to give it time to pass.

For the first few days at home, Benny continued to squirt out bright yellow poop in his sleep, like he had on Brad's lap in the hospital on the day we brought him home. As a result, we made sure he always had a pee pad underneath him. Fortunately, if he had to go during the night, he would pop up in his bed, which would wake us up, and Brad would take him outside.

The first day Brad went into the office and I had to give Benny all his meds by myself, I was like a frantic, frazzled, sleep-deprived mother of a colicky newborn. Even pulling out all the tricks Andrea had taught me, it still took me almost two hours to get Benny to take his pills. When he wouldn't eat them in pill pops, I wrapped them in turkey, but he kept spitting out the pills and eating the turkey. Eventually, I used the shooter with a chaser of water to get him to take a few, but the rest I had to crush, mix with broth, and squirt down his gullet with a syringe. That last method wasn't fun for either of us because when I inserted the syringe in his mouth, he clamped down his jaw on my finger. I quickly learned my lesson and kept my fingers farther back on the syringe, so he bit it instead of me.

Andrea called during the day to check on Benny, so I told her about the difficulty I was having giving him his pills. She emailed me a little while later, stating that she'd discussed it with Dr. Hui, and he'd prioritized Benny's meds in order of importance so I knew which ones to give him first and which ones could be skipped if need be. That was a huge help.

Since Benny had come home, we'd been giving him several small meals throughout the day rather than just feeding him twice a day like we had prior to the surgery. We were giving him about an eighth of a cup of turkey and the same amount of rice four or five times a day, which didn't seem like much. On this particular day, after I fed him a snack around four o'clock, he still seemed hungry, so I gave him a little bit more. But shortly after that, he started whimpering and whining again, like his tummy hurt, only this time, he also started drooling. He'd never done that before, so I frantically typed another email to Andrea.

She replied right away, stating that the taste of the meds could cause him to drool; however, it had been hours since he'd had any pills, so I didn't think that was the problem. She also said it could be due to his elevated kidney values, but given everything he's been through, it could just be normal. She also encouraged me to keep giving Benny the Cerenia, the antinausea pill. Ultimately, I think he just ate too much too quickly and had a bellyache.

The next day, I had some difficulty getting Benny to take his meds again, but eventually, he took all but one in turkey. The other one, he spit out three times, so I decided to try again later and finally succeeded. After Brad got home from work, he got Benny to eat some apple and one of his cookies, so it seemed like Benny was starting to get his appetite back and enjoy his favorite foods.

We also noticed that since Benny had come home, when we'd take him outside on sunny days, he would sort of flinch and stumble, like the sun was bothering him. A few days later, I noticed a milky film on Benny's left eye, so I added it to my list of questions to ask Dr. Hui at our follow-up visit.

On Monday, February 12, Brad and I had a phone consultation with an animal nutritionist whom Dr. Hui had recommended. She said that given Benny's conditions (no gallbladder, chronic kidney disease, allergies), she suggested a low-fat novel protein, but he also needed to be on a protein-restricted diet for the kidneys. Therefore, most of his calories would come from carbs, like pasta, rice, and veggies. Given all this, she advised switching him to pork—or possibly salmon or tilapia—and said he should be getting about 380–400 calories a day, which on his current diet, would be about one cup of turkey, one cup of rice (she said white was better than brown for him), a quarter teaspoon of canola oil, and some veggies. She also said we needed to add vitamin and mineral supplements to his food. When I mentioned that he was eating the turkey but picking out the rice, she proposed grinding them up together. *Genius! Why didn't I think of that?*

By the end of the conversation, Brad and I were committed to a home-cooked diet for Benny, but we were on the fence about pork. I'd always heard that pork is one of the most common proteins that dogs are allergic to; plus, it has a reputation for being higher in fat. However, the nutritionist assured us that she would recommend leaner cuts.

Since the weekend, Benny's appetite had declined slightly, but the day after we talked to the nutritionist, it disappeared altogether. Despite giving him the appetite stimulant, he wouldn't eat anything or take his pills.

When he still hadn't eaten by two thirty, I called the VCA and asked if I could bring Benny in for his follow-up with Dr. Hui the next day instead of waiting until Friday. They said yes, but it would be a drop-off appointment.

Of course, after I changed the appointment, Benny took his meds in a pill pop; it was the first time he'd eaten one since his surgery. However, when it came time for his bedtime meds, he refused the pill pop. So, I quickly cooked up a sweet potato and hid the pills in small chunks. It worked like a charm! I still wanted Benny to see Dr. Hui sooner rather than later, though, because he wasn't as interested in the turkey as he had been when he first came home from the hospital, and he needed to eat.

The next morning—Valentine's Day—Benny and I arrived at the VCA around eight. When Andrea came to get him from me in the lobby, I told her that he'd been doing pretty well with the turkey, but then, all of a sudden, his appetite disappeared. I also pointed out the film on his eye. She made notes for Dr. Hui and said he would call me when Benny was ready to be picked up. I transferred Benny into her arms, then went to run a few errands close by.

I finished my shopping around eleven, so I headed back to the hospital, let the front desk clerks know I was there, and waited in the lobby, reading a book on my tablet. Around 12:45 p.m., Dr. Hui called. When I told him I was in the lobby, he replied, "Oh. I'll come get you and we can talk in a room."

When I met him in the hallway, I thanked him for agreeing to see Benny a couple days early. "It's no problem," he said. "Benny is like family at this point." It meant a lot to hear him say that. By then, the entire internal medicine staff and most of the ER staff recognized us when we came in. But hearing Dr. Hui say Benny was like family set my heart at ease because I knew he was getting the best care in the Indianapolis area—probably in the entire state.

For the next twenty minutes, Dr. Hui and I sat in a room and discussed the results of Benny's latest blood work and his treatment plan going forward.

"Benny's ALT was 314 when he left the hospital, but it's up to 668 today," Dr. Hui began. "However, he's off fluids now, so that part I'm not too concerned about."

"What's it supposed to be?" I asked. Even though we'd discussed these levels numerous times, I could never keep track of what they should be.

"It's supposed to be under 120," Dr. Hui replied. "But his bilirubin, which was high at 1.6 last time and had been over 7 at one point, is normal now."

"Oh, that's good," I said, happy for some positive news.

"Yeah, that part is good. Like I said, I'm not too worried about the ALT right now because it can fluctuate, especially since he's still recovering from the liver biopsy and because his bilirubin is normal now. The problem is his kidney values."

"Oh," I groaned.

"When Andrea told me you wanted to come in earlier for a follow-up, I had a feeling it might be his kidneys. And sure enough, his creatinine has jumped from 2.7 when he left to 3.4 today."

"And what's normal?"

"Normal is 1.4. So, it's not what I would like to see, but it's also not through the roof. I was worried that it was going to be 5 or 6 or something. The problem is, his BUN was 61 when he left, and now it's above 180."

"What should it be?" I sounded like one of those toy dolls from my childhood that you pull a string on its back to make it talk, but it can only say a few phrases.

"It's supposed to be less than 25. So, when the increase in the creatinine and BUN aren't proportionate, I worry that he still has some kidney injury from the surgery and that he's also experiencing some degree of dehydration, which would make sense," Dr. Hui explained. "He already had kidney issues prior to the surgery, and since he's been home, he hasn't been eating well and maybe isn't staying as hydrated as he should be—not through any fault of your own—but he's just not staying sufficiently hydrated.

"The other thing I wanted to ask: what medications have you been able to get him to take consistently?"

"We've been able to give him all his medications, but I'm not going to lie, it hasn't been easy. Like yesterday, I wasn't able to get him to take his *morning* pills until midafternoon," I confessed. "So they're not necessarily exactly twelve or twenty-four hours apart like they're supposed to be, but we have been able to give him all of them. Sometimes I have to dilute them in water or broth and squirt them in his mouth, though, and neither of us like that."

At that point, Dr. Hui and I went through Benny's meds, one by one. In the end, he kept Benny on the doxycycline (antibiotic), mirtazapine (appetite stimulant), Cerenia (antinausea), Prilosec (antacid), and prednisone. He decided to hold off on the rest, including Baytril and metronidazole (two other antibiotics), Entyce (appetite stimulant), ursodiol, fenofibrate (used to treat high cholesterol and triglycerides in the blood), and clopidogrel, which is used to prevent blood clots. Regarding the latter, the thought was that Benny was two weeks post-op, so a blood clot seemed unlikely.

"That should leave you with only five meds to deal with, which will be much more manageable. It'll be less stress for both you and Benny, and it's going to make him more likely to eat. Once he starts eating well and getting better, we can add some of those back in if we need to. But right now, it's all about the bare essentials."

"I'm game for that!"

"We'll do one more week of the doxy, and then hopefully we can be done with that too. Those antibiotics can be a bit rough, so by taking him off the metro and the Baytril, he should start to feel better—and even better when he's done with the doxy."

Neither of us spoke momentarily while Dr. Hui looked at his notes. Then he broke the silence. "And now . . . ," he sighed heavily, "here's the part I don't want to talk to you about, but I will."

I braced myself for him to mention a DNR again, but instead he said, "Do you think you could give Benny fluids underneath the skin?"

Relieved that he hadn't asked about a DNR, but nervous about his request, I inhaled deeply then let out my own anxious sigh as I responded, "I have done it before with my childhood dog, Arnold, but that was over twenty years ago."

"Really?" Dr. Hui sounded surprised.

"Yeah, I think so. Is that where I insert an IV under his skin, like behind his neck, and then we just sit there and let the fluid trickle in?"

"Exactly."

"Then, yeah, that's what I did for Arnold."

"Well, I think it would be beneficial for Benny ... especially right now."

"Okay. Then I'll do it." There was nothing I wouldn't do for my little boy.

"I'm sure you're wondering if it's temporary or long term. I'm not going to lie. I honestly don't know yet," Dr. Hui admitted. "The plan is to put him on the fluids and see if he starts to feel better and eat better. Then we can recheck his numbers and see if he's improved. If he has, then we can probably back off on the fluids and see how he does."

"Sure," I agreed. "But will Andrea or someone give me a refresher course on how to do it?"

"Of course."

With that out of the way, Dr. Hui and I turned the discussion to Benny's diet and the consultation Brad and I had with the nutritionist.

"Her suggestion was either to continue with turkey and rice or switch to pork, which is a novel protein for him," I said. "I'm a little leery about pork, though, so I wanted to get your take on it. Plus, is now the best time to do a food trial given that he's on a lot of meds and still recovering from surgery?"

"If she okayed the turkey, and he eats the turkey, then I think it's fine," Dr. Hui weighed in.

"When he has an appetite, he goes to town on the turkey," I commented. "He had been picking out the rice, but the nutritionist suggested grinding it all together, so since I started doing that, he's eating the rice too."

"Switching to the mirtazapine twice a day should help with his appetite, so I think it's fine to stick with the turkey."

"Okay," I said. Then after a beat of silence, I added, "Oh, did you notice his left eye?"

"Yeah. It looks like he has a corneal ulcer."

"Oh, dear. What does that mean?" I wondered.

"He's got a calcium deposit in his eye. You know that kind of whitish stuff in his cornea? He just has some ulceration of it. It's usually caused by a bacterial infection," Dr. Hui elaborated. "We'll start him on some eye drops. It's just a superficial ulcer, meaning it's just on the top layer, but if it progresses, it can become a deep ulcer and rupture the eye, so we need to watch it."

Yikes! I thought. *What's next?* But I knew better than to verbalize that negative thought and put it out there in the universe because I didn't want anything else thrown at Benny. Poor little guy already had enough on his proverbial plate.

A moment passed before Dr. Hui said, "I wish he was doing better."

"You, me, and Brad too."

"But it could be worse, to be honest. So we'll give it a little more time. I'll be interested to see how he does and what his numbers look like after he starts the fluids and once we can get him off all the antibiotics. Either I or someone from my staff will call you next week for an update, and I'd like to see him again in two weeks."

When Dr. Hui stood up to leave, I said, "Thank you, Dr. Hui. Take care."

"You're welcome. Fingers crossed we'll get him through this."

A few minutes later, Andrea came in to show me how to give Benny the fluids. Back when I'd administered subcutaneous fluids to Arnold, we had to sit still for half an hour or more, letting gravity do the work as the liquid slowly moved through the tubing and into him via an IV. For Benny, the process would be much quicker. First, as Andrea demonstrated, I would draw the fluid into an enormous syringe with a large, eighteen-gauge needle. Next, I would remove that needle from the syringe and replace it with the cap end of the tubing, which connected to a smaller "butterfly" needle. Then came the hard part: inserting the butterfly needle into Benny and physically pushing down on the syringe to get the fluid flowing into him. Sounds easy in theory, but when Andrea asked if I wanted to give it a whirl or let her perform the task while I watched, I opted for the latter.

"Hopefully, he doesn't give you too much of a fuss, but I know he's a sensitive little guy," Andrea said while drawing the fluid into the syringe. Andrea was tall and slender with a pretty face, kind eyes, and a caring heart. "If he starts eating better, you can give him a little snack or treat when you do the poke, and he might not even notice."

"If the needle poke does hurt him, can I numb him up with an ice cube first? That's what we did when we gave him his allergy shots."

"Absolutely," she responded. "Are you still giving him allergy shots?"

"No. They weren't really helping, so we stopped them last fall."

Next, Andrea showed me the best way to insert the needle into the skin on his back. "Take your thumb and index finger and pull up the loose skin to make a triangle, like a door to a tent. The needle goes right in that door, right between your fingers."

"Is up by the scruff of his neck too high?"

"I find that to be a little too high because if he moves his neck, it'll be uncomfortable for him. Plus, the needle could come out or you might poke through his skin."

As I held a snoozing Benny on my lap, Andrea, who was sitting in the chair next to me, prepared to insert the needle. Just as the needle punctured Benny's skin, he moaned and jerked his neck a bit, so I squeezed him a little tighter.

"Oh, Benny Boy! I'm glad you're feeling better!" Andrea said sweetly.

"You're okay, Baby Boy," I comforted. "Mommy knows you're sensitive, but this will make you feel better."

"Benny, you surprised me!" Andrea continued. "I knew you were a sensitive guy, but I didn't think you were going to react like that. Good job, Benny!"

As Andrea slowly pushed down on the syringe, I could tell the fluid was going in because a little hump started forming on his back. Andrea assured me that the fluid doesn't burn or sting; it just feels a little weird going in. I've had IVs before, so I could relate to that.

"It can be pretty tough to push the syringe down, and my hands get weak and tired, so I like to set it on a flat surface for leverage," she said as she placed the bottom of the syringe on the chair. "Depending on where you give Benny his fluids, you can use your counter, a table, the floor, or whatever to help you push it."

With the needle in and the fluid flowing, I had a little more courage, so I decided to try pushing down on the syringe. Andrea wasn't kidding: I could tell right away that it was stiff and would take some effort to push the fluids through. But literally, within thirty seconds of me taking over, the syringe was empty. "Well, I guess I just caught the tail end of that," I quipped.

"Yeah, even pushing as slowly as we were, it only takes a couple minutes. Then you just pull the needle straight out like this," she said as she gently removed the needle and rubbed the little camel hump on Benny's back. "Sometimes there might be a bit of leakage or a spot of blood, but that's totally normal. He's got a nice little fluid pocket, which will absorb as the day goes on."

"Okay," I sighed. "That seems fairly straightforward and much quicker than when I did it for Arnold."

"I think you guys will be fine. Some people just aren't comfortable with needles and it can be difficult for them to poke their own pet."

"That's my husband," I replied.

"Oh ...," Andrea said, a bit concerned.

"I practically had to distract *him* with treats so we could give Benny his allergy shots."

Andrea laughed heartily then said, "Well, hopefully you guys get into a routine. The hardest part will be the needle poke, so once you get past that, you'll be all set. And, worst-case scenario, you can bring him in and we can do it for you."

I was grateful to have that as a fallback, but I felt confident we could do it on our own.

Andrea handed me a bag with a week's worth of supplies and reminded me to use new needles every day for safety and cleanliness and because the butterfly needles could dull with repeated use, which would make the poke even more painful for Benny. She also advised me to put the caps back on the used needles and return them to the VCA so they could properly dispose of them.

Before we left, Andrea said, "I think these subcutaneous fluids are really going to help Benny perk up and start eating and feeling better."

I told her I hoped so, thanked her profusely, and then Benny and I headed home.

Despite getting some not-so-good news about Benny's kidney values, a weight was lifted off my shoulders after meeting with Dr. Hui. I felt like part of the team as we went back and forth discussing Benny's meds and diet, and I had faith that Benny was on the right path, especially with adding the subcutaneous fluids to his regimen.

But that evening, Benny suddenly decided he no longer liked turkey. "What happened to my little boy who would eat practically anything?" I said to Benny, holding my hands in the air in mock frustration and surrender. "You've suddenly become such a picky eater, like the little girl from the PediaSure ad from years back, who, while grocery shopping with her mom, would annoyingly say, 'I don't like that! ... I don't like that!' What am I gonna do with you, Benny?"

Chapter 32

The Return of Our Super-Duper Pooper

"Hi, Dr. Hui. This is Jennifer Schaeffer, Benny's mom. Last night, Benny decided that he no longer likes turkey, so I'm wondering what to give him as his protein source. We're still on the fence about pork, but we're open to trying it or salmon, tilapia, or a prescription canned food if it would be better for him. Give me a call when you get a chance to discuss this, or email me if that's easier. Thanks! Have a great day!"

Dr. Hui responded to my voice mail message later that day and said he recommended pork or tilapia. I did some research on the two, and since we didn't know which cuts of pork would be best in Benny's case, Brad and I chose tilapia. However, due to a traumatic childhood experience, I don't eat anything that lives in the water and the smell of fish makes me gag, so Brad agreed to be in charge of cooking it. If it got Benny to eat and helped him live as long as possible, I could deal with the house smelling like a seafood restaurant.

Brad went to the grocery store and picked up a package of fresh tilapia from the seafood section. When he got home, he prepared it while I made some rice. When everything was cooked, I ground it up in a mini food processor I'd inherited from my grandma and presented it to Benny in his bowl. Lo and behold, he licked his bowl clean and was looking around the kitchen floor to see if we'd dropped any morsels.

"Great job, Buns!" Brad and I praised in unison then laughed at the fact that we think so much alike. We've always had this uncanny ability to read each other's minds and often have the same thoughts at the same time.

Seeing Benny excited to eat and have an appetite again warmed my heart and helped me relax a bit. That alone was worth the fishy smell.

I emailed Dr. Hui the next day with the good news. "That's great to hear!" he wrote back. "I'm glad our little Benny is doing better. Fingers crossed that he keeps eating well."

Between the subcutaneous fluids and the tilapia-rice combo, Benny started eating like a champ. After a few days, I emailed the nutritionist and told her we'd decided to move forward with a homemade diet of tilapia and pasta. (We ultimately chose pasta because, although Benny was eating rice after I'd started grinding it up with the protein, it was coming out just as it had gone in, so it was clear that he wasn't digesting it properly.) The nutritionist said she'd have a recipe ready for me soon and told me where to order the supplements.

That weekend, Benny seemed to be moving in the right direction. In fact, he had his first solid poo since January 28! Since he was on the mend, Brad and I left him alone for the first time since before his surgery and went to a concert just a few miles from home. We checked on our little guy periodically from the Benny cam, and he seemed to be resting peacefully. He didn't even have to wear the cone when left alone because he hadn't been licking or chomping his paws.

But as soon as we pulled into the garage, I heard, "OW ROO! ... OH ROOOAR!"—the sounds of our little Howler Monkey making it known that he was disgruntled and dismayed. We'd only been gone about three hours, but he acted like it had been three days. However, he soon settled down as we cuddled on the couch to watch a show and exchange Valentine's Day gifts.

Over the next ten days, the three of us settled into a routine, just as Andrea had predicted. Benny was sleepy and sluggish in the mornings, but after I got the fluids in him, he'd liven up a bit. He wasn't quite as energetic as he was before the surgery, but the fluids were definitely helping.

After some back and forth, the nutritionist sent Benny's specially formulated recipe for a home-cooked diet, which included a few select fruits and vegetables, based on Benny's preferences. But Brad and I were surprised that the recipe only allowed Benny 30 grams (one ounce) of tilapia *per day*, which was a fifth of what we'd been giving him, and she'd made it with rice instead of pasta as we'd requested. We still hadn't received the special vitamins and supplements we'd ordered, so while we waited, we cooked up the recipe without them.

After dinner on February 27, Benny had to fast because he had a follow-up appointment with Dr. Hui the next day. But around 4:30 a.m. on the twenty-eighth, we woke up to him having dry heaves. He later vomited during his appointment, but Dr. Hui said it was just bile because he had nothing in his stomach.

Overall, the appointment went relatively well. Most of Benny's numbers were improving: His creatinine and bilirubin had both dropped and were within the normal range. His phosphorus, ALP, and BUN were still high, but they were lower than they had been two weeks prior. However, Benny's ALT liver enzyme had actually gone up since his last visit, which was concerning.

At that point, Benny had been on the doxycycline since the beginning of February, so Dr. Hui said to finish up what we had left, which was six days' worth, and then we'd be done with it. He also switched Benny from eye drops to an antibacterial eye ointment and wanted us to follow-up with Dr. Budelsky, the ophthalmologist on staff.

The subcutaneous fluids seemed to be boosting Benny's energy level, but Dr. Hui needed to know whether his kidney values were improving because his kidneys were healing or because of the fluids. As such, he instructed me to cut back on the fluids and only give them to Benny on Mondays, Wednesdays, and Fridays.

"I'll be very interested to see what his numbers look like and how he acts after you decrease the sub Q fluids to three times a week," Dr. Hui said.

"Is it bad to have him on the fluids every day?" I asked, looking down at Benny and running my fingers through his fur as he patiently sat on my lap. "Does that mean his kidneys aren't functioning properly?"

"It's not necessarily bad, but if he doesn't need them, I'd prefer to have him off them. Obviously, if his kidney values go back up or you notice that he's just really slowing down without them, we'll put him back on them."

When we discussed Benny's diet, I was shocked to learn that he'd lost a tiny bit of weight (five ounces) since his last visit. He'd been eating so well that Brad and I were convinced he'd actually gained a little. However, at the same time, I felt the amount of tilapia that the nutritionist had recommended just wasn't enough. But, then again, I wasn't a doctor or nutritionist.

When I asked Dr. Hui's opinion, he was on the fence. He thought Benny's diet could still be too high in fat, and that was driving the elevated ALP.

"Too high in fat?!" I exclaimed. "What's lower in fat than whitefish?"

"I'm not sure. It's pretty lean," Dr. Hui admitted. "It could either be the fat content or it could be that even though he's eating it well, his body doesn't like the fish protein.

"For now, just keep doing what you're doing and don't reduce the amount of tilapia yet. Let's see what his kidney values look like next time after we've weaned him down on the sub Q fluids. If his kidney values go back up, it means the sub Q fluids are just diluting the numbers, so it's probably necessary to give him less tilapia or something lower in fat. But if we wean down on the fluids and his kidney values stay steady, he can probably get a little bit more tilapia.

"I also want you to start giving him a small meal before you go to bed so he has something in his stomach overnight. That should prevent the dry heaving.

"I'd like to see him again at the end of next week. We might think about decreasing his prednisone then. It's probably driving his appetite a bit, but a lower dosage will be better for his body in general. That said, I'm not gonna change it now. .... It's very tricky. It's kind of like a Jenga tower, and I don't want to pull out the wrong block."

"Yeah, right," I responded with a slight laugh at his spot-on analogy.

"So we'll see. So far, we've been lucky. He's a trooper."

"Yes, he is," I agreed as I pulled Benny close and kissed the top of his head.

That night, we gave Benny a bedtime snack, and he slept peacefully without any tummy troubles. The next morning—Leap Day—he seemed a little more tired and unsteady on his feet than he had in the past week or so, but per Dr. Hui's instructions, I skipped the sub Q fluids. Benny also didn't drink much on his own that day. He took a big drink for Brad around six in the morning, but he didn't drink anything else until three thirty in the afternoon—even when I put the water bowl right under his nose. He had one more drink after dinner, but that was it.

Benny's appetite was also seesawing. He ate all his breakfast around ten thirty, but when lunchtime rolled around, he wasn't hungry. However, he'd also had a treat each time he went potty outside, which was about four times.

Around four thirty, Benny threw up. It was mostly foamy, yellow bile. Thinking it was because he had an empty stomach, I once again offered him lunch, and this time he ate it.

He polished off his dinner and bedtime snack, but around two o'clock in the morning, we once again woke up to him gagging and retching, his body convulsing as if he were going to puke, but nothing came up.

In the previous week or so, Benny's poops had pretty much gone back to normal, but on the morning of Friday, March 1, he had watery diarrhea with rice particles in it, which was similar to when he'd first come home from the hospital and was eating turkey and rice. Even so, he ate most of his breakfast.

After that—even before we gave him his fluids—he was a little perkier and more steady on his feet than he had been the day before. I sent Dr. Hui a note to let him know how he was doing and asked about switching him to pasta. I explained that I wasn't sure why the nutritionist had made his recipe with rice when we'd told her he no longer liked it and couldn't digest it well, and she'd been the one to suggest pasta in the first place.

That afternoon, Benny ate about half of his tilapia, rice, and apple for lunch, but then he vomited a few minutes later. Again, it was mostly yellowy liquid with a few pieces of food. I didn't want to be a pest, but I sent Dr. Hui another update and asked him to call me because I needed to know what to do over the weekend. He called back before he left for the day and said to switch to the pasta, go back to giving Benny Cerenia to stave off nausea, and give him fluids again the next day but skip Sunday.

After getting his fluids on Saturday, Benny was more energetic and his appetite was so strong that he devoured the tilapia, pasta, and green beans we prepared. I didn't even have to grind it up into a "casserole."

On Sunday, he snarfed down his breakfast, but after that, things started going downhill again. As the day progressed, he seemed to get weaker and more lethargic. He was very wobbly and struggled to walk, plus his back was arched. Brad took Benny outside at 3:15 p.m. and he peed, but it was dark yellow in color. When they came back in, we discovered that Benny had had an accident on the floor at some point, which he'd only do if he wasn't feeling well.

For lunch, he picked the tilapia out of his bowl and turned his nose up at the pasta and green beans. He ate all his dinner but then refused his bedtime snack altogether.

As Dr. Hui had instructed, we had skipped the fluids that day. Benny drank an average amount of water, but given the dark yellow urine and the way he was acting, Brad and I were concerned that he was dehydrated. By bedtime, I wanted to do something, but I knew from experience that if I called the VCA, they wouldn't give me any advice over the phone, nor would they call Dr. Hui; they'd just tell me to bring Benny into the ER. So at eleven, I called my sister Lori, who's a dialysis nurse, and asked if she thought it would be all right if we gave him a half dose (30 milliliters) of his fluids. She said that should be fine, so we did. After receiving the fluids, Benny immediately perked up a bit, but he still wouldn't eat or drink anything before bed.

On Monday morning, Benny ate almost all his breakfast, but he wouldn't drink any water. Even after getting his fluids, he was unsteady on his feet, arched his back, and seemed to get more lethargic as the day wore on. And when I offered him a cookie, he seemed like he was too weak to chew it. Eventually, he dropped it on the floor, gave up, and walked away.

For lunch, he picked out the tilapia and still refused to drink. By 5:15 p.m., I emailed Andrea at the VCA with an update and to let her know that Benny had refused water all day. I ended the note by saying: "Brad and I aren't sure what to do. We feel like something is definitely not right, but we don't know what. We're debating whether we should bring him in tonight, tomorrow, or see if Dr. Hui can see him on Wednesday instead of Friday. My concern is that he's in kidney failure. As I mentioned before, my childhood dog had kidney failure, and I feel Benny's symptoms are similar. But I'm sure those symptoms could be something else too. What do you suggest?"

She wrote back to say that Dr. Hui would like me to bring Benny in the next day at 10:00 a.m. to recheck his kidney values. "It'll just be a technician appointment because Dr. Hui isn't in on Tuesdays, but we'll text him the results of Benny's blood work, then he'll reach out to you with a plan."

That night, Benny ate some tilapia and noodles out of Brad's hand, and he finally drank about half a cup of water. A couple hours later, he got another drink, but after about ten minutes, he started shaking and whining like he was in pain. We all moved to the couch, but Benny couldn't get comfortable. After about fifteen minutes of him crying, moaning, trembling, and trying to get comfortable, he let out a loud, human-sized burp and then was fine. We hated to see him in pain, so when he seemed all right after a huge belch, we laughed with relief.

"C'mon, Buns. We gotta go," I told Benny the next morning. He was at his food station, staring at his bowl. "Sorry, but you can't have any breakfast yet. You have to get your blood drawn."

I pulled his parka over his Mommy's Boy sweatshirt then carried him to the back seat of the SUV and clipped his seat belt to his harness. He was shivering, but it's difficult to say whether that was due to the frigid temps or because he knew he was going to the vet. Probably both.

I gripped the steering wheel tightly as I drove slowly and methodically toward the VCA. It was snowing heavily and, with the swirling winds, it was difficult to see and the roads were slick. Despite the weather, I had allowed enough time that we actually arrived about ten minutes early, which was good because we needed it.

"Holy cow!" I exclaimed. "The parking lot is jam-packed!" I made a couple laps around the lot, but there wasn't a single spot to be had. *Should I park at Wolfie's?* I thought to myself. *Probably not. They'll be opening for lunch soon, so I'm not sure that's allowed.* I continued creeping around the parking lot until someone exited the hospital, then I stalked them for their spot.

As I was waiting in the lobby for Benny to get his labs drawn, an announcement came over the loudspeaker: "Attention, if you're parked at Wolfie's, you need to move your vehicle right away." *I'm glad I didn't do that.*

A few minutes later, I heard a commotion at the front door. I looked up from my tablet to see two people rushing in, carrying a Jack Russell who was lying limp in his owner's arms with his tongue hanging out. As the owners handed their fur baby to a tech, I heard them say he'd been attacked by a big dog. My heart ached for the poor little guy and his parents, so I said a prayer that he'd make a full recovery.

When Benny and I got home, he inhaled his breakfast. Dr. Hui called around three with Benny's results. "All of Benny's numbers are elevated again and he's dehydrated, so I want you to resume giving him the fluids every day, which should also help stabilize his phosphorous level. I want to recheck his labs in two weeks. At that point, we'll see if we can cut back on the fluids."

We had finally received the vitamin and supplements that the nutritionist recommended, so I asked if we should start them. "No," Dr. Hui said. "Hold off on giving them to Benny for the time being."

When Brad got home from work, we gave Benny his fluids. About an hour later, while I was making his dinner, Benny peed on the floor. He'd been following us around the kitchen as I prepared his dinner and Brad got stuff out for us, so I just figured he was hungry and wanted to keep an eye on us in case we dropped some food. But after Benny peed on the floor, Brad said, "I thought he might have to potty."

"Then why didn't you take him out?" I said with surprise.

"I don't know," Brad replied. "I guess I just hadn't gotten around to it."

I shook my head, rolled my eyes, and told Benny that one wasn't his fault.

This time, I ground up the pasta and green beans then cut the tilapia into teeny tiny pieces and mixed it all together, and Benny ate every bite of his dinner. We were so proud of him that we may have gone a little over-the-top with our praise party because he looked at us like we were losing it.

But the celebration didn't last. When I took Benny out in the morning, his eye seemed to be bothering him again because he was doing the herky-jerky thing with his head as the sunshine glared off the glistening snow. When we came in, he didn't want his breakfast, so I started with his fluids. But he seemed a bit ornery because every time I started to numb the area, he'd get up and move to a different part of his bed. After several tries, I decided to try his breakfast again, but he still wouldn't eat.

His eye continued to bother him, even indoors, so I wondered if the light could be giving him a headache or migraine. Bright lights often trigger my migraines, so it made sense. After I turned off the lights, he ate about half his food.

I was finally able to get his fluids in him around one thirty, while he was napping. He woke up just as I was finishing, so I offered him the rest of his breakfast, but he didn't want it. He did eat a couple cookies, though. Around three thirty, he went to his food station and stared at the place where his food bowl would be, so I fed him lunch, plus an apple slice. That night he ate all his dinner and most of his bedtime snack, so we were hopeful that the fluids were doing their job and getting him back on track.

The next day, Benny definitely had more pep in his step and he ate well, nearly finishing each of his four meals and having a bonus apple slice as an afternoon snack. He also had three solid poos, which was a good sign that our super-duper pooper was back!

Chapter 33

"A Celebration"

Friday, March 8, 2024, was the tenth anniversary of the day Benny and I first met. That morning, Brad had to give a presentation at work, which always makes him nervous, so after taking Benny out a little after six, he held Benny close, gave him a hug, and confided to him his apprehension. He said it always helped him feel more calm and relaxed. That was one of Benny's superpowers—to make people feel less anxious and stressed with his mere presence. In fact, the last time we were at the assisted living facility where my dad was living, one of the residents wanted to pet Benny. When she was done, she beamed, "You made my day!" That was the Benny Effect. He offered emotional support to Brad and me, and we did the same for him.

Despite having a doctor's appointment, Benny didn't have to fast, and he ate almost all his breakfast and did both potties before we left to see Dr. Budelsky, the ophthalmologist at the VCA.

Dr. Budelsky and his staff were downright jovial. With his quick wit and sense of humor, I was able to relax in his presence, which is something I'd never been able to do at the VCA before. As much as I'd come to adore and appreciate Dr. Hui and his staff, Dr. Budelsky's side of the hospital seemed much less stressful and more lighthearted than the side with the ER, ICU, and internal medicine department, which was naturally a welcomed relief.

Benny stood calmly as Dr. Budelsky examined him and shined a bright light in his eyes. "I wish all my patients were this good," he said.

That's my boy!

However, by the time Dr. Budelsky finished his exam, Benny was shaking, which, knowing him, was less about the exam itself and more about the height of the table. I scooped him into my arms, pet him as he trembled, and spoke softly into his ear, "You're all right, Baby Boy. You're all right. You did a great job!"

Dr. Budelsky said to continue with the antibiotic ointment and give Benny artificial tears to lubricate his eyes. He also added a different eye drop, called EDTA, to break up the mineral deposit in Benny's left eye, but it would need to be ordered from the online pharmacy they used.

I'd always wondered how animal ophthalmologists could assess a pet's vision, so I took the opportunity to ask. Dr. Budelsky quickly deadpanned, "We just have them read an eye chart."

I burst out laughing, and as Dr. Budelsky chuckled, he added, "I wish we could because it's tough. In general, unlike humans, it doesn't take a lot of vision for dogs to get around. Some of it's simply about how easy it is for me to see to the back of his eye. Because if I can look in easily, he should be able to look out easily.

"I can get glimpses of the back of Benny's good (right) eye, but it's hazy, which is age-related. So if Benny were a human, he'd probably need bifocals. However, that blurriness doesn't affect dogs as much because they don't read or drive like we do. Benny does have some scattered cataracts, which are likely affecting his vision a little bit, but it's nothing I can realistically make better with surgery."

As much as I would've liked Benny to have twenty-twenty vision, I couldn't bear the thought of putting him through another surgery, so I appreciated Dr. Budelsky's candor.

"I'd like to see Benny in three to four weeks for a follow-up, but you can call or email me with any questions or concerns," Dr. Budelsky said. "Or if you're here for an appointment with Dr. Hui and have a concern about Benny's eyes, I can pop in and take a quick look."

After we got home from the VCA, Benny ate all his lunch, but his ornery streak had returned.

"Buns, you have to sit still so Mommy can give you your fluids. They'll make you feel better, I promise." After getting the fluids, tubing, and needles set up, every time I tried to numb him, Benny would move away from me. "Ugh . . . I give up," I groaned dramatically after the sixth or seventh attempt. Despite my frustration, I could only laugh and took it as a sign that Benny was feeling stronger and less lethargic because he was alert enough to know what was going on. Finally, when Brad got home around five, Benny settled down enough to get his fluids.

Benny gobbled up his dinner and a slice of apple, had good potties all day, and ate all of his bedtime snack after we watched *Walk the Line.* As I tucked Benny into bed, I told him the story of the day we first met, recounting: "You were at an adoption event in my neighborhood that day. I'd already been preapproved to adopt you, but we had to meet first. Your name was Boo back then, and as soon as I stepped inside the little boutique pet store, I looked to my left and there you were.

"I said, 'Is this Boo?' and when the woman with you said yes, I squatted down and you put your paws on my knees and looked up at me with those big, brown, puppy dog eyes. It was just like you were saying to me, 'Hi! You're gonna be my mommy. You wanna get out of here?'

"The lady watching over you asked if I wanted to take you for a walk, so we grabbed a leash and walked around the block. You were such a good boy! You didn't pull or anything; you just did your business and sniffed a bit. When we went back inside the store, I told the lady that I was ready to proceed with the adoption. But much to my disappointment, she said I would have to wait. I could tell you were sad that I was leaving you behind and you must've been wondering why, so I tried to explain that I would see you the next day. To be continued tomorrow. Love you, Baby Boy. Night night."

The clanging of my alarm woke me up on Saturday, March 9. I wasn't ready to get up, so I pulled Benny next to me for morning cuddles, something we'd often do on weekends or days when I wasn't feeling very motivated. As I reflected on the past ten years with Benny, Brad came back to bed and joined us for a few minutes. As I lay there with Benny in my arms, the hypnotic effect of watching his little chest move up and down with each slumberous breath made my eyelids heavy. It was such a precious moment that I just wanted to preserve it forever and hold him in my arms all day.

Unfortunately, I had to break the spell because my bladder was about to burst, and I had to make Benny's birthday card and wrap his presents. It was his twelfth birthday, and we had a lot to celebrate!

Benny ate all his breakfast and lunch, including an apple slice with each, and he had several healthy poops throughout the day. When Brad was bringing him back from a potty break during the afternoon, Benny actually hopped up all three steps on his way into the house. With some get-up-and-go and his appetite improving, it seemed like he had overcome his post-op obstacles and was finally getting back to normal.

I finished my tasks around two and spent the rest of the afternoon snuggling with Benny and Brad on the couch. While we watched qualifying for the next day's IndyCar race, I sifted through photos of Benny and wrote a Facebook tribute to him for his birthday and to celebrate our first ten years together. After submitting the post, I sat back and relaxed with my boys and watched TV.

While we were cuddling, Benny crawled on top of me, stood on my chest, and smothered my face, neck, and ears with kisses, even getting my glasses. "Thank you, Bunny! That was wonderful! I can't see now, but I don't mind. I love Benny kisses!"

I'd often whine because lately, for some reason, he seemed to favor giving Brad kisses rather than me. Perhaps it was because Brad eats more meat, fish, and peanut butter than I do. Either way, I was grateful for the kisses, and Brad captured the moment in a series of photos.

Brad was planning to give Benny a bath, but later in the afternoon, he said, "I'll give you a tubby tomorrow, Buns. It's your birthday, so let's enjoy some cuddles and family time."

After eating all his dinner, Benny still seemed hungry, so I gave him two more apple slices, which was the end of his allotment for the day. As he was finishing them up, I thought, *Darn it. . . . I wanted to record the cute little sound he makes when he crunches the apple. I'll have to remember to do it tomorrow.*

After dinner, Benny opened his gifts. He didn't seem as interested in opening them as he used to be, but he wasn't completely uninterested either. He especially loved the pumpkin and blueberry Fruitables that the nutritionist had recommended. After giving him a few of the tiny treats, I put them on the counter.

By then, I had stacked his present stash against the wall, so he walked down his ramp and started sniffing them, looking for the Fruitables. He even sniffed Brad's legs and feet because earlier in the day, Brad had kneeled on the floor and used the kitchen mallet to break up some crunchy treats to fill Benny's cookie jar, so he must've still had some powder from pulverized cookies on his slippers. In fact, until Brad took a shower, Benny followed him everywhere, relentlessly licking his feet and legs.

After Benny finished opening his presents, we snuggled together on the couch, watched the previous night's episode of *Dateline*, and talked about how well Benny had been doing lately.

"Benny seems to have really turned a corner this week," Brad observed.

"Yeah, since we went back to giving him the fluids every day, his appetite has improved and he's had more energy," I added. "He's made a remarkable turnaround just in the last six days. Remember how lethargic he was last Sunday when I called Lori at eleven about giving him half a dose of fluids?"

"Yeah," Brad recalled. "Those fluids really seem to help. . . . Can you believe he's been home from the hospital for a month?"

"Has it really been that long?" I said. "It feels like the past month went by quicker than those eight days he was in the hospital! It's been a long road, but it seems like he's on his way to making a full recovery. Thank God!"

Just before midnight when Brad and Benny returned from bedtime potties, Brad announced, "We've got a double pottier!" meaning that our super-duper pooper had performed his duties . . . or doodies.

"Great job, Bunny!" I called out from the kitchen, where I was preparing his bedtime snack.

"Thanks, Mom," Brad said in his Benny voice as Benny breezily sauntered into the kitchen then wolfed down his snack.

Once upstairs, I tucked Benny in before I got ready for bed. I took off the red, buffalo-plaid flannel shirt he'd been wearing along with this "Birthday Boy" bandana, placed him in his bed on top of our bed (his bed-in-a-bed), and started to tell him his regular night nights.

"Oh, I almost forgot!" I said. "I need to read you the Facebook post I made for your birthday." I pulled it up on my phone and read it to him. "Ten years ago today, I brought my baby boy home for the first time. Although we'd met the day before and it was love at first sight, the rescue group made me wait until the following day to take him home. It was supposed to be a foster-to-adopt with a seven-day trial period, but I knew right away that Benny—or Boo as they were calling him—was meant for me. So far, this year has had its medical challenges, but Benny is a strong little guy, and I'm so proud of him for fighting to survive. And I'm praying for at least ten more healthy happy years with him. He's brought me love, joy, and happiness every single day of the past ten years, and in doing so, he literally changed my life. I'm so blessed that God chose me to be his mommy. I don't know his exact birthday or age, so we celebrate today as his birthday, and I just guess that he was two when he came into my life. So Happy 12th Birthday, Benny Boo Bear! You are my sunshine! Wishing you a healthy, happy year to come! Love you, Baby Boy!"

We also looked at the photos and video clip I'd posted. When we watched the video, I said, "This is from your birthday five years ago, Bunny. Let's get you back into fighting shape like you were in this video as you tore into your presents."

After that, I recounted for Benny the day I brought him home as I do every year on March 9. "Aunt Karen came with me to pick you up, but when you walked into the room, you remembered me from the day before, hopped onto my lap, and knew I was your mommy. . . . You were truly heaven sent, Benny. You've changed my life in so many positive ways and brought me joy each and every day." Then I kissed the top of his head and said, "Night night, Munchkin. Love you, see you in the morning. Sweet dreams. God bless you. Mommy loves you. Happy Birthday, Baby Boy! I hope you had a great day! I love you. Night night."

As I lay in bed, I thought about what a great day the three of us had together and how much Benny had improved in the past few days. I really believed he was on the road to recovery, and as long as we could manage his kidney disease with his diet and fluids, he could live another five to ten years—Dr. Hui had even said as much. Then I said my prayers and read for a while. Around one o'clock (which was actually two because it was the night we flipped the clocks ahead an hour for daylight savings time), I put away my tablet, caressed Benny's head—he was snuggled in between Brad and me, about midway down the bed—and told him again that I loved him.

Chapter 34

The Nightmare Begins

A little before five, in the early morning hours of Sunday, March 10, 2024, I shot up in bed. "What's wrong, Bunny? Do you have to potty?"

I'd been startled awake when Benny stood up, stepped out of his bed-in-a-bed, and began walking toward the edge of the big bed, near my feet, as if he were sleepwalking. I grabbed him just before he tumbled to the ground.

"Brad, wake up. . . . Benny needs to go outside," I said, nudging him.

"Hmm. . . . Okay," Brad said groggily then hopped out of bed and started getting dressed.

When Benny let out a little whine, I figured he was letting us know, "I really have to potty *NOW*!" I picked him up to put him back in his bed and said soothingly, "Hang on, Buns. Daddy is getting dressed to take you outside."

But while I was holding Benny, he started wriggling around like he was trying to escape my hold. Then he howled, "OH ROOOAR!"

"What's wrong?" Brad asked with concern.

At first I thought maybe Benny had caught one of his claws on his collar because that had happened before, and whenever it did, he'd shriek and scream like a cat in heat. But this time, I knew that wasn't the case.

"I don't know," I said, the pitch of my voice rising. "He's not wearing his collar, so his nail isn't caught on anything, and I can't tell if something else is wrong!"

Just then, as I was still holding Benny, I realized that he wasn't trying to worm his way out of my arms, he was having a seizure. At the moment I made this connection, Benny peed and pooped simultaneously. My chest tightened as I called out to Brad, "He just peed and pooped! I don't know what's wrong, but I think he's having a seizure!"

The seizure only lasted maybe fifteen seconds, but it seemed like an eternity. After Benny's body stopped flailing, I carried him into the hallway, still thinking we'd take him outside. But when Brad turned on the light, I knew something was seriously wrong. Benny was lying on his back in my arms, breathing laboriously with his tongue hanging out of his mouth. By then, my heart was pounding double-time and I was starting to feel lightheaded, so I sat down on the ottoman to think.

"Should I take him outside to see if he has to do more potties?" Brad asked, still half asleep. In his drowsy state, I don't think he was fully grasping the gravity of the situation.

"He already went! I think he had a seizure! We need to get him to the hospital!" I cried.

Hearing the sense of urgency in my voice, Brad agreed, so he grabbed my glasses, my phone, and Benny's bed. When he returned to the hallway, I had him call the VCA because we weren't sure what to do if Benny had another seizure. The only thing I knew to do was keep him from swallowing his tongue, so I made sure it was hanging out of his mouth. Brad held the phone to my ear while I tried to explain to the young woman on the other end what was going on. "This is Jennifer Schaeffer. My dog, Benny, is a patient of Dr. Hui's. I think he just had a seizure and we don't know what to do if he has another one."

She responded with the same spiel I'd heard the front desk clerks say so many times as I sat in the lobby, "If you want to bring him in, that's fine. Just know that it'll be $183 for an exam, and that doesn't include any tests or treatments."

Tears trickled down my face as I became frantic. "I know that!" I barked. "We're coming in. I just need to know what to do if he has another seizure on the way!"

She just repeated her lines as if she were an automated message.

"Just hang up," I grumbled to Brad, deflated and annoyed at the woman.

Still in my pajamas, I rushed downstairs with Benny in my arms as Brad grabbed his wallet and keys. It was only in the twenties outside, but I didn't even put on my coat because I didn't want to set Benny down. Somehow I managed to slip into my sneakers.

Brad opened the door on the passenger's side of the SUV so Benny and I could get in, then he placed Benny's bed in my lap and helped me clasp my seat belt. As I held Benny, his breathing continued to be ragged and his tongue remained hanging out of his mouth. I didn't know if I should attempt CPR or if that would make things worse. That's what I was hoping someone at the VCA could tell me, but the desk clerk was of no help.

As Brad sped south down Keystone, I cradled Benny in my arms and told him how much I love him, "Benny, you and your daddy are the loves of my life, and I love the two of you more than anything in this world. I love you, Benny, and your daddy, Braddy, so much—SO MUCH—that my love for the two of you is infinite. That means it has no beginning and no end; it's always been there and always will be, and there's so much of it that my heart bursts with love for the two of you. You know, some people say, 'I love you to the moon and back,' but I love you and your daddy, Braddy, to the sun and back because that's a lot, lot farther.

"Hang in there, Benny. Keep fighting to survive and be Schaeffer Strong," I encouraged. "We're taking you to the hospital to get help."

At some point along the way, Benny had a second seizure. When that happened, Brad turned on the dome light on my side so I could see Benny better. His breathing was shallow, so I did my best to do CPR, tapping vigorously on his little chest to keep his heart beating.

As we passed 116th and Keystone, Benny let out a gasp. I was staring into his eyes, and when he exhaled, I literally saw the light go out of them, like a veil had been draped over them. One second they were dark brown pools of chocolate and the next, I could see right through them. It was 5:15 a.m.

My entire body went limp, and if I hadn't been sitting, I surely would've fallen to the ground. Barely able to breathe, I surprisingly calmly whispered, "I think he's gone."

"No! Benny, no!" Brad cried out. "Hang in there, Buns!"

"I don't think he's breathing," I murmured. I instructed Brad to pull off at the next exit, so he did, but we didn't know if we should continue to the VCA or go home. Brad went around the roundabout once, then I saw a church on the southwest side of 106th. "Let's pull in there."

While we sat in the church parking lot, Brad stroked Benny and thought he felt a pulse. We were both touching him, looking for signs of life, and that's when Brad realized it was actually his own racing heartbeat he was feeling, not Benny's. We sat there for what felt like five to ten minutes, trying to decide what to do before I finally said, "Let's just go home. There's nothing they can do at the VCA, and if we go there, we won't be able to say goodbye on our own terms. Plus, they may take him from us and make us cremate him, and I'm not ready for that."

As we drove home in silence under the indigo sky, I couldn't believe what was happening. It felt so surreal, like an out-of-body experience. Between the trauma of what had just happened and the fact that I normally wasn't up before dawn, the moment had a dreamlike quality. But this wasn't a dream. As I held Benny's lifeless body in my arms, reality hit and a river of tears spilled from my eyes.

Back at home, we placed Benny in his bed then cuddled with him on the couch, cried, told him how much we love him, how much he'd changed our lives, and how life would never be the same without him. I buried my face in his fur and cried deep, heaving sobs. Grief grabbed me by the throat like a menacing beast and choked me so hard I could scarcely breathe. *How is it possible that just a few hours ago we were celebrating Benny's birthday? He was doing so well, he'd been improving, and had such a good day yesterday! This CAN'T be happening! This isn't real! This is just a terrible dream, and when I wake up, I'm going to hold Benny tight and tell him how much I love him. Please let me wake up from this nightmare! PLEASE WAKE UP!!!*

But I wasn't asleep; I was actually living this nightmare.

After a while, Brad and I did a three-way call with my sisters. As soon as I texted to see if we could talk ASAP, Denise knew. She replied and asked if it was about Benny, but I didn't want them to find out via text, so I didn't respond. When I broke the news, they both said I gave Benny the best life he could've ever had, and I appreciated that, but I wanted more time with him, and he deserved more time on Earth. Denise said she was going over to see Dad, so she'd tell him since he often didn't hear his phone ring.

After talking to my sisters, we called Brad's parents and let them know. They were also very sympathetic but were practically speechless, which is odd because they always know the right things to say.

Later in the day, I called my dad. Denise had said she'd tell him about Benny, so it seemed strange that he hadn't called to check on me or express his condolences or anything. I'm not going to lie—that hurt. When he answered the phone, the first thing he said was, "Don't cry. Hold it together." That's pretty much the story of my life. All I could think was, *How does he expect me to hold it together? My son literally just died in my arms a few hours ago!* It brought back painful memories of him saying to me, "You're too close to Benny. You're really gonna have a difficult time someday when he's gone." Back then, I thought, *What am I supposed to do? Put a limit on how much I love him? I can't control who I love or how much I love them. And just like when I was younger and you didn't like my boyfriends, YOU can't control who I love or how much I love them.* We only talked for about five minutes or so. That's all I could handle.

A little while later, we called my cousin Jim. After my mom passed away in 2005, he'd become like a brother to me. He and I are a lot alike in terms of our sensitivities, our passion for books and writing, and our love of dogs, so I knew he'd understand what I was going through. Of course, he was shocked and saddened because he loved Benny. Everyone who ever met Benny loved him. He touched so many lives.

As expected, Jim understood exactly what I was feeling. We talked about how some people don't always understand getting so attached to a pet that it feels like your child. But particularly when you can't have children, it's hard not to develop that kind of bond.

Throughout the day, I'd been beating myself up, wondering, *What if I hadn't taken Benny to the vet in Illinois who put him on hydrocortisone long-term? What if I'd pushed Dr. Hui to run more tests back in November when I'd first told him that Benny had been vomiting more frequently? Maybe he would've done an ultrasound then and diagnosed the mucocele early enough that it could've been treated with antibiotics rather than surgery? But on the other hand, if Benny still had to have surgery, would he have died sooner?*

"You can't burden yourself with these what-ifs," Jim said soothingly. "It was God's doing, not yours. You gave Benny the best life you possibly could. You gave him so much love and the best care possible."

Brad agreed as he pulled me close in a comforting embrace. "He had the best medical care in Indiana. We did all the right things. You, especially, are not to blame."

Deep down, I knew they were right, but I've always blamed myself when something goes wrong, even when it's obviously not my fault or was completely out of my control. After being in therapy for a while, I'd realized this was the consequence of having two parents who—as much as I love them—could never admit any wrongdoing. When you grow up with two parents who are never wrong, you start to internalize things and think, *If they're not wrong, then I must be. If they're not to blame, it must be my fault.* And over time, that carries over to every relationship you have. It took a long time for me to overcome that. I guess, in some ways, I'm still working on it.

Jim talked about losing Reggie, his beloved schnerrier who passed away in 2009, just a few weeks shy of his seventeenth birthday. Jim had found Reggie floating in the pool, so he thought that somehow his neglect had cost his beloved pooch his life. But the vet said there was no water in Reggie's lungs, so he hadn't drowned; he'd died before he fell into the pool, likely due to a heart attack or stroke. Eventually, Jim stopped blaming himself and focused on all the blessings Reggie had brought and all the positive memories they shared.

"That's what Brad is trying to focus on too," I replied, "but he's much better at it than I am. All I can think about is how I wanted more time with Benny. We really thought we'd have at least five more years with him—even his doctor thought so. And he was doing *so well* this past week."

"Take comfort in knowing that Benny's last day was a really good one," Jim encouraged, "and that he likely didn't suffer."

Jim also confided that he still dreams about Reggie and said he actually had a dream about him around four or five o'clock that morning.

"Are you sure it was Reggie?" I wondered. "Because that's about the time when Benny passed away."

"I just *assumed* it was Reggie, but it could've been Benny," Jim said. He and his sister, Deb, have always been more attuned to communicating with those on the Other Side.

"I would love for Benny to come visit me in my dreams or anytime, really," I confessed.

Later, when I saw Benny's apple container in the fridge, I remembered wanting to record him crunching an apple slice. Through my tears I wailed to Brad, "I didn't know there wouldn't be a tomorrow!" It was the end of tomorrows with Benny.

Chapter 35

Memories of Our Ambassador of Love

On Monday, March 11, I woke up around nine, when the morning sunlight began creeping through the curtains so brightly that I thought Brad had left the overhead light on. We'd slept in the guest room because I couldn't bear to sleep in our bed without Benny, but also because we'd neglected to wash the sheets after Benny had pottied on them when he'd had his seizure. Truth be told, part of me didn't want to wash them because I felt like I'd be washing away Benny.

Sunday had felt like the longest day of my life; it was definitely the saddest. Despite being physically and emotionally exhausted, I still had trouble sleeping, which isn't out of the ordinary for me. I'd read until I was falling asleep with my tablet landing with a thud on my chest, but when I put it away, sleep still evaded me, so I took a melatonin. I was a bit disappointed that I didn't dream about Benny because I'd asked him to visit me whether I was awake or asleep. After talking to Jim, I really thought Benny would find a way to let me know he was okay.

After dragging myself out of bed and forcing myself to eat breakfast, I wanted to take a shower, but I was so tired and depleted just from walking up the stairs that I lay back down and took a nap. Just as I was drifting off to sleep, I had a sensory dream in which I could distinctly hear Benny's cute licking sounds and actually feel him gently kissing my face. I firmly believe he was visiting me from the Other Side to say a proper goodbye.

When I finally dozed off, I had a really vivid dream about Benny. I was lying on my left side in the guest room, facing the closet, just like I was in real life. In the dream, I said, "Benny, come cuddle with me," as I pulled him up next to me. It was so realistic that I could feel his soft fur.

In the dream, we lay in bed cuddling while watching an old episode of *Grey's Anatomy*. After a while, when a guard from heaven came and told me it was time for Benny to go, I cried out, "Please don't take him! Please let him stay!"

The guard replied, "He can't stay, but we can give him a special pass so he can come back whenever he wants."

"Yes! Please do that!" I begged.

The guard brought in God, and they gave Benny a tag for his collar. But when I looked at the tag, it had a different name on it, so I said, "That's not his name. His name is Benny." They gave him another tag, but when I looked again, it still didn't say "Benny." I was frustrated, but I didn't want to cause any problems, so I conceded, "That's fine. I'll call him whatever you want me to call him as long as he can come back to visit."

I thanked the guard and God, shook their hands, and said, "Thank you SO much! Thank you for letting me visit Benny and for letting him come back anytime." And then my alarm went off.

When Brad came in, I told him, "I just had this amazing dream about Benny. It seemed SO real. I want to try to go back to sleep to keep it going." But as is usually the case, that didn't work.

After I hauled my butt out of bed and mechanically took a shower, Brad suggested we take a walk around the neighborhood. He was working from home that week so he could mourn in private and also be there for me. I had a little more energy after my shower, so I said yes.

Brad always sees the glass as half full and tries to find a silver lining in things. I also try to do that, but he's much better at it, especially in situations like this. "We need to be there for each other and let each other know what we're thinking and needing," he stressed.

I agreed, but deep down I was thinking, *I know I'm going to need more from you than you will from me, and I don't want to burden you or weigh you down with my grief.* He'd never given me a reason to think that, but that's just how my brain works.

It was a cloudy, crisp, windy day in the low fifties, but I was numb to the temperature—numb to everything, really. As we strolled the perimeter of our neighborhood, Brad reminded me of a walk we'd taken with Benny after a big snowstorm in early 2021, the first winter we'd spent in our house. "It was a chilly and breezy but sunny day, and we took some selfies right over there," Brad recalled, pointing down the road. "And on the way back, Benny walked through a 'snow tunnel,' where one of the neighbors had cleared a path on the sidewalk."

"I remember that," I replied with a half-hearted smile. "It was so cold that day! And the snow was over a foot high on each side, so it towered over Benny as he trotted through the canyon in his cozy, blue parka."

"I'm trying to stay positive and think about fun things we have coming up," Brad said a little while later to fill the silence, "like visiting my parents next weekend for my mom's birthday then your family the weekend after for an early Easter celebration."

"Yeah, I know. But I keep thinking about how Benny won't be with us when we do those things," I replied as my voice cracked and tears trickled down my face. "You're much better at putting a positive spin on things than I am."

As we rounded a corner back into our subdivision, Brad continued, "I keep thinking of all the ways Benny inspired me. Like if I was nervous about a presentation at work or a medical issue or whatever, I could always tell him about it. Even if I didn't say the words out loud, he just had this way of helping me relax."

I agreed and added, "That's one way Benny literally changed my life. Before him, I was really shy and had some social anxiety, but he helped alleviate some of that. That's part of the reason I liked to take him with me everywhere. That and I just didn't want to be away from him. Even when he couldn't be with me, like on our early dates and when I first met your parents, somehow I was able to channel that sense of calm he gave me, so I could just be myself and not feel anxious or as nervous. . . . Plus, I could tell him anything and he just listened and never judged or gave unwanted advice. You know, he was the first one I told about having feelings for you."

"Really?"

"Yeah. It was the week after we remet in Chicago, so early June of 2017, and we started messaging on Facebook. I would write to you while reading before going to bed, and one night, I said to Benny, 'Can I tell you a secret? I met a guy at the U2 concert last week, and he's really cute and sweet and smart and funny . . . and I think he might like me too. But I don't want to tell anyone else because I don't want to jinx it.'"

A little while later, I sniffled through my tears as I admitted, "In many ways, this is harder than losing a human. When my mom and Margaret and Dr. Bob died, it was really painful, but at the same time, they'd all been battling cancer and Dr. Bob was in his nineties, so their deaths weren't completely unexpected. But this happened so quickly and right when Benny was starting to do better. Plus, Benny just gave unconditional love, and he was always my source of comfort during tough times. Who do you lean on when you lose your source of comfort?"

"We lean on each other," Brad replied poignantly as he held my hand and kissed it.

"It's just so hard because I was with him practically every day the past seven years. And when I couldn't be—like when we'd take a trip or I'd go up north to take my dad to an appointment—I wanted to be with Benny and missed him fiercely."

"I know. I remember how difficult it was for you to leave him last year when we went to Vegas and when you went back with your sisters."

"Yeah, I just always knew that I had a limited amount of time with him—that days I spent away from him were days I couldn't get back—so I made a conscious effort to cherish every moment I had with him. But we just didn't have enough time together, and it went by so fast!" I wailed.

After a pocket of silence, Brad said, "Some of my first memories of Benny were from when you'd pick me up at the bus station on Friday nights then we'd stop at Olive Garden or that Mexican place near your town house for a late dinner. When we'd get back to your place, Benny would be lying quietly in his crate, watching Steve Harvey on *Family Feud*."

"And when we let him out of the crate, he'd be all wiggly and so excited to see us that he'd show his teeth and go grab a toy and squeak and squeak," I added with a smile, even though my heart was breaking, knowing that I'd never hear him squeak a toy in delight or see his toothy grin or his adorable little wigglebutt again.

As I lay in bed Tuesday morning, too emotionally drained to move, I thought about how Benny was my doggie soulmate. This wasn't a new revelation; I'd known it from the moment I first brought him home and I thanked God every day for bringing him into my life. But I realized then that Benny was probably Brad's doggie soulmate too.

Sure, Brad had Sam and Lilah when he was a kid, but they were almost never allowed in the house, so Brad hadn't developed as close of a bond with them as he had with Benny. Plus, Benny was the perfect amalgamation of Brad and me. If we were able to have human children, I don't think they could've possibly been a better blend of the two of us than Benny was. He was so like the two of us in many ways: He had a big heart, the ability to love uncondi-tionally, the ability to quickly forgive, an old soul, allergies, and a love for cuddles and naps. He was also shy, extremely loyal, and emotionally and physically sensitive. Plus, whatever Brad and I were eating, Benny wanted some. Brad's the same way; whenever I'm eating something, he suddenly craves the same thing.

Brad came into the bedroom a little while later and lay down with me. "I was just thinking how much Benny taught me about love," he said as he held me in his arms. "He was such a cuddle bug and a love bug. He was an ambassador of love. And he was so compatible to both of us."

"I know! I was just thinking about that!"

Later in the day, Brad and I took another walk around the neighborhood. Back in February, Punxsutawney Phil had predicted an early spring, and this year, the famous groundhog got it right. It was sixty degrees and sunny on the twelfth of March, which felt like a heat wave. We saw so many squirrels on the walk—more than we'd ever seen since moving to the suburbs—that we couldn't help but be reminded of Benny. He would've gone berserk chasing them. *Perhaps he's sending us a sign,* I thought.

On the walk, I told Brad that I want to keep Benny front and center in our hearts and minds. "Even someday when we get another dog," I said, "I don't want to take down Benny's photos or move his Christmas ornaments to the side of the tree like I did with Arnold's after I got Benny." Brad agreed.

I also mentioned an epiphany I'd had the night before while trying to fall asleep. "There should be ambulances for pets."

"Yeah?" Brad said with a chuckle.

"I'm serious. When you're in an emergency situation, every second counts. If there was a pet ambulance service with a vet tech or veterinarian on board that could've been giving Benny CPR or meds or whatever on the way to the VCA, who knows? Maybe they could've saved his life."

"And even though I'm grateful that we were both with Benny when he passed, I'm sorry that you were driving and weren't physically touching him when it happened," I added.

"We had no idea that was going to happen," Brad assured me. "I'm just thankful we were awake and with him and he wasn't alone or in the back room of the hospital."

"I am too, but I still can't help but wonder, Was he scared? Was he in any pain? Did he suffer? Did he know what was happening? Did he cry out because he knew he was slipping away from us? Like, did he see the white light and the angels I'd always told him to avoid—even though they're family and we love them? Did he see them and not want to go, but he didn't have a choice?"

"We'll never know, but I'm sure he went the way he wanted to: with us rather than by himself or at the hospital. You have to hold on to the positives," Brad encouraged.

On Wednesday, three days after Benny passed, I was still numb. I'd wake up in the middle of the night and reach down by my feet to pet Benny, but he wasn't there. And in the morning, the first thing I'd do is look at his picture on my phone. I still couldn't wrap my head around the fact that he was really gone. It was like I was trapped in a nightmare that I couldn't wake up from.

I was still crying all the time, sometimes to the point where I was heaving, taking short, hitching breaths, and almost hyperventilating. I was also napping during the day and couldn't concentrate on much of anything. Memories of Benny kept coming at me one after another, like pulling tissues out of a box. As soon as one surfaced, another one would pop up, and so on.

But that day, I found the strength to gather up some of Benny's unused supplies. I'd reached out to Benny's doctors on Monday to let them know of his passing, and I'd learned we could donate unused, unopened supplies to the VCA. I emailed Andrea and asked if she had some time to talk with us later in the day when we dropped off the items, and she said to have the front desk let her know when we got there and she'd make time.

Brad and I arrived at the VCA around five thirty that afternoon. As we waited in a room for Andrea, I noticed our family Christmas photo card among others on the bulletin board on the wall. Benny and I had been in that room many times before, and I always held him up to show him our photo to help calm him. But this time, I took seeing his cute little face staring back at me as a sign that he was there with us.

Andrea joined us a few minutes later. She was teary-eyed and visibly choked up as she talked about Benny and shared stories of her own dogs who had passed. She spent about half an hour with us, and it was comforting to speak to someone who knows what it's like to love a dog as if it's your child and then to lose that dog. In fact, she said, "It's been proven that the relationships humans have with their pets are comparable to relationships with a human child. I know people who don't have pets or have different relationships with their pets, and they don't necessarily feel that way, but it's been proven to be true. So don't downplay your emotions or question how you're feeling because it is literally like you lost a child."

"I don't. I just feel like some people don't understand it," I admitted.

"A lot of people don't, and I find it almost offensive because I know how I feel and I know the truth behind it," she added.

What I took from that is if someone feels the need to judge me because of my feelings over losing Benny or says I should get over it quicker because he was "just a dog," then that's their problem. And perhaps I should feel sorry for them because they've never experienced the type of special bond that I did with Benny, or maybe they aren't emotionally capable of experiencing such love.

When I told Andrea my idea of having pet ambulances, she informed us that she'd recently read an article about a man who'd started that kind of service because he saw a need for it; however, it was in California.

"Not only does he do emergency-type stuff, but he also helps people, like the elderly, who aren't able to lift their pets to get them into the car to go to the vet. So he does all sorts of transportation," she continued, "but he mainly focuses on the emergency services. He has a team and they do exactly what you were saying, administer to the pet's needs while on the way to the hospital."

Before she left, Andrea teared up as she said, "I'm just so, so sorry. The entire time I've known you and Benny, we always knew if there was something we could do to give him a fighting chance, you guys would do it. You always made sure Benny had what he needed. You took absolutely exceptional care of him, and I find situations like this to be extra crappy because not only has something horrific happened, but you guys did your part. And we don't have a good reason for why it didn't work out the way it was supposed to."

Before Andrea went back to work, I gave her a hug. Over the past couple months, whenever she was Benny's tech, I'd found myself wanting to be her friend, if I knew how to make friends as an adult. I still sometimes struggle with shyness, so I have a difficult time getting to know people. Plus, I'm an introvert, so a lot of times I'm fine doing things by myself. But sometimes it would be nice to have a female friend to talk to, go shopping with, or get mani-pedis. I haven't had someone like that nearby since I left the Chicago area in 2020.

Dr. Hui came in to speak to us a few minutes after Andrea stepped out of the room. Andrea had briefed him on what had happened to Benny, but he wanted to hear it from us, so I began by describing the pep in Benny's step on Friday, went through our day on Saturday, and then recounted the traumatic events from early Sunday morning.

When I was finished, Dr. Hui weighed in with his theories. "I would say it was one of a few things. One, he might've thrown a blood clot that went to his brain. Two, he had a brain bleed, which would basically mean a stroke. A clot is when platelets obstruct a blood vessel, whereas a bleed is like an aneurysm. It's when the vessel ruptures and there's a bleed in the area.

"A third possibility is that he had some kind of cardiac episode, whether it was an arrhythmia or a clot to his heart, and he experienced a seizure secondary to low blood oxygen levels to his brain. Or lastly, he might've had a slow-growing brain tumor. If a patient is already on steroids, like Benny was, those decrease inflammation, so it's usually undetectable until it's really bad. A brain tumor could cause a seizure or a brain bleed or something associated with it."

The thought of Benny experiencing any of those things was unbearable to me. I simply gulped down my tears and eked out, "Okay."

"But from what you're describing," Dr. Hui continued, "I would say it was likely some sort of clot or bleed, whether it was from a tumor or from somewhere else, like his heart, and the brain didn't get enough oxygen."

"Because he couldn't just die from a seizure alone, right?" I asked.

"No. As dramatic as it can be, a seizure alone would not be fatal. The only time patients die of seizures is when they've been seizing for hours and hours, like while the owners are away at work. So I can almost guarantee you there was something else that led to the seizure, and that's what he passed from."

"If he had a blood clot, what might've caused it?" I wondered out loud.

"For him, it could've been a lot of things," Dr. Hui answered.

"With everything he had going on, was he more at risk for a blood clot?" Brad asked.

"Exactly. He was very at risk with all his issues, like general inflammation, protein loss due to kidney disease, and the prednisone could predispose him to it a little bit. But he also had risk factors for a bleed. As dogs get older, just like in people who have aneurysms, the vessels in the brain are delicate and they tend to be weaker. So anything else going on systemically that'll make them sicker is going to make them more likely to bleed."

I wasn't sure if I wanted to know the answer to my next question, but it had been weighing heavily on my mind, so I had to ask. "I don't even know if you can answer this question, but when he cried out and yelped, do you think he was in pain? Do you think he suffered? Do you think he knew what was happening?"

"It's hard to say for sure. But a lot of times, when animals are having a seizure or finishing a seizure, they often vocalize during what's called the postictal period, which is a time when they're not quite aware of what's going on and they may be a bit confused. Because of that confusion, they often vocalize and bark, as if saying, 'What's going on?' That's probably what caused the vocalization rather than him being in pain."

Months later, Brad and I were watching an episode of the 1990s police drama *Homicide: Life on the Street* when a scene triggered a flashback to the final moments of Benny's life. In the episode, Detective Frank Pembleton, played by the late Andre Braugher, is interrogating a suspect in "the box" when he suddenly screams, grabs his head, and starts seizing before collapsing on the floor in a heap. As I watched the scene unfold, I froze as I remembered the ear-piercing howl Benny emitted right before his body began flailing in a seizure. And when I held him in my arms afterward, his body was limp and motionless, just like Frank's on TV. When it was revealed later in the episode that Frank had suffered a stroke, I said to Brad, "That's exactly what happened to Benny. If that's what happens during a stroke, then Dr. Hui was right that that's probably what caused Benny's death."

With all our questions answered, Brad offered his gratitude, "We really appreciate everything you did for Benny over the years. We think you guys helped extend his life and his quality of life for multiple years and we're very grateful."

I seconded the motion.

"You're welcome. And you guys took great care of him. He was lucky to have you two, for sure," Dr. Hui reciprocated.

"We were lucky to have him," I sniffed.

"You guys were a perfect fit," Dr. Hui added. "You know, obviously, it was really sad to hear that Benny had passed, but I was happy to hear that he had such a good day on Saturday."

"Yeah, we can always look back on that as a positive," said my perpetually optimistic husband.

"He made it to his birthday by a whisker," I said, choking back sobs.

"And you were with him when he passed. That's important too," Dr. Hui reminded us.

"Maybe Benny will help other dogs in the future. Hopefully, you can think back on Benny and how he recovered from multiple rounds of things," Brad suggested.

"Yeah, he definitely taught us a lot," Dr. Hui responded.

As we all stood up to leave, I gave Dr. Hui a hug and Brad shook his hand. "Thank you again for everything you did for Benny," I said.

"You guys are very welcome," Dr. Hui replied. "If you have any more questions, just let me know. We'll miss Benny. He was a good guy."

"Yeah, he definitely lived up to his namesake, Benny Goodman," I concurred. "And he was a fighter."

"Definitely," Dr. Hui agreed. "He was 100 percent a fighter."

It was good to get Dr. Hui's expert opinion on what likely happened to Benny in his final moments and to hear that we did everything right. As we were exiting the hospital, a handful of pet parents anxiously waited in the lobby, but one lady was visibly crying. Without even thinking, I walked up to her and said, "Can I give you a hug?"

After she nodded, we embraced and cried together, then I said, "We just lost our little guy, and I hope your fur baby is going to be all right." She thanked me and said she was sorry about Benny. She said she knew what we were going through because she'd lost her other dog a couple years earlier. Before we left, I said, "I'll say a prayer that your little one will pull through." And I did.

It was nice to speak to Andrea and Dr. Hui, but it had been another emotionally taxing day. Later, as Brad and I crawled into bed and told each other good night, I said, "Thanks for being my rock, Babe."

"You're welcome," he replied. "You're my rock in a world of sand."

"That's really profound. Where did you hear that phrase?"

"I just made it up right now," he laughed.

Chapter 36

Signs, Guilt, and a Tsunami of Grief

On Thursday, I received a text message that a package from Chewy was out for delivery. "I don't believe this!" I griped to Brad. "Despite my profound sadness, on Monday I called Chewy, along with the other pharmacies that filled Benny's meds, and asked them to cancel his auto-refills. And now, just a few days later, I get a text that a shipment is arriving from Chewy today! Did they not understand and send out a refill anyway?"

When the package arrived, Brad went to retrieve it from the front porch. "Oh my God!" he exclaimed.

"What is it?" I asked curiously from the living room.

Brad didn't say a word; he just came in and showed me the box. Chewy had sent flowers and a sympathy card. Brad and I were both floored. As we opened the box and gently unpacked a dozen bright yellow sunflowers, we both commented that we'd never had a company—outside of an employer—send flowers when a loved one had passed. If I didn't have a black thumb and was in my right mind, I might've realized that we could've planted the seeds of those flowers to have a beautiful, living reminder of Benny for years to come. But it didn't even occur to me until months later.

Over the next few weeks, we received dozens of sympathy cards and emails from family members, friends, Benny's doctors, some of my author clients, and even the manufacturer of his probiotic. Some folks even made donations to animal charities in honor of Benny.

As I read each message, it was like I was watching a commercial for the ASPCA—you know the one where malnourished dogs and cats gaze desperately into the camera from behind the bars of a cage, while Sarah McLachlan's "I Will Remember You" plays in the background. In other words, I bawled my eyes out. But my heart overflowed with gratitude from the outpouring of love, compassion, and thoughtfulness. It really hit home how many lives Benny had touched. Everyone loved him from the moment they met him; even strangers we'd meet on the street or at the pet store would fawn over his angelic face and calm, gentle demeanor. *Why did you take him away when he brought joy to so many?* I beseeched God.

The weekend after Benny passed, Brad and I went to visit his parents for his mom's birthday. When I stepped out of the car, my mother-in-law, Ann, enveloped me in a long hug and told me how sorry she was about Benny. I did my best to stifle my tears, even as we sat on the couch and recounted Benny's final birthday party, what had happened on the morning he died, and Dr. Hui's theories as to what actually caused his death. Brad's parents were very supportive, but they said they simply had no words to express how sorry they were for our devastating loss.

Sunday, before we headed home, we met Brad's best friend, John, and his wife, Laura, for lunch. It was St. Patrick's Day, and everyone around us was in a festive mood and a state of revelry, but I felt broken inside. Laura immediately pulled me in for a warm embrace and told me how sorry she was about Benny. Tears spilled from my eyes, but I somehow managed to hold it together and not make a scene.

When John and Brad branched off into their own conversation, Laura asked, "So how are you *really* doing?"

"I guess I'm still in shock," I confessed. "It's so hard for me to believe and accept that Benny is actually gone. . . . It sort of feels like he's just in the hospital and we're really bad parents because we haven't been visiting him."

I also lamented my concern that a lot of people won't understand that, to me, Benny truly was my son. Like Brad and me, John and Laura's dogs are their kids, so I knew Laura could empathize.

As I replayed the details of Benny's final minutes, Laura took my hand and we cried together as I relived those traumatic moments.

It was good for me to get out of the house, visit with family and friends, reminisce, tell stories, and even laugh, but I still felt like I was trapped in the longest nightmare and couldn't wake up. After we got home, Brad and I opened the card and gift John and Laura had given us: a framed photo of Benny in his suit on our wedding day. As we placed it on the mantel, all the emotions I'd been suppressing over the weekend erupted like lava from a volcano.

Brad went back into the office on Monday for the first time since Benny had passed, but I struggled to get out of bed. My head felt like a lead balloon, and there was such a weariness in my bones that I could barely move. I slept until eleven then finally washed our bedding, knowing it was time to move out of the guest room. After summoning the strength to take a shower, I sat on the soft carpet in our closet, silently crying as I caressed Benny's clothes and inhaled his scent before storing them in vacuum-sealed bags, hoping to preserve his aroma.

As I made my way downstairs, the house no longer seemed quite like a home without Benny there. It was especially cold, empty, and filled with a deafening silence, the only sound coming from the hum of my laptop's fan. I tried to stay busy, but I missed Benny so much that I literally ached inside. I was totally devoid of energy and felt like I'd gone ten rounds in the ring with Mike Tyson. That feeling wouldn't go away anytime soon.

Over the course of the next few weeks, I also started feeling more anxious and panicky. My limbs tingled and I could hardly catch my breath. One time, I worked myself into a tizzy, thinking about the fish oil supplement that we were supposed to give Benny with his homemade diet. Tilapia was the protein source, so it didn't seem imperative that he take the fish oil right away. The nutritionist hadn't said that it was, so I planned to start giving it to him the day after his birthday. Obviously, I didn't get the chance, so I began to worry, *What if not giving him the fish oil right away caused a blood clot that eventually killed him?* I couldn't stop thinking about whether my negligence had somehow played a role in his death. I was so fraught with guilt that I felt nauseous.

I tried to reassure myself that it wasn't my fault—that nobody had mentioned the possibility of a blood clot, plus he was eating whitefish, which is high in omega-3s. However, when I read online that tilapia isn't as high in omega-3s as some other types of whitefish, my guilt returned. *But if the nutritionist knew that,* I rationalized, *she should've said, 'I don't have a problem with you feeding him tilapia if he likes it, but it's not as rich in omega-3s as some other forms of whitefish, so it's absolutely essential that you give him a fish oil supplement every day to prevent blood clots.'* If I'd had any inclination that Benny was at risk for blood clots, I would've done whatever was necessary to prevent them and keep him alive.

I knew I needed to stop blaming myself. And deep down, I recognized that God took Benny away from us; it wasn't something I did or didn't do. And knowing that I had the fish oil in my possession and was going to start it that morning, God could've prevented Benny from getting a blood clot or aneurysm. I may always wrestle with some amount of guilt over this and struggle with the what-ifs, but the bottom line is that God called him home, and there was nothing I could do to stop it. Lord knows, I would've if I could've.

Another time, my anxiety literally led me to go postal. A couple weeks after Benny died, I became panicky and short of breath as I packed up the supplement packets that the nutritionist had us order. We never got a chance to use them—in fact we never even opened the box—so the company agreed to refund our money when I called to inform them of Benny's passing. We just had to pay return shipping.

Brad was working from home that day and offered to go to the post office for me, but I knew he was busy with work, so I said I'd do it. Besides, I was planning to drop off an unopened package of Benny's thyroid meds at Dr. Steve's office and stop at the grocery store.

When I arrived at the post office, my face was moist with tears and I was on the verge of a breakdown, just being there to return Benny's stuff. I had purposely opened the box in case the postal clerk said I could use the lighter bubble envelope I'd brought to make the shipping less expensive. But as I stepped up to the counter, the young man—a little twerp about my height, who looked like he was about sixteen—said, "You'll have to tape up the box first.

We sell rolls of tape, or if you want to send it Priority Mail, there's tape over there on the counter."

I'd already priced Priority Mail and knew it was much more expensive, so I didn't want to go that route, and I swear I've seen dispensers of clear tape there for customers to use. But the clerk was adamant that I'd have to purchase my own, so I said, "Fine. Just tell me how much it is and I'll mail it from home."

"Oh no! You can't do that!" He seemed shocked that I'd even suggest such an outrageous thing.

At that point, I lost it. I grabbed the box off the scale and growled, "Fine. . . . Just give me the damn thing!"

He raised his arms up as if to say, "Don't shoot," which I found comical, but I was too pissed to laugh. As I stormed toward the door, he sarcastically called out, "Have a nice day, ma'am."

I hated throwing a temper tantrum in public, which is something my dad would do, but all the emotions from returning Benny's stuff just pushed me over the edge. My anger was probably the only thing preventing me from dissolving into a puddle of tears as I drove across the street to Dr. Steve's office.

I could hardly find the words when I stepped inside. Typically, Dr. Steve's front-desk clerks recognized me and Benny, but I'd never seen the two young women there that day. As I placed the Chewy box on the counter, I muttered, "My dog, Benny, was a patient of Dr. Steve's, and he passed away before he could use these meds, so the package has never been opened. I was told I could donate them."

They nodded and gaped at me as tears filled my eyes. I think they offered their condolences, but I just turned and walked out the door.

When I arrived at home, Brad jovially asked, "How did it go?"

"You're gonna have to take these to the post office," I grumbled. As I rehashed the scene at the post office, I slammed the package on the counter, got out our roll of packing tape, placed the supplement packets in the bubble envelope, and sealed it up, all the while cursing the postal clerk, describing him, and saying to Brad, "Be sure to tell the little shit that your wife says he can go F himself!"

Brad went upstairs to grab his wallet, and by the time he returned, my rage toward the postal clerk had boiled over into tears. I was sitting on the stairsteps shaking and sobbing. It was a deep, visceral cry that had been building up for days, with tears streaming down my face and snot dripping from my nose. After grabbing a paper towel, Brad sat next to me on the stairs, wiped my nose, and held me tight. Although I'd cried every day—sometimes multiple times a day—since Benny's passing, this was the hardest cry I'd had in over a week. I think the anxious, panicky feelings I'd been experiencing had combined with my anger at God for taking Benny too soon, and it all bubbled to the surface when the postal clerk fueled the fire.

Brad ended up going back to the post office and sent the package without incident. When I asked him how it went, he said, "The little shit waited on me."

"Did you tell him that your wife said he can go F himself?" I asked, knowing Brad would never say that.

Brad shrugged and said, "In my head I did."

That night, as had become the norm, I couldn't fall asleep because invasive thoughts bombarded my mind. Things that had never occurred to me or didn't seem to matter before suddenly filled me with sadness and regret, like the fact that Benny never got to see the ocean. As I tossed and turned, I struggled to get comfortable, wavered between being hot and freezing, and had difficulty breathing. The air felt thick, as if all the oxygen had been sucked out of the room. If I was on my back, I felt like someone was lying on my chest, smothering me. If I was on my side, I felt like my lungs were being crunched together, constricting my breathing. If I was on my stomach, it was slightly better, but it still felt like each breath was a chore.

I'd felt short of breath several times since Benny's passing. In fact, the same thing had occurred after Margaret died in late 2022. As I lay there desperately trying to fall asleep, I wondered if it could be broken heart syndrome. My sister Denise and our cousin Deb had told me there really is such a thing.

Rather than tossing and turning and staring at the ceiling, I grabbed my tablet from the nightstand and googled "broken heart syndrome." I learned that it's technically called Takotsubo cardiomyopathy and can be caused by an emotionally or physically stressful event, such as the death of a loved one, a sudden illness, or an unexpected loss. When this occurs, "the heart's main pumping chamber changes shape, affecting the heart's ability to pump blood effectively," resulting in symptoms such as shortness of breath, fainting, rapid heart rate, and chest pain. According to what I read online, this condition usually goes away on its own within a few weeks to a couple months, and while prescription medications are available to treat it, many patients experience relief from good, old-fashioned aspirin. I took an aspirin and soon fell asleep.

Although the aspirin helped remedy the shortness of breath and panicky feelings associated with broken heart syndrome, I was still erupting into a torrent of tears at random times. I'd be fine one minute, then a memory of Benny would pop into my head, and with the flip of a switch, I'd be overcome with a wave of sorrow and would just weep uncontrollably and cry out to God in anguish.

In early April, I was watching an episode of *Chicago Med* that I'd recorded from earlier in the season. When I saw that the episode had aired on January 31, it was like a dam broke. Tears flooded my face as I realized that Benny was still alive then. He was in the hospital following his surgery, but he was still alive.

Later, during the same episode, Dr. Charles, a psychiatrist, consoled Maggie, one of the nurses, as she burst into tears, thinking of her impending divorce. As he consoled her, Dr. Charles said spontaneous weeping was natural for people going through a divorce. When he said that, it was like a light bulb went off in my head, and I realized that I was experiencing spontaneous weeping over the loss of Benny. Although it didn't help stop the deluge, it was nice to have a name for what was happening to me and know that it's natural during the grieving process—at least according to a TV show psychiatrist.

A few weeks later, an episode of *Grey's Anatomy* filled me with guilt, panic, and grief. During the episode, Teddy Altman, one of the doctors, collapsed when her heart stopped. They resuscitated her, replaced one of her heart valves, and determined that it happened due to bacterial endocarditis, which was most likely caused by a dental infection. But then she got a blood clot in her leg from the valve replacement surgery and had to have an embolectomy to remove the clot before it traveled to her lung or brain or split into multiple clots. While she was in that surgery, neurosurgeon Amelia Shepherd explained it this way, "An infection in Teddy's mouth led to severe damage to her heart. Two parts of the body completely separate from one another." They were able to successfully remove the clot, but this made me wonder, *Could I have done more on the way to resuscitate Benny? If we had pet ambulances here, would Benny have survived?* All the angst from these emotions percolated to the surface and soaked my face with salty tears.

I'd also read that dental disease can lead to kidney disease in dogs. *Is that what caused Benny's chronic kidney disease?* I worried. *Did a painful tooth cause him to stop playing with his toys? Did me choosing not to get Benny's teeth cleaned due to my fear of him undergoing elective anesthesia play a role in him dying young?* I'll never know for sure, but I'm racked with guilt over the possibility that, in my quest to keep Benny alive as long as possible, I somehow caused him pain or discomfort or my actions led to his untimely death. Thinking about those things sent me spiraling into a dark hole of grief and guilt that left me bawling so hard my eyes felt like they were bulging out of my head.

Even something as innocuous as a comedic film caused the waterworks to flow. One night, Brad and I watched *The Guilt Trip*. At the beginning, in a flashback, Barbra Streisand's character tells her little boy, "If all the little boys in the world were lined up, I'd still pick you." It reminded me of what I always said to Benny about being the luckiest mommy in the universe because he was my little boy. She said it again to her grown son (Seth Rogan) at the end of the movie, and he replied, "I would pick you." At that point, a tsunami of grief crashed over me because it reminded me of the day Benny and I met, how he seemed to pick me, and how he knew instantly that I was his mommy. Brad tried to console me as my body shuddered with big, heaving sobs, the tears gushing from my eyes and snot streaming from my nose.

"We did everything we could for him. You gave him the best life he could've possibly had," Brad soothed.

Through my tears and sniffles, I squawked, "I know, but it seems like just yesterday I brought him home for the first time. Our ten years together went by in the blink of an eye. We just had the perfect life, the three of us, and now it's gone. He's gone and he's never coming back, and I'm just having such a hard time accepting that."

Songs were actually my biggest trigger. Two weeks after we lost Benny, Brad and I were on our way up north to visit my family when the song "Forever Young" by Alphaville came on the radio.

At first, I was excited to hear the song and told Brad that it was David Ross's walk-up song during the magical 2016 season for the Chicago Cubs. But as I listened to the lyrics, particularly the chorus, tears began spilling from my eyes.

Brad saw me crying and asked if I was thinking about the Cubs. Through my sobs, I choked out, "No. . . . I was thinking about Benny when he was younger, especially during our early days together when he had so much puppy energy and would try to climb trees while chasing after squirrels and would run the length of our apartment, tearing after a toy that I'd thrown."

Another time, I was driving home from a day trip up north to tour a new assisted living facility for my dad with my sisters. The day had been taxing, so I decided to listen to a playlist from Lifehouse, one of my favorite bands. When "Broken" came over the speakers, the tears started to flow. I know it's a breakup song, but the lyrics—particularly the chorus—described exactly how I'd been feeling. And when "From Where You Are" played, I blubbered so fiercely that I had to exit the highway and compose myself. Every single word of the song made me think of Benny. Just listen to it. You'll see what I mean.

Everything reminded me of Benny, not just love songs and breakup songs. On April 10, one month after losing my sweet baby boy, I was mindlessly wandering up and down the aisles of the grocery store when "Ebony and Ivory" began to play over the Muzak. Of course, it made me cry, but it also brought a smile to my face as I remembered Benny and Binky walking together in harmony back in Chicago a decade earlier. I took that as a sign from Benny that he was still with me.

Every night after Benny's passing, I'd stare at his photo and tell him goodnight. I'd also ask him to communicate with me and send me signs to let me know he's still with me and that he's all right. A couple weeks after he left us, he came to me in a dream in the early morning hours. I saw him sitting on his Snoopy blanket and in the sweetest, childlike voice he said, "I'm okay, Mommy. I'm okay."

I woke up right after the dream and felt an enormous sense of peace wash over me. "Thank you, Benny," I whispered. "Please visit me anytime, all the time. I love you, Baby Boy."

Two days later, I was lying in bed, drifting back to sleep after Brad got up for work, when I heard my mom say, "Benny didn't suffer. When he cried out the first time, it was because he thought he had to potty. The second time was because he didn't want to leave you and Brad, but he didn't have a choice."

It would seem that, at least subconsciously, I was starting to accept that Benny was gone, but a month or so later, I began having dreams that Benny was still alive. In one, Andrea, Dr. Hui's tech, had come to our house to discuss Benny's meds. While she was there, she called Dr. Steve's office for a refill, and I could hear the person on the other end of the line say, "We thought Benny had passed away." Andrea replied, "That's what we thought too, but he's alive and well." My heart was filled with joy knowing that Benny was still alive, but then I woke up and had to face reality.

Months later, I had a dream that Benny and I were taking a walk through our old neighborhood in Hanover Park, and he started running really fast. He didn't seem to be chasing anything, but he was dragging me along behind him, so I was hustling to keep up with him. I giggled with delight as I said to him, "It's great to have you back and see you so spry and healthy with so much energy, Bunny! Your daddy and I didn't think we'd ever see you again. We thought you were gone forever." The dream felt so real, like Benny was still alive and the past few months really were just a bad dream. But then my alarm went off and woke me from my blissful slumber, and when I reached for Benny at the foot of the bed, I realized that he'd just been visiting in my dreams.

But Benny didn't just come to me in dreams. Sometimes I physically felt or heard his presence. One time I was awakened from a sound sleep when I heard him bark or yelp. In life, when he was dreaming, his whole body would twitch and he'd frequently let out soft little cries. So as I always did, I sat up in bed, reached out to comfort him, and said, "Mommy's here. You're okay. It was just a bad dream." But this time, it was Brad's leg, not Benny, that I was petting.

Another time, I had the sensation that Benny was "fluffing" or repositioning the blankets in bed to get comfortable. I woke up because I literally felt the bed moving. I asked Brad if it was him, but he was in a deep sleep and hadn't moved.

Of course, whenever I see a dog that resembles Benny, I'm reminded of him and it tugs at my heartstrings. But one in particular felt like something more—like Benny had actually appeared in the flesh. In mid-April, Brad and I took advantage of the lovely spring weather and decided to venture to the subdivision across from ours for a walk. While we were meandering through the neighborhood, we came across a house on a corner, where a small white dog was sitting by himself, under a tree in his front yard. He was so still and calm that at first I thought it was a statue.

"He looks like Benny!" I said with a gasp. And he did except that his hair had a little curl or wave to it.

The dog and I locked eyes, and as Brad and I walked by, the little guy and I just stared at each other. Usually on our walks, the dogs we encounter bark and chase after us from their side of the fence, but this sweet boy sat quietly and never took his eyes off me—just like Benny. As we continued down the street, I kept turning back to look at him, and he was still watching me. It reminded me of one of the sympathy cards we'd received, which had the line, "If you see me in the distance, that's me."

Sometimes I would see Benny in the most unlikely places. Shortly after we moved into our house in 2020, I pointed out to Brad that some of the swirls in our bathroom tile formed images that looked like Benny, so every time I take a shower, I'm reminded of that adorable face. But when we visited Brad's parents just a week after Benny's passing, his face appeared in an unusual source.

Brad's parents were showing us a poster-sized aerial photograph of their property that was taken in the late 1970s, shortly before their house was built. As my father-in-law, Dick, pointed out landmarks on the property that Brad was familiar with but I wasn't, I started tuning out. I just gazed deeply at the photo as if staring at one of those Magic Eye posters that were popular in the 1990s. Then, all of a sudden, an image of Benny's face popped up in the photo. The eyes and nose were actually a small copse of trees on a bare spot on the land, but all I could see was Benny's adorable little face, including his perked-up ears. As if in a trance, I fixed my eyes upon Benny's visage and spoke to him telepathically, thanking him for materializing to me.

As I continued scrutinizing the photo, I saw Benny in two other places in different poses. When Brad's parents left the room, I whispered conspiratorially, "You know how we sometimes see Benny in the bathroom tile?" When Brad said yes, I continued, "I see Benny in at least three places in this photograph." Brad didn't notice them until I pointed them out, but when he did, he was as bowled over as I was.

During another trip to see Brad's parents, they took us out to dinner at a swanky restaurant reminiscent of the supper clubs of the 1940s. As soon as I sat down, my eyes were instantly drawn to a poster of Benny Goodman aka "The King of Swing," my Benny's namesake.

Signs of Benny's presence were all around. Bunny was one of his many nicknames, and over the summer, we'd see bunnies hopping around in our backyard almost every evening. Then one night, we saw two bunnies frolicking and chasing each other in the grass. I'd learned earlier in the day that Benny's buddy Chewee had passed at age seventeen, so I knew in my heart that the playful bunnies symbolized Benny and Chewee, long-lost friends reunited in heaven.

Another time that summer, Brad and I were unloading groceries from the back of the SUV when we heard the faint melody of an ice-cream truck approaching. We'd never seen an ice-cream truck in our neighborhood before, so it seemed out of place. But as the truck's dulcet tune grew nearer, my heart clenched. The truck was playing "You Are My Sunshine," the song that I often sang to Benny. My eyes began to burn and I felt a warm tightness in the back of my throat as I tried, unsuccessfully, to hold back tears.

But not all of Benny's visits left me in tears. Since my mom passed away in 2005, I've continued to talk to her almost daily. Sometimes, I think she likes to play tricks on me and things go missing. When that happens, I say, "Mom, please help me find XXX," and suddenly, it'll appear in a place that I'd already searched. I'm pretty sure my mom was teaching Benny these shenanigans one night in May when I stayed up late to finish making Brad's birthday card.

Using my Cricut die-cut machine, I'd already cut out all the pieces, so I just needed to assemble them to make the card. For the front, I'd cut individual cursive letters to spell out "Happy Birthday to My Husband." But as I was gluing the letters onto the background, the *t* from *to* and the *y* from *My* were missing. For about ten minutes, I looked everywhere. I hunched over the kitchen island, my makeshift workspace, and eyeballed every square inch. I even got on my hands and knees and crawled all over the kitchen and attached dining room floor, sifting through the rug underneath the dining room table with my fingers. The letters were nowhere to be found.

Exasperated, I finally said, "Benny, if your Grandma Judy is showing you how to play tricks on Mommy, that's not cool. *Please* help me find these letters. I don't want to make new ones."

After pleading my case, I looked at the floor again, and right between my feet, just below the island, I found the *t*. "Thank you, Benny. That's a good boy! Now help me find the *y*."

I began my search anew, combed over all the same places again, and even shook out my hair, which was pulled back in a ponytail. Nothing. Near tears, I begged, "Benny, it's now officially Mother's Day. Please don't play tricks on your mommy on Mother's Day. Please help me find this last letter."

After that, I surveyed the area one more time and found the *y*. It was on the floor between Brad's chair and the island, right where I'd been searching a minute earlier and it wasn't there.

"Aha!" I shrieked with surprise as I picked up the tiny letter with my tweezers. "Thanks for not being a stinker, Bunny! I love you!" Then I finished the card.

In recent years, when Benny began having chronic health issues, I made a vow to myself that I wouldn't immediately get another dog after he passed. I know people who have, and I don't judge them, I just know that wouldn't work for me. So as much as I've longed for the companionship of another dog, I've been keenly aware that the void in my heart is for Benny. Therefore, getting another dog to try to fill that void wouldn't be fair to a new dog, and I feel it would be disrespectful to Benny to quickly try to replace him. Benny is irreplaceable. He was my doggie soulmate. And like human soulmates, the love and the bond that he and I shared only happens once in a lifetime, so I can't imagine loving another dog as much as I love him. I'm sure Brad and I will get another dog someday, but I don't want it to be a rebound dog that we only adopt to fill the gaping hole in our hearts that Benny left behind. Yes, I'm sad, lonely, and sometimes a bit anxious when Brad is at the office and I'm alone, working at home all day. But I can manage until the time is right to welcome a new dog into our home.

Thoughts of Benny often pop into my mind as I'm drifting off to sleep or when I'm in a semiconscious state, right before waking up in the morning. I'm always grateful for these visits from Benny, but one in particular seemed especially poignant. In June 2024, Benny communicated a message to me that when Brad and I do get another dog, it'll be another small white dog, possibly a Maltese, but this time, it'll be a girl. We'll name her Pearl, and she'll have a role in my editorial business, just like Benny did, sharing trivia and/or publishing-related tips that we'll call "Pearls of Wisdom." I guess we'll wait and see what the next chapter holds.

Epilogue

Lessons from Benny

In the days following Benny's passing, I felt like I was just existing, not really living. I simply couldn't believe or accept that he was really gone, and I continuously struggled to focus on anything other than memories of my sweet baby boy. Brad could usually find a way to make me smile and even laugh, and walking, getting out of the house, and attending virtual pet grief support groups helped (the closest one to Indianapolis was nearly an hour away). I certainly wasn't happy that the people in these groups had also lost a beloved pet, but there's something deeply comforting in communal grief. Hearing the group members' stories helped me realize that other people felt exactly like I did—that their fur babies were akin to children and they were grieving them as such. It made me feel seen and heard, like I wasn't alone and that nothing was wrong with me because of the intensity of my grief over losing Benny.

Day by day, a slideshow of Benny memories clicked through my mind as if I were peering at them in a ViewMaster, so I began writing them down so I wouldn't forget. I've always wanted to consistently keep a daily journal, but there never seems to be enough hours in the day. But in the spring of 2024, all I seemed to have was time—time to grieve, time to write, time to heal.

As the weeks crept by, I realized that my journaling could be the outline for a memoir about my time with Benny, so I sifted through photos and the recesses of my mind and started making notes to chronicle our journey together. Brad wholeheartedly supported my endeavor, even though, to really commit to it, I'd have to forgo taking on any editing projects while I was writing, which would prevent me from contributing to the household finances.

As soon as I started writing the actual manuscript, the words effortlessly flowed out of me as I typed them on the keyboard. Instantly, a sense of peace radiated through my body, like that's what I was meant to do. Reliving my time with Benny—especially when he was younger and more playful and energetic—was certainly therapeutic, but there were moments when uncontrollable spasms of grief racked my body, causing me to tremble as I let out an anguished wail from the depths of my soul. When that happened, Brad would question whether writing was helping or hindering my healing process, so I'd reassure him that I knew from experience that I had to feel the pain in order to heal the pain. Whatever traumas we've endured, we need to take the time to properly grieve and feel those feelings—no matter how difficult it is and how much it hurts—because if we purposely suppress or unconsciously repress those emotions, they will manifest in other, unhealthy ways. In other words, as famed psychiatrist Carl Jung is attributed as saying, "What you resist persists."

While researching for this memoir, it became evident to me in hindsight that after his first hospitalization in September 2020, Benny never fully bounced back. That summer, despite the chronic diarrhea and tummy troubles he was dealing with, he was still very vibrant, spunky, and energetic, vigorously squeaking his toys and dragging me on walks to chase squirrels and chipmunks near Brad's condo. But after recovering from his bout of pancreatitis, he lost some of his mojo. He was no longer interested in his toys or chasing varmints—although, in his defense, after we moved to our subdivision in the burbs, we rarely saw squirrels and never chipmunks. We certainly had many more good times as a family after that, but I'll always look back on the summer of 2020—when we were living together at Brad's condo as a blissful family of three and Benny was his chipper little self—as the last of the halcyon days.

Benny may have slowed down a bit and lost that puppy playfulness, but his love for Brad and me never diminished and his desire to be right next to us only increased. I never wanted to be away from him either, so I often joked that Benny and I had separation anxiety for each other. It was true, though. That's why I know in my heart that Benny did not cross over to the Other Side willingly; he wouldn't have left me unless he had no choice. His physical body may have been taken away, but his soul is still here with me.

In reliving my time with Benny, I realized that, in many ways, I was reborn when he came into my life. The magnet I have that says: "Who rescued who?" is so true (albeit not grammatically correct). In her book *The Memoir Project,* Marion Roach Smith says, "Dogs do things for people that people cannot do for themselves." That's exactly what Benny did for me. He was a beacon of light in a storm, entering my life during a sad, lonely, and dark period. When I was drowning in the depths of loneliness and lacking self-confidence, Benny was my savior, a furry little paw reaching out to pull me from the abyss and lift me above the water and into the light. He was my security blanket and a source of emotional support, but at some point, without either of us really noticing, he helped me brave the world and embrace love and life on my own, without the encumbrances of the anxiety and shyness that had held me back for so long.

All my life, I believed I couldn't be happy unless I got married and had children. Benny made me see that I most certainly could be happy without those things—that although I *wanted* them, I didn't *need* them. Taking a cue from The Beatles, he taught me that all I need is love.

From Benny's example, I learned to be my goofy, silly self, nap when I need to, love without limits, and enjoy my favorite things in life. Not only did he fill my life with unlimited unconditional love and unbounding affection, he also made me realize that I was worthy of love and taught me how to accept it. In all those ways, Benny literally changed my life because he helped me become the person Brad—my human soulmate—fell in love with and married. As a result, my lifelong dream of becoming a wife and mother came true—albeit not in the traditional sense. But Benny helped me see that being a dog mom can be every bit as fulfilling as being a mother to a human child.

At times I still feel like I don't know how to live in a world without Benny. I got 3,653 days with him (exactly ten years, including three leap years), but it was nowhere near enough. The time Benny and I spent together blew by in a blur, like an IndyCar speeding by at 200-plus miles per hour. Benny gave me a purpose and a reason to get out of bed in the morning. Even during times when I was in between work projects and didn't have much to do, I felt useful because I had to take care of him. And just like my friend Nicole had predicted more than a decade earlier when she suggested I get a dog, I had to get dressed to take him outside, so I couldn't mope around all day in my PJs.

As these memories and realizations hit me, the most difficult thing for me to process was—and still is—the moment he passed away. Even though I can picture myself in the SUV, holding Benny in my arms as the light went out of his eyes and his soul slipped from his body, it's still difficult for me to comprehend that it actually happened. It feels surreal, like I watched it happen to someone else. And when I picture it in my mind, it's like I'm looking at us from above, as if I had an out-of-body experience. It's like *my* soul also slipped out of *my* body and hovered above, while his soul departed and ascended to heaven, taking a piece of me with him.

I've always believed that everything happens for a reason. I know now that the Desi Debacle and not being allowed to adopt other dogs I applied for in early 2014 happened because I wasn't meant to adopt them. The universe was waiting for me to find Boo/Benny because he and I were destined to be together. I firmly believe that. What I haven't been able to reconcile is why Benny was taken from us so soon. Why couldn't I have more time with him? What is the lesson there? To cherish each and every moment? I would've done that whether I had ten days with him, ten years, or a hundred. I know ten years is much more than a lot of people get with their pets, and I'm truly grateful for every single second I had with Benny, but I wanted more. If that makes me greedy or selfish, so be it. It's only human nature to want more time with our loved ones, especially after they're gone.

What I have realized is that time slips through our fingers like grains of sand. Losing Benny has made me keenly aware of how precious life is—and it's even more so for our beloved pets—so we need to suck the marrow out of each and every day. I've started making a concerted effort not to put things off and to start checking things off my bucket list. Since you're reading this, I've obviously checked writing a book off that list, and Brad and I are finally planning to take a honeymoon. I'm making an effort to meet up with my best friend from high school more often too. We lost touch for decades and reunited a few years ago. Although she only lives an hour away from me, we don't see each other often, so I'd like to remedy that. I think it's important for me to make some new friends as well. I also need to get back to taking photos and videos of the people and events I want to remember and hold on to for posterity. And I always say "I love you" to my loved ones before hanging up the phone or going our separate ways—even if I know they know it—because you never know when it'll be the end of tomorrows.

Every night after Benny's passing, I'd look at his picture and tell him how much I love him, remind him how he changed my life, and ask him to send me a sign about which dog to adopt next. About a year after we lost Benny, Brad and I decided it was time to open our hearts and our home to another dog. As I dipped my toe into the search on Petfinder, I focused my attention on female dogs. I didn't want our next pooch to remind me of Benny in any way (other than in color so I could keep my business name: White Dog Editorial). Plus, Benny had indicated in a dream that our next dog would be a girl.

I also wanted an older dog because it's often more difficult for them to get adopted. When Brad saw my search parameters, he surprised me by saying he'd like to get a puppy. But I put my foot down and said, "Uh . . . no. You're not the one who'll be home all day and will have to potty-train a puppy!" He knew it was true, so that was the end of the puppy conversation.

Recalling Benny's severe separation anxiety, Brad and I also decided to get two dogs this time, hoping that having a sibling would make it easier for them when home alone. So, I kept an open mind about getting a male dog, as long as he didn't look like Benny, aside from the white fur.

In late March 2025, Brad and I were approved to adopt two female Maltese through a rescue group near Indianapolis. They weren't biological sisters, but they'd spent their entire lives together, so even though the organization didn't require them to be adopted together, we felt they should be. Besides, I'd always dreamed of having twin girls. We set up a meet-and-greet with the girls for a Sunday afternoon. I was so excited that I brainstormed a dozen possible girl names and ordered pink and purple collars, leashes, and harnesses in anticipation of bringing them home. But I refrained from buying cute little dresses until I knew their sizes.

The day before the meet-and-greet, Brad and I had to make a trip up to South Bend for a family function. Not wanting to risk missing our appointment to meet the girls, we weren't planning to stay overnight. However, on the two-hour drive to the family function, we received word that we'd been approved to adopt Cassidy, a two-and-a-half-year-old male Bichon in Fort Wayne, which is about two hours northeast of Indy and two hours east of South Bend. We'd been applying for dogs for a few weeks with no responses, then suddenly, we were approved to adopt three in a matter of hours! Brad and I talked it over and decided to stay overnight in the South Bend area, then go meet Cassidy on Sunday morning. If we didn't adopt him, we'd still go meet the Maltese "sisters" in the afternoon.

When Cassidy came out to greet us, he warmed up to me right away, but he was a little skittish around Brad. That reluctance evaporated when we took him for a walk around the property. As he zigged and zagged back and forth across the sidewalk, I said, "Maybe we should name him Ziggy." I liked the name Elliott, but Ziggy seemed to suit his personality much better.

By the time we finished our walk, Cassidy and Brad were buddies, so there was no doubt we were adopting him. But while we were signing the paperwork, my eyes fell upon a white puppy on the other side of a glass-enclosed room.

"Oh my God," I gasped, staring into a pair of soulful brown eyes that were so familiar to me. "He looks just like Benny!"

"Would you like to hold him?" the adoption coordinator asked.

Completely entranced and feeling like a powerful, invisible force was pulling me toward the pup, I replied, "Yes, please."

As we entered the room, my heart began to pound. When a volunteer handed me the twelve-week-old furball, he snuggled in my arms and licked my face. He was so calm and chill—just like Benny.

"I want him," I whispered to Brad, my heart overflowing with so much love for this tiny Benny doppelganger that I was practically choking back tears.

"Both?" Brad questioned, somewhat shocked and undoubtedly worried that I'd changed my mind about Cassidy.

"Yeah," I assured him. "You said we could adopt two this time."

"I know, but I thought you wanted a girl and you said you *didn't* want a puppy," Brad reminded me with a laugh.

"I know . . . , but forget what I said before. I truly believe Benny sent us here to find this little guy. And you know I always wished I could've gotten Benny as a puppy."

"If you're sure, then let's do it!" said my awesome husband.

Unfortunately, we couldn't take the puppy home that day, so I agreed to pick him up four days later, after he'd been neutered. However, before then, he was exposed to parvo and had to be quarantined for two weeks.

In the meantime, when we got the newly christened Ziggy home, it was as if he'd always lived there. He made himself comfortable on the couch, right between Brad and me, and gratefully licked our hands in exchange for rubbing his belly. Like Benny, Ziggy was terrified of our stairs and insisted on being carried up and down them. It also took him a couple days to accept the toys and treats we offered, but eventually he did and his kooky personality emerged. One night, just after he and Brad returned from a walk, Ziggy began barking and yapping as he enthusiastically ran laps around the kitchen and living room. The elation on his giddily grinning face was contagious as he spun in circles on the hardwood floor like a whirligig.

Brad and I just stood and stared at him wide-eyed, wondering what had gotten into the sweet little guy. "I've read about dogs doing 'zoomies,'" I said. "Maybe that's what this is?"

Brad replied with a laugh, "Either that or he's gone completely loco!"

When Puppy was finally in the clear, Brad, Ziggy, and I drove to Fort Wayne and brought him home. Ziggy had enjoyed his time as an only child, so at first he wasn't pleased with the idea of having a baby brother. But once they started playing, they quickly grew to love each other, albeit in a Wrestlemania sort of way. Ziggy showed him the ropes and taught him where to potty outside and how to play with toys, bark at the doorbell, and lift his leg to pee. (Although in his own unique fashion, Puppy preferred to lift his front leg rather than his rear one.)

Puppy taught Ziggy a few things too. Unlike Ziggy, Puppy had no fear of the stairs, hopping up and down them like a kangaroo. After a couple days watching the little tyke navigate the stairs with ease while he was being carried, Ziggy faced his fear and followed in Puppy's footsteps.

We named the puppy Joey due to the aforementioned kangaroo-like antics and because, when we first brought him home, I occasionally carried him in a little pouch strapped to my chest, like a kangaroo and her joey. Plus, he was born around New Year's Eve like Joey McIntyre from New Kids on the Block.

Joey and Ziggy reignited a spark in me that was extinguished when Benny passed. Sometimes I still do a double-take, thinking Joey is Benny. Like Benny, Joey is very affectionate and loves to smother my face with kisses. But the calm and chill demeanor he displayed when we first met, which reminded me so much of Benny—it's gone. With his boundless energy, Joey bebops around the house like Tigger, loves to eat paper, and plays in his water bowl as if he's bobbing for apples, even blowing bubbles through his nose. I'm amazed at the wonder in his eyes as he discovers new things, and as a puppy, literally *everything* is new to him. I can't wait to see how he reacts when he encounters his first squirrel.

Every day, Brad and I still wish Benny were here with us, but it's so wonderful to be dog parents again and be on the receiving end of the unconditional love they offer so willingly. I truly believe Benny is here with us in spirit and that he guided us to Joey and Ziggy. I didn't think I wanted a puppy, another male dog, or one that reminded me of Benny, but, as always, God and the universe provided exactly what I needed.

Photo Gallery

Welcome home, Little Boy Boo!
March 9, 2014

Watch out, Bono—there's a new kid in town.

Benny's first haircut.
March 2014

Mommy and her
baby boy.

We're getting married!

Basking in the sun and about to do roly-polies.
Summer of 2020

**Benny and Braddy,
soon-to-be Daddy.**
Summer of 2020

**Our handsome boy in his
wedding suit.**
September 25, 2020

Benny could've been a model.

Showdown with a squirrel.

Morning cuddles.

Rub my belly! Rub my belly!

I'm watching your
speed, Dad!

I'm all ears!

Benny and Monkey.

Mommy's Boy in his Mommy's Boy sweatshirt.

The day Benny walked through the snow tunnel.
February 20, 2021

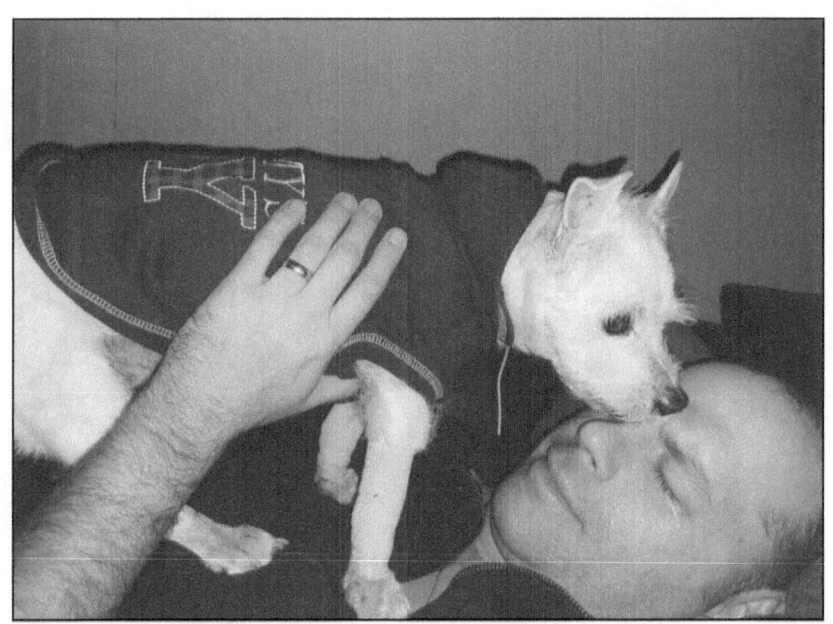

Thunderbolt gives Daddy kisses.

Mommy gets Benny kisses.

Hi, I'm Benny and I'm a Pisces.
I like chasing squirrels, eating, sleeping,
and cuddling with my parents.

I'm all ready for bed.
Goodnight!

Acknowledgments

First and foremost, to my husband and soulmate, Brad Schaeffer, I extend all my love and heartfelt thanks for your unwavering support and encouragement, not only while I wrote *Mommy's Boy*, but also while I grieved (and continue to grieve) the loss of our precious Benny. You are my rock, and I truly would not have made it through this most difficult time without your constant love and emotional support. You championed this book from the moment I first pitched the idea to you; you held me when the writing became so difficult that I sobbed while typing; you offered feedback on my early drafts and helped me fill in some memory gaps; and you never once complained that I'd taken a sabbatical from my editorial business to pour my heart and soul into this project. You're the best thing about me, and our love is bigger than anything in its way. I love you, always and forever.

To my sisters, Lori Bonnici and Denise Berkland, life made us sisters, but love made us friends. I may not enjoy talking on the phone quite as much as you do, but I love spending time with you. Thank you for the many times you babysat for Benny. I'm so lucky to have the two of you in my life and in my corner.

To my dad, Jim Huston, you instilled in me a love for dogs, helped me convince Mom to keep any stray that found its way to us, and I'm sure were instrumental in Mom allowing Arnold to be an inside dog. Thanks for watching Benny when Brad and I couldn't take him with us on our travels. I know it wasn't always easy following his feeding instructions and keeping "Hoover" away from Lulu's food.

Many thanks to my cousins Rich Deuitch and Jim Pauley—my brother from another mother—for graciously allowing us to stay with you when we're in town. We always have a blast with you guys, but when are you gonna get another dog?

I'm forever grateful to Ann and Dick Schaeffer for raising Brad to be the loving, supportive, and amazing man that he is; for welcoming Benny into your home; for immediately putting me at ease and making me feel like part of the family; and for always inquiring about the book.

My sincere appreciation to the friends and family members who offered condolences after Benny passed away and showed genuine support for this book by asking for updates, following me on social media, and sharing my posts. It means more than you know.

To Bill Taylor and Kathryn K. ("Nicole"), thanks for encouraging me to get a dog, even before I was ready. You were right, but so was I. Haha! Special thanks to Karen Soll Aleo, who was there when I brought Benny home and spoiled him like a good auntie should. I'm deeply grateful to the Davila family, for allowing me to have a dog in my apartment, encouraging me to get one, and taking Benny out and watching him before I got home from work.

Heartfelt appreciation to my dear friends Margaret Hartsough and Scott Hampton for your unwavering support and friendship and for doting on Benny as his aunt and uncle. You two comforted me during my many heartbreaks, were there when I met Brad, came along on our first few dates, and stood by us during our "first wedding" in Vegas.

Profound thanks to Michael Acres who introduced Brad and me to each other—not once, but twice—and encouraged me to keep the lines of communication with him open. When we met outside the Bradley Center in Milwaukee on September 25, 2005, I never would've imagined in my wildest dreams that you'd introduce me to my soulmate and I'd marry him exactly fifteen years later.

Of course, I must give a shout out to U2, those incredibly talented men from Ireland, who led Margaret and I to Scott, then to Mike, and ultimately to Brad. Your music has inspired me, been a balm to my soul during the darkest times, and brightened my days in countless ways.

I'm indebted to my editorial team, Debbie Almgren-Horwitz and Steve Grundt, my former coworkers and two of the savviest and most detail-oriented editorial professionals I've had the pleasure of working with and proudly call my friends. I'm beyond grateful to my beta readers, William Croyle, Anna Dergan, Lisa Rimmert, and Dan Schaeffer, for finding the time to offer invaluable feedback and encouraging me to go even deeper. Your thoughtful insights tremendously improved my manuscript.

Many thanks to my designer, Michelle Argyle Park of Melissa Williams Design, for working your magic to bring my vision for the cover to life, for sticking with me even after I changed the subtitle three times, and for your patience when my perfectionism caused me to make numerous changes after the book was in layout. I'd also like to acknowledge Barbara Delage of Springboard Literary for your expert marketing and PR advice as we consoled each other over the loss of our fur babies.

Endless thanks to Benny's care team: Dr. Steven Nichols, Dr. Lori Thompson, Dr. Timothy Hui, Dr. Timothy James, Dr. Carl Budelsky, Dr. Jessy Leto, Dr. Gina Santiago, Andrea Tillison, Karen Dietrich, Jessie Brown, and all the other techs and staff members at the VCA in Fishers, the Integrative Veterinary Clinic in Westfield, and the Animal Allergy & Dermatology Center of Indiana. You all provided Benny with the best possible medical care and treated him like part of the family. For that, I will always be grateful.

To Heather Owen, Anna Friedman, and all the foster parents and volunteers at One Tail at a Time, who rescued Benny so he could rescue me: thank you for the wonderfully compassionate work you do to help animals find their forever homes.

Much gratitude to Anne Strohm for encouraging me not to give up my dog search and to check out OTAT. I hope you know what a profound impact you had on my life.

To the rescue groups that wouldn't let me adopt because I worked full-time outside the home: you were right, those dogs weren't right for me, and in the end, it all worked out for the best because it led me to Benny, the best dog in the history of the universe. But let's be honest, you could've handled the situation better.

I'd also like to acknowledge Jessica Ricker of the Michigan State University Pet Loss Support Group. Thank you for all you do to help grieving pet parents during a most difficult time of their lives. You provide an invaluable service, and your work is appreciated immensely. To all the other grieving pet parents I've met through this group and other online support groups, I offer my sincerest condolences and hope this book helps you find some comfort on your healing journey. You are not alone.

I'd also like to thank my English and creative writing teachers through the years, including Cathy Connell, Ada Barr, Ann Orth, and Tracey Thompson, for praising my writing and encouraging me to stick with it, despite my lack of self-confidence. It took more than three decades, but I finally did it. And to Nancy Hain, who expanded my reading horizons—although she was scarily strict and required her third-grade students to read books with an eighth-grade reading level. However, I do blame my need for glasses at age eight on reading so many books with tiny print.

To Jane Friedman, Marion Roach Smith, Mary Karr, Polly Campbell, Ann Kroeker, Myra Levine, Brooke Warner, Jane Roper, Shayla Raquel, Angela Ackerman, and Becca Puglisi—your collective expertise in creative writing, memoir, and publishing provided a creative spark and helped me dig deeper as I poured out my memories and emotions.

Heavenly thanks to my dad's beloved dog Sweetie and all the dogs I've had throughout my life: Arnold, Snoopy, Candida, Mopsy, Fezzy, and Gigi, my first dog, who may have actually been my imaginary dog since nobody else in my family remembers her.

Love and gratitude to my guardian angels who are always watching out for me and are surely showering Benny with cuddles and kisses: Margaret; Dr. Bob Fenstermacher; my brother, Steve Klopfenstein; my brother-in-law, Bernie Berkland; my grandparents, aunts, and uncles; and my mom, Judy Huston who fostered in me a love for reading at a very young age and always encouraged me to follow my dreams.

And last, but certainly not least, Benny, my sweet baby boy, you enriched my life in countless ways and filled my heart with more love and joy than I ever could've imagined. Your love truly rescued me, and you were and always will be my sunshine.

About the Author

Jennifer Huston Schaeffer is an author, editor, and the owner of White Dog Editorial Services. She grew up surrounded by cornfields in a bucolic small town in southwestern Michigan, where she developed a love for reading, writing, and, of course, dogs. After graduating from Purdue University, Jennifer moved to Chicago and began working in the publishing industry in 2002. She adopted Benny, her doggie soulmate and the inspiration for *Mommy's Boy*, in 2014. When she's not editing other people's books, she enjoys reading, writing, crafting, and watching true crime documentaries and classic game shows. Jennifer is a member of the Indie Authors Association, the Midwest Independent Publishers Association, the Central Indiana Writers Association, and the Editorial Freelancers Association. She is also the author of *U2: Changing the World Through Rock 'n' Roll*.

Follow Jennifer on:

Facebook: Jennifer Huston Schaeffer: Author
Instagram: @AuthorJenniferHustonSchaeffer
Website: www.whitedogeditorial.com/blog

If you enjoyed *Mommy's Boy: How My Doggie Soulmate's Love Rescued Me*, please leave a review on Amazon and/or Goodreads. It would mean the world to me because it helps other readers discover the book, builds my connection with readers like you, and motivates me to keep writing. Thank you for taking the time to share your thoughts.

With gratitude,
—Jennifer Huston Schaeffer

Amazon

Goodreads

www.ingramcontent.com/pod-product-compliance
Lightning Source LLC
Chambersburg PA
CBHW030911120626
46554CB00001B/108